D0064802

Healthy Cities and Urban Policy Research

Edited by Takehito Takano

Spon Press
Taylor & Francis Group

LONDON AND NEW YORK

First published 2003 by Spon Press
11 New Fetter Lane, London EC4P 4EE

Simultaneously published in the USA and Canada
by Spon Press
29 West 35th Street, New York, NY 10001

Spon Press is an imprint of the Taylor & Francis Group

© 2003 Takehito Takano, selection and editorial matter; individual
chapters, the contributors

Typeset in Times by GreenGate Publishing Services, Tonbridge, Kent
Printed and bound in Great Britain by
The Cromwell Press, Trowbridge, Wiltshire

British Library Cataloguing in Publication Data
A catalogue record for this book is available from the British Library

Library of Congress Cataloguing in Publication Data
Healthy cities and urban policy research / edited by Takehito Takano.
    p. ; cm.
  Includes bibliographical references and index.
  ISBN 0-415-28844-4 (alk. paper)
  1. Urban health–Congresses. 2. WHO Healthy Cities
Project–Congresses.
  [DNLM: 1. WHO Healthy Cities Project. 2. Urban Health. 3. Health
Policy. 4. Urban Health Services–organization & administration. WA
380 H43482 2003] I. Takano, Takehito, 1949–
RA566.7.H432 2003
362.1 '042–dc21
                                                    2003004325

ISBN 0-415-28844-4

Contents

List of tables, figures and boxes

Tables

Figures

Boxes

Notes on contributors

Frances E. Baum is Professor and Head of the Department of Public Health, Flinders University of South Australia, and Foundation Director of South Australian Community Health Research Unit.

June Crown is Chair of WHO European Region Healthy Cities Profiles and Indicators Group at Department of Public Health Sciences, Kings College London.

Jill L. Farrington is Deputy Head, Centre for Urban Health and Governance, World Health Organization, Regional Office for Europe.

Colin Fudge is Professor, Dean and Pro-Vice Chancellor at the University of the West of England, Bristol and Chair of the European Commission Expert Group on the Urban Environment.

Irene S. M. Lee is Postdoctoral Fellow, United Nations University, Institute of Advanced Studies and Affiliated Researcher in the Department of International Health in the Division of Public Health, Graduate School of Tokyo Medical and Dental University.

Evelyne de Leeuw is Director of the School of Public Health of the University of Southern Denmark (Odense/Esbjerg). She previously was Director of WHO Collaborating Centre for Research on Healthy Cities at Universiteit Maastricht.

Keiko Nakamura is Associate Professor and Head of the International Health Section in the Division of Public Health, Graduate School of Tokyo Medical and Dental University and Secretary General of the Promotion Committee for Healthy City Tokyo.

Hisashi Ogawa is Regional Advisor in Environmental Health at World Health Organization, Regional Office for the Western Pacific.

Takehito Takano is Professor of the Department of International Health Development in the Division of Public Health, Graduate School of Tokyo Medical and Dental University, and Director of WHO Collaborating Centre for Healthy Cities and Urban Policy Research.

Agis D. Tsouros is Head, Centre for Urban Health and Governance, World Health Organization, Regional Office for Europe.

Preface

Half of the world's population lives in urban areas. The United Nations estimates that 1995's urban population will double by 2025. By 2015, the world is expected to hold 33 megacities, 20 of them in Asia.

Urbanisation affects human health in unprecedented ways. Attempts to improve the health of citizens necessitate the development of comprehensive schemes integrating a wide range of factors pertaining to urban issues. Therefore, the World Health Organisation has engaged in the Healthy Cities Project since 1986 to institutionalise a system to ensure and promote the health of urban residents.

This book will provide readers with the solid basics of the Healthy Cities Project and help practitioners and researchers bring the project up to a higher level. Furthermore, the book gives clear explanations of the project, practical guidance and directions to those wishing to launch a Healthy Cities project. It can also serve as a supplementary reading for university students in urban planning, public policy, community development and public health.

This book is a collection of eleven papers by leading experts from academia or international organisations who have long been involved in the Healthy Cities movement. This book is a product of a March 2000 conference and is unique as it is perhaps the first academic work to combine public health with urban planning. I hope that this book gives you a better understanding of the Healthy Cities movement and that it gives you a scientific foundation that will improve your urban health planning and policy formation.

Takehito Takano

Chapter 1

Development of Healthy Cities and need for research

Takehito Takano

GLOBAL URBANISATION AND POPULATION HEALTH: BACKGROUND FOR HEALTHY CITIES

Increase in urban population

Urbanisation has been rapidly progressing worldwide in recent years, and this trend has been particularly prominent in Asia and other developing regions. According to United Nations' statistics (United Nations 1999), urban populations roughly doubled in the industrialised nations and quadrupled in the developing nations during the latter half of the twentieth century. Today, approximately half of the global population of 6 billion people live inside urban areas. The world population is projected to increase to 8 billion over the next 30 years or so, and the number of city dwellers will clearly surpass 6 billion. In other words, in three decades, over two-thirds of the global population will reside within urban areas. In the industrialised nations, over three-quarters of the population already live in urban areas, and this percentage is projected to continue to gradually increase.

Asian urbanisation is characterised by the formation of megacities including Tokyo. Demographers forecast that there will be more than 30 such megacities ten years from now, and that about two-thirds of these will be located within Asia (United Nations 1999).

Together with the globalisation of the economy and the development of new technologies, the worldwide advance of urbanisation is radically changing people's living environments and living conditions. For residents' health, these developments offer both new potential benefits and numerous challenges. The acceleration of urbanisation and the development of urbanised societies will have an increasingly severe impact on the global environment, and will influence the very conditions for humanity's survival. Rapid urbanisation underscores the critical need to adjust course toward achieving a cyclical and sustainable society.

IMPACTS ON POPULATION HEALTH

Urbanisation affects determinants of health in unprecedented ways. On one hand, urban development produces a number of benefits including increased land values, capital gains, and a more active local economy. A number of key factors in urban society improve health levels of the population. On the other hand, although it creates economic growth, infrastructure development, and a sophisticated lifestyle, urbanisation also triggers new problems and issues bearing on multiple aspects of urban life, including food security, housing, employment, living environment, health of future generations, increasing levels of crime, violence, sex trafficking, drug abuse, and vulnerability to natural disasters. Urbanisation also increases the importance of crisis management for natural and man-made calamities and disasters such as outbreaks of infectious diseases.

Problems originating in an urban area can well spill over its borders and encroach on the entire society, as exemplified by urban overcrowding and rural underpopulation, and imbalance between production and consumption. Urban problems, furthermore, impact the world community by affecting populations, resources, economics and the environment. For these reasons, attempts to improve the health status of citizens necessitate the development of comprehensive schemes integrating a wide range of factors pertaining to urban issues.

Urbanisation and the agglomeration of megacities do not necessarily improve living standards. In fact, the number of people concentrated in informal settlements, including squatter areas and other squalid unimproved city districts in developing nations, has risen, and is continuing to increase rapidly (World Bank 2001). Even in industrialised nations, systems sometimes result in a relative decline in health levels in urban areas (Takano and Nakamura 2001b), and these health levels are closely related to the quality of urban living environments (Takeuchi et al. 1995; Tanaka et al. 1996; Takano et al. 2002).

Rapid urbanisation tends to exacerbate disparities in living conditions. The inability of urban infrastructure to keep pace with urbanisation results in a deterioration of living environments and an insufficient supply of essential services, posing severe public health and sanitation problems. And when urbanisation is not accompanied by sufficient economic growth, it expands the ranks of the urban poor, increases the factors that cause social instability, and prevents overall improvements in urban health levels (Asian Development Bank 1997).

Growth in the number of urban poor is evident in the industrialised nations as well and poses diverse social medicine issues: deterioration of living environments, mismatch in supply and demand for essential services, diminished socioeconomic vitality from an aging society and lower birthrates, increased crime and social unrest, and a growing number of homeless people and others with no fixed residence. Moreover, the characteristics of urbanised societies are intimately related to such health issues as the emergence, re-emergence, and spread of new and existing infectious diseases, supply of safe food, stress, and psychological health. Efforts to address traditional urban problems such as air pollution, garbage disposal, safe water and food supply, and the creation, maintenance and management of housing and living environments meet increasing difficulties in megacities with wider income disparities (World Health Organisation [WHO] 1997).

Demands for an integrated activity framework

Urban problems with their related health issues have the aspect of a structural problem, and therefore we need structural solutions to tackle them. That is why we need an integrated policy framework in which to undertake activities.

The conditions of the diverse health determinants in urban areas are becoming increasingly complex, indicating that solutions will by no means be easy. On the whole, the varied health problems challenging cities in recent years are intricately interrelated with the background of general urban problems. Just as rural health activities were developed to improve low health levels in farming districts and industrial health activities to address high health risk workplaces in the past, we now need to develop urban health activities to cope with the numerous health problems suffered in urban areas.

To date, nationwide public health measures have been subdivided into individual systems for maternal and child health, elderly health, psychological health, communicable diseases countermeasures, environmental health, and other fields. With the trend toward decentralisation of government authority to the municipal level, municipal government bodies are now being called upon to develop new city health frameworks to address urban health problems effectively in an integrated manner.

The majority of urban problems directly impact on residents' health, and close cooperation among governments, residents, businesses, and other bodies will be essential to solve these challenges. A new collaborative approach is needed to bring together a partnership of the public and private sectors and the community to focus on urban health and to take a broad approach in dealing with health issues. The complex problems, increased responsibility of city governments, and the possibility of partnerships have created demands for a new integrated framework like 'Healthy Cities'.

EVOLUTION OF 'HEALTHY CITIES'

WHO Healthy Cities Project/Programme

The Healthy Cities concept emerged in the 1980s on the basis of a new public health movement (Kickbusch 1989; Ashton 1992; Baum 1998), the Ottawa Charter (WHO 1986), and the Health for All strategy (WHO 1981). It is an innovative means for improving urban living conditions and the health of the population (WHO Regional Office for Europe 1992). According to a number of WHO publications, Healthy Cities projects require a holistic approach by emphasising the importance of intersectoral collaboration and community participation to create environments supportive for health (Tsouros 1990; WHO Regional Office for Europe 1992; WHO 1995a, 1995b; WHO Regional Office for the Western Pacific 2000).

The publication entitled *WHO Healthy Cities: A Programme Framework* (WHO 1995a) stresses several key concepts including intersectoral collaboration, a partnership approach (among NGOs, private companies, community organisations and groups), a supportive environment, and 'settings' approach. A supportive environment for health has been defined as one which helps to improve physical, economic, and social conditions supportive of health. Municipal Health Plan (MHP) was recognised as follows:

> MHP promotes collaboration between sectors and serves to generate awareness of health and environmental problems by municipal authorities, non-government agencies, and communities; and mobilizes resources to deal with the problems.
>
> (WHO 1995a)

According to *Twenty Steps for Developing a Healthy Cities Project* published by WHO: 'A healthy city is one that improves its environments and expands its resources so that people can support each other in achieving their highest potential.' Healthy public policy, an important characteristic of Healthy Cities, can be achieved through political decisions, intersectoral action, community participation, and innovation (WHO Regional Office for Europe 1992).

The WHO chose Healthy Cities as the theme for World Health Day 1996, and encouraged a global network among cities (Goldstein and Kickbusch 1996). The fourth International Conference on Health Promotion held in Jakarta, Indonesia, in July 1997, recognised the global Healthy Cities movement and announced the 'Statement on Partnership for Healthy Cities'. Monitoring and analysis have been raised as an important topic in the publication *Building A Healthy City: A Practitioners' Guide* (WHO 1995b).

Many cities are now trying to develop Healthy Cities by respecting individual cities' characteristics as well as regional ones. Further development of Healthy Cities will be encouraged by participation of various cities and by efforts towards appropriate research development.

A setting-based approach

'Healthy Cities' derives from a concrete application of the principles and strategies of the Ottawa Charter for Health Promotion in urban settings (WHO 1986); it is a comprehensive setting-based approach.

While settings are simply 'areas', such as schools, workplaces, markets, shopping districts, and city blocks, the Healthy Cities approach does not view settings as just physical locations. Rather, the settings are understood from a wider perspective as venues for daily activities, for the actual manifestation of diverse environmental conditions, and above all as the concrete objects of intensive health-related policies. According to the WHO's *Health Promotion Glossary* (1998), a setting for health is defined as:

> the place or social context in which people engage in daily activities in which environmental, organisational and personal factors interact to affect health and well being. A setting is also where people actively use and shape the environment and thus create or solve problems relating to health. Settings can normally be identified as having physical boundaries, a range of people with defined roles, and an organisational structure. Action to promote health through different settings can take many different forms, often through some form of organisational development, including change to the physical environment, to the organisational structure, administration and management. Settings can also be used to promote health by reaching people who work in them, or using them to gain access to services, and through the interaction of different settings with the wider community. Examples of settings include schools, work sites, hospitals, villages and cities.

The advantages of the setting-based approach include greater ease in securing community participation by identifying specific areas within cities, in forming linkages and clarifying the division of work among related institutions, organisations and wide-ranging concerned parties, and in integrating individual policy measures. As a result, the setting-based approach facilitates the effective utilisation of personnel, goods, budgets, and other limited resources. Settings where the Healthy Cities concept has been introduced are called, for example, 'healthy schools', 'healthy markets', and 'healthy towns', with Healthy Cities as the overriding, comprehensive concept.

Healthy Cities as a strategy to develop a comprehensive policy package

The term 'Healthy Cities' as used by the WHO does not actually refer to cities whose residents enjoy a high level of health, but rather to cities that have introduced Healthy Cities programmes, and to the methodologies that they are developing. The Healthy Cities approach began in the latter 1980s, mostly in Europe. At that time, these efforts were referred to as Healthy Cities projects. In line with the greater emphasis on Healthy Cities as an overall concept, the recent trend has been away from referring to specific efforts as individual projects, and toward adopting titles such as Healthy Cities programme, Healthy Cities policy or Healthy Cities approach. In many cases, urban governments are simply referring to their policy strategies as just Healthy Cities.

The Healthy Cities strategy was initiated amid the rapid progress of urbanisation worldwide, in both industrialised and developing nations. The advance of urbanisation poses new challenges for maintaining human health. While urbanisation results in economic development, improved urban infrastructure, and more sophisticated lifestyle technologies, it also presents varied challenges in such diverse areas as food supply, the production and distribution of foodstuffs, housing, and changes in the living environment. City problems are by no means limited to urban areas alone, but rather constitute issues for an entire society (including rural regions), such as excessive population density in some areas and depopulation in others, and the overall structure of production and consumption. Moreover, urbanisation has international repercussions via demographic shifts, allocation of resources, economics, and the environment.

To respond to these types of changes in living conditions from the effect of urbanisation on human health, and to boost the physical, psychological, and social health levels of urban residents, it is necessary to establish a framework to secure the health of city dwellers by espousing the Healthy Cities approach and supporting Healthy Cities programmes. These efforts are based on a recognition of the need to secure the conditions required to maintain human health in urban environments and involve people who have conventionally been perceived as outside the purview of the medical and healthcare sector.

With their dense and complicated structures and functions, cities need to adopt comprehensive strategic policies to promote the health of their residents. The development of Healthy Cities is based on recognition that there is a common structure within urban problems that lies behind individual health issues, and that it is difficult to promote the health of city dwellers via public health policy alone, as narrowly defined (Takano and Nakamura 2001a). Accordingly, the Healthy Cities principle is being developed as a key pillar to advance the overall health of urban residents, primarily at the individual city level, by ensuring that health aspects are incorporated into all city policies and works, including urban development, planning, administration, and management – that is, as a citywide structure to support residents' health.

The Healthy Cities approach, which is based on but transcends conventional health promotion measures, is becoming established as an effective means of realising sustainable urban development and the formation of healthy, stable, high-quality local societies in and around cities through the introduction of urban environmental management and other novel methodologies.

In practice, the Healthy Cities approach takes the form of Healthy Cities programmes. These are comprehensive, integrated policy packages encompassing all the major factors for sustaining urban health, ranging from the formation and implementation of healthy public policy to vision sharing, a high level of political commitment, the establishment of structural organisations, strategic health planning, intersectoral collaboration, community participation, a setting-based approach, the creation of a supportive environment for health, the preparation of city health profiles (which serve as an urban health index database), the establishment and use of active national and international networking, utilisation of participatory research, the establishment of periodic monitoring and evaluation processes, and the design of mechanisms to ensure the sustainability of projects.

Since Healthy Cities as a strategy spread to diverse cities worldwide and experience has been accumulated from individual cities adopting model approaches, Healthy Cities is developing into a comprehensive policy package to carry out individual projects and activities effectively and efficiently.

THE NEED FOR RESEARCH TO ADVANCE HEALTHY CITIES

Healthy Cities has now grown into a comprehensive policy package to resolve urban health and environmental issues practically and effectively. With experience accumulated via efforts in cities across the globe, emphasis increasingly came to be placed on the urban environmental aspects and on city management and administration.

What is more, in recent years the scientific underpinnings of Healthy Cities have become clearly established. Thus Healthy Cities is gaining substance as a scientific strategy supported by empirical evidence, possibly because Healthy Cities has come to be used as a framework for the collection of facts, analysis of causes, and utilisation of prior experience, with feedback mechanisms for ongoing refinement. Facts are being collected from the experiences of Healthy Cities worldwide, linked together via national and international networks, with the WHO providing the support structure. The accumulated data (including examples of failures) are being examined from diverse viewpoints by experts in many different fields who are conducting analyses toward making Healthy Cities more effective. These feedback mechanisms are resulting in reports of more and more Healthy Cities success stories, and the Healthy Cities approach is becoming highly attractive as a new, multidisciplinary research field.

When Healthy Cities do succeed with their comprehensive approach, the effects are great indeed. However, many difficulties are encountered along the way to making Healthy Cities a reality. Healthy Cities proponents sincerely hope that a greater number of experts from more diverse fields will become involved to develop and advance Healthy Cities further.

De Leeuw *et al.* reviewed the prior research on Healthy Cities, and, taking notice of the relationship between researchers and Healthy Cities, divided the studies into four categories: research for Healthy Cities, research in Healthy Cities, research on Healthy Cities, and research with Healthy Cities (de Leeuw *et al.* 1992). The first category, research for Healthy Cities, refers to basic and applied research that is useful for building up Healthy Cities. Research in Healthy Cities refers to research conducted by the parties actually developing Healthy Cities. Research on Healthy Cities refers to research conducted on Healthy Cities projects themselves as the research topic. Finally, research with Healthy Cities basically refers to the participatory research methods that are frequently emphasised in the implementation of Healthy Cities projects.

'Participation' is a key word for Healthy Cities research. Such research may be jointly conducted by project implementation parties and local residents, for example, to identify the issues, analyse and interpret data, and consider the conclusions that are reached. This approach, known as participatory research or action research or a 'Doing Research Together' activity (Takano 1999), deepens the understanding of all those involved regarding actual conditions, and clarifies facts that would be difficult to confirm by outsiders. Moreover, community participation itself affords an excellent opportunity for everyone involved to deepen their understanding of Healthy Cities, and improves their analytical abilities. Also, participatory research leads to facts-based research that provides a solid basis for developing Healthy Cities, as well as research to secure new skills and technologies that are necessary for developing Healthy Cities.

It is crucial for us to acquire evidence of how Healthy Cities have changed people's living and health. Exchange of experiences is useful at the country level, at the city level, as well as at the community level. Examples of intersectoral collaboration, community participation, action plan formation, and evaluation with people in the community need to be gathered and analysed. Sharing a database of evidence among various actors at the global level will contribute to the worldwide development of the Healthy Cities Project.

References

Ashton, J. (1992) The origins of Healthy Cities. In Ashton, J. (ed.) *Healthy Cities*. Milton Keynes: Open University Press.

Asian Development Bank (1997) *Asian Development Bank Annual Report 1996*. Manila: Asian Development Bank.

Baum, F. (1998) *The New Public Health: An Australian Perspective*. Melbourne: Oxford University Press.

de Leeuw, E., O'Neil, M., Goumans, M. and de Bruijn, F. (1992) *Healthy Cities Research Agenda. Proceedings of an Expert Panel*. Maatricht: Research for Healthy Cities Clearing House.

Goldstein, G. and Kickbusch, I. (1996) A healthy city is a better city. *World Health*, 49: 4–6.

Kickbusch, I. (1989) Healthy Cities: a working project and a growing movement. *Health Promotion*, 4: 77–82.

Takano, T. (1999) *Integration viewpoints and 'doing research together' activity*. In Proceedings of the WHO Meeting on Health Protection and Health Promotion Harmonizing Our Responses to the Challenges of the 21st Century. Manila: WHO Regional Office for the Western Pacific.

Takano, T. and Nakamura, K. (2001a) An analysis of health levels and various indicators of urban environments for Healthy Cities Projects. *Journal of Epidemiology and Community Health*, 55: 263–70.

Takano, T. and Nakamura, K. (2001b) The national financial policy and the equalization of health levels among prefectures. *Journal of Epidemiology and Community Health*, 55: 748–54.

Takano, T., Nakamura, K. and Watanabe, M. (2002) Urban residential environments and senior citizens' longevity in megacity areas: the importance of walkable green spaces. *Journal of Epidemiology and Community Health*, 56: 913–18.

Takeuchi, S., Takano, T. and Nakamura, K. (1995) Health and its determining factors in the Tokyo megacity. *Health Policy*, 33: 1–14.

Tanaka, A., Takano, T., Nakamura, K. and Takeuchi, S. (1996) Health levels influenced by urban residential conditions in a megacity. *Urban Studies,* 33: 879–94.

Tsouros, A. (1990) *World Health Organization Healthy Cities Project: A Project Becomes a Movement.* Copenhagen: WHO/FADL.

United Nations (1999) *World Urbanisation Prospects: The 1999 Revision.* New York: United Nations.

World Bank (2001) *World Development Report 2000/2001: Attacking Poverty.* New York: World Bank/Oxford University Press.

World Health Organisation (WHO) (1981) *The Global Strategy for Health for All by the Year 2000.* Geneva: WHO.

WHO (1986) Ottawa Charter for Health Promotion. *Health Promotion*, 1: iii–v.

WHO (1995a) *WHO Healthy Cities: A Programme Framework.* Geneva: WHO.

WHO (1995b) *Building a Healthy City: A Practitioners' Guide.* Geneva: WHO.

WHO (1997) *Health and Environment in Sustainable Development.* Geneva: WHO.

WHO (1998) *Health Promotion Glossary.* Geneva: WHO.

WHO Regional Office for Europe (1992) *Twenty Steps for Developing a Healthy Cities Project.* Copenhagen: WHO Regional Office for Europe.

WHO Regional Office for the Western Pacific (2000) *Regional Guidelines for Developing a Healthy Cities Project.* Manila: WHO Regional Office for the Western Pacific.

Chapter 2

The third phase (1998–2002) of the Healthy Cities Project in Europe

Agis D. Tsouros and Jill L. Farrington

This chapter is based on the presentation given by Jill L. Farrington on the occasion of the International Conference on Healthy Cities and Urban Policy Research in 2000 (but figures have been updated to match the situation as of December 2002).

INTRODUCTION

Healthy Cities is a dynamic concept. It has its solid foundation in the principles of Health 21 and Agenda 21. It has evolved over three phases: 1988–92, 1993–7 and 1998–2002. Its success and appeal is due to a great extent to its ability continuously to re-invent, adjust and re-position its strategic agenda. Healthy Cities in Europe developed and sprang through an extraordinary period of political and socio-economic change. This was also a period of global change and of the emergence of global strategic agendas. The core aspects of Healthy Cities could be summed up as follows: action that addresses the root causes of ill health and equity that is based on inter-sectoral partnerships and community empowerment; recognition of the key role of local governments in health and sustainable development; recognition of the importance of the urban and local dimension in health development; and networking for innovation, learning and cooperation at national and international levels under a widely-known label. The Healthy Cities movement in Europe consists of 30 national networks (and several sub-national at regional/provincial levels), which involve more than 1300 cities and towns, and the World Health Organisation (WHO) network of designated cities.

PHASE III

The WHO network consists of highly committed cities, which were designated by WHO to be WHO project cities. Phase I (1987–92) involved 35 cities in the network of WHO project cities. The accent was on creating new structures to act as change agents and introducing new ways of working for health in cities (Draper *et al.*

Fig. 2.1. WHO Healthy Cities network phase III (1998–2002) in the WHO European region

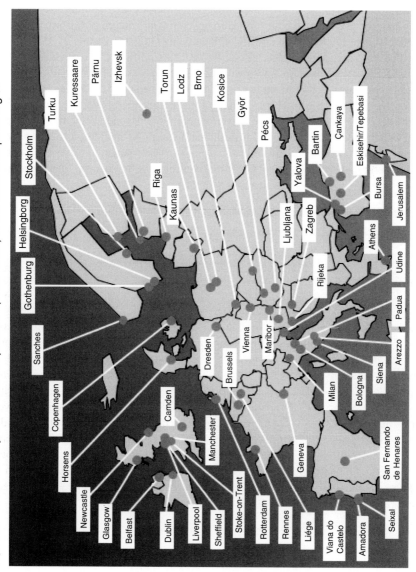

Turku
Kuressaare
Pärnu
Izhevsk
Torun
Lodz
Brno
Kosice
Stockholm
Győr
Pécs
Bartin
Çankaya
Eskisehir/Tepebasi
Helsingborg
Riga
Kaunas
Yalova
Bursa
Gothenburg
Ljubljana
Zagreb
Jerusalem
Sanches
Athens
Rijeka
Udine
Copenhagen
Dresden
Vienna
Maribor
Padua
Arezzo
Horsens
Brussels
Siena
Camden
Milan
Bologna
Newcastle
Manchester
Geneva
San Fernando
de Henares
Glasgow
Belfast
Dublin
Liverpool
Sheffield
Stoke-on-Trent
Rotterdam
Rennes
Liége
Viana do
Castelo
Amadora
Seixal

1993). Thirty-nine cities were involved in the second phase (1993–7) of WHO project cities, including thirteen that had not participated in such a network in Phase I. This phase was more action-oriented with a strong emphasis on healthy public policy and comprehensive city health planning (WHO Healthy Cities Project Office 1993). The third phase (1998–2002) involved 55 cities. Its main aim was partnership-based policies and a plan for health development with emphasis on equity and the social determinants of health and strategic links to local Agenda 21, community development and regeneration initiatives (WHO Centre for Urban Health 1997). Phase III was supported by a political declaration, the Athens Declaration, and was founded on a set of criteria and requirements which provided the basis for assessing and designating applicant cities. These criteria are grouped under the four strategic elements of Healthy Cities action: political commitment (endorsement of principles and strategies); mechanisms and institutional reforms to support partnership work, community engagement and to manage change (establishment of project infrastructures); strategic and integrated planning (commitment to specific goals, products

Fig. 2.2.   National Healthy Cities networks in the WHO European region

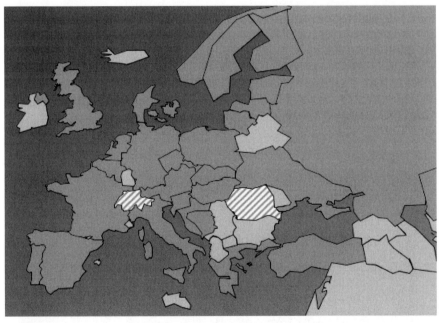

Key:

◼   Countries with national Healthy Cities networks

▨   Countries with developing national Healthy Cities networks

☐   Countries with no national Healthy Cities networks

and outcomes); and active networking (investment in formal and informal networking and cooperation). It should be noted that from the outset the implementation and the further development of Healthy Cities work was founded on a very strong political presence and involvement.

THE ATHENS DECLARATION

The Athens Declaration provides the policy and strategic framework for the third phase of Healthy Cities. It was signed at the Athens Conference in 1998 by the mayors and senior politicians from 110 European cities and it was endorsed by the members of the Regional Committee of the European Office of WHO. The Declaration has since then been translated into fifteen languages and signed by several hundreds of mayors in thirty European countries. Box 2.1 presents extracts from the Athens Declaration.

Box 2.1.   The Athens Healthy Cities Declaration

[Extracts]
We the Mayors and Senior Politicians attending the International Healthy Cities Conference in Athens, June 1998 ...

We now understand better how health in the urban environment is determined by social and economic conditions and also by gender, age and ethnicity. We know that health should never be the exclusive concern of any one political party or professional discipline. We are aware that health must become a vital element in the core values and mainstream plans of our cities.

We will create the preconditions for change and commit our cities to these specific actions for health through leadership and empowerment; through partnerships and infrastructures for change; through integrated planning for health and sustainable development; as well as through networks. We pledge to assist in taking the health for all approach beyond cities to rural areas, localities, provinces, regions and other levels of sub-national government.

1. **Leadership and empowerment**
    We pledge to make equity, health and sustainable development central values in our vision for the development of our cities. We will give political commitment and strong leadership to bring together and implement strategies for health for all and local

agenda 21, paying particular attention to the need to provide leadership opportunities for women and minority groups. We will mobilize people and resources to attain Healthy City goals and fully engage local communities.

2. **Partnerships and infrastructures for change**
    We will support strategic city-wide alliances for health and sustainable development involving the public, voluntary and private sectors. This cooperation should involve other agencies including universities. We will put in place adequate support structures to coordinate and support work towards the goals of the Healthy City Project. Access to public health expertise should be ensured through the maintenance of an appropriate public health infrastructure at local level.

3. **Integrated planning for health and sustainable development**
    Drawing on relevant expertise, we will develop city health development policies, strategies and plans that set out to improve the social, environmental and economic determinants of health, setting targets and timetables for improving health while acknowledging the special contribution of each sector of city life and every agent of change. We will especially address issues related to: health needs of children and young people, women, ethnic minority groups and older people; links between poverty and health; needs of populations at risk; dangers which arise from tobacco abuse, addiction to drugs and alcohol, pollution, and violence; and other concerns connected to urban planning, ecological management and social support.

4. **Networks**
    We give a specific commitment to phase III of the WHO Healthy Cities Project as a project city or national network city. At the local, national, regional and international levels, we will contribute as active members to strategic alliances for promoting health for all and sustainable development into the twenty-first century. We will work in cooperation with international bodies involved in tackling the problems faced by cities. Active support for the European Cities and Towns Campaign, in cooperation with other major networks and associations, will provide a further opportunity to advance the goals of Healthy Cities Project and promote the agenda of health for all and sustainability.

5. Monitoring and evaluation

We will monitor closely the impact of actions taken as a result of the adoption of the Healthy Cities philosophy and ensure that both processes and outcomes are evaluated against health targets. The Healthy Cities project has played a major role in uncovering the determinants of health and has an important role to play in promoting and publicizing effective ways of reducing health inequalities and improving the quality of life for all.

Action by others

Cities cannot act alone. Within the European Region, the national and regional governments of Member States have a key role to play. They influence the pace and sustainability of modernization, industrialization and the pattern of urban development. They also provide the legislative and fiscal framework for health.

We therefore **call on national governments** within the European Region:

- to recognize the importance of the local dimension of national health policies and acknowledge that cities can make a significant contribution to national strategies for Health For All and Agenda 21;
- to use, in their national health strategies. the experience and insights of cities in analysing and responding to local health conditions using intersectoral approaches;
- to examine ways in which additional resources could be made available in support of Health For All and sustainable development policies;
- to support national networks of healthy cities in their coordinating and capacity-building role; and
- to encourage the participation of local government representatives in Member States' delegations to meetings of WHO's governing bodies and other relevant international fora.

Welcoming the development of the WHO European Centre for Urban Health, **we look to the WHO Regional Office for Europe:**

- to provide leadership and strategic support in work towards the goals of phase III (1998–2002) of the WHO Healthy Cities Project;
- to promote capacity-building and networking for healthy cities in all Member States of the European Region, especially those that

have not been involved so far in the movement, including the Newly Independent States and Member States in the Balkan region;
- to provide technical support and guidance for better integrated city health planning, evaluation and monitoring;
- to promote and encourage the development of local action components in all of WHO's technical areas; and
- to promote synergy between sectors and settings, harmonizing the skills and experience of local and national governments.

We are convinced that the combined efforts of local, regional and national governments and of WHO will bring about changes that will substantially improve the health and well being of our citizens.

Source: WHO, Regional Office for Europe, Athens Declaration of Healthy Cities (endorsed at the Athens International Healthy Cities Conference), 23 June 1998

PHASE III REQUIREMENTS

Cities are designated to the WHO network on the basis of specific requirements. In their applications they are asked to provide evidence of political commitment, adequate capacity and resources and a number of preconditions relating to the way they address the health of their population. The full Phase III package also includes explanatory comments on each of the requirements and details on the eligibility and designation process. The Phase III requirements are:

A   Endorsement of principles and strategies
- Cities must have sustained local government support and support from key decision-makers in other sectors to the principles and goals of the project.
- Cities must have in place mechanisms which ensure an integrative approach to health planning, with links being made between their health policies and other key city-wide strategies, and their health strategies and city-based work on Agenda 21.
- Cities should develop policies and strategies based on health for all for the twenty-first century. Particular emphasis should be placed on the three issues of 1) reducing inequalities in health, 2) working to achieve social development, and 3) commitment to sustainable development.
- Cities should select *at least one* additional target of health for all for the twenty-first century, which has particular local importance. Progress towards this target should be carefully monitored.

B   Establishment of project infrastructures

- Cities must have an intersectoral steering group involving political/ executive-level decision-makers.
- Cities must have a full-time identified project coordinator or equivalent and administrative/technical support for the project. The project coordinator must have proven fluency in English.
- Cities must identify and give commitment to the package of resources required to implement the strategies and action plans for Phase III.
- Cities should review project management processes and implement a programme of action to address identified weaknesses.
- Cities should demonstrate increased public participation in the decision-making processes that affect health in the city, thereby contributing to the empowerment of local people.
- Cities should establish mechanisms for the engagement of the business sector in local action for health, at both policy and operational levels.
- Cities should implement a communications strategy, involving a range of communications mechanisms, to stimulate visibility for health issues and public health debate within the city; this strategy should be evaluated to assess its impact; *and/or*
- Cities should implement an ongoing programme of training or capacity-building activities for health and healthy public policy-making; this programme should have two strands: involving key decision-makers across the different sectors in the city, and involving local communities and opinion leaders; the impact of this programme should be evaluated.

C   Commitment to specific goals, products and outcomes

- Cities must produce and implement a city health development plan during the third phase, which builds on previous integrative city health planning and reflects the values, principles and objectives of health for all for the twenty-first century and Local Agenda 21; relevant national health strategies; and local city-specific priorities. This plan must have clear long term and short term aims and objectives and a system on how the city will monitor whether these objectives have been met (indicators and evaluation framework). The city health development plan should take a broad perspective so that actions taken in different sectors, at different levels and by various players hang together to provide an integrated approach to health and development. Its added value is integration and the mobilisation of the total resources of society for health development. It should be people-focused and tackle the determinants of health.
- Cities should implement a programme of systematic health monitoring and evaluation, integrated with the city health development plan, to assess the health, environmental and social impact of policies within the city. In addition, cities should strengthen health accountability mechanisms and measures.

- Cities should implement a programme of action targeted at reducing health inequalities within the city.
- Cities should carry out a programme of action to promote healthy and sustainable urban planning policies and practice within the city.
- Cities should develop and implement a tobacco control strategy, in line with WHO's identification of tobacco as a strategic priority.
- Cities should implement and evaluate a comprehensive programme of activity to address *at least one* of the following priority topics: social exclusion, healthy settings, healthy transport, children, older people, addictions, civil and domestic violence, accidents.

D   *Investment in formal and informal networking and cooperation*

- Cities must give executive and political commitment for the attendance of the project coordinator and nominated politician at WHO business meetings and symposia. At each, the city should be represented, as a minimum, by the coordinator and politician responsible.
- Cities should ensure that their mayor (or lead politician) attends the mayors' meetings at start of the phase (1998) and midway through it (in the year 2000).
- Cities should be connected to the Internet and electronic mail, and ideally should have access to video-conferencing facilities.
- Cities should participate actively in different networking activities (thematic, sub-regional, strategic, twinning, etc.) during the phase, including the development of close links with national networks. Cities should demonstrate practical contributions to these networks throughout the phase.

EPILOGUE

The road to intersectoral and integrated policy and strategic planning is lengthy and complex. Factors such as local organisational culture, remit for health, ability to manage and provide leadership are very important in this process. Cities are at different starting points when they join the Healthy Cities movement. In broad terms progress with the WHO Healthy Cities project could be described as a sequence of five stages.

Achieving a higher stage does not preclude parallel activities that would correspond to a lower one. However, the cities joining Phase III had to show evidence of a general approach to health corresponding at least to stage 3. Throughout Phase III WHO cities, represented by their politicians and coordinators, met approximately every eight months to discuss progress, to exchange experiences, to debate and learn new concepts and methods and to develop strategies for the future. Networking has proven to be a very effective means for accelerated development, capacity building and legitimisation of the process of change and innovation.

Box 2.2.   Implementing the Healthy Cities approach: Five stages describing progress from traditional to advanced approaches

Stage 1: *Focus*: Health education and disease prevention activities mainly within the health sector.
Approach: Traditional public health.

Stage 2: *Focus*: Increased volume of disease prevention and limited number of health promotion activities. New actors involved.
Approach: Traditional public health.

Stage 3: *Focus*: Health promotion and disease prevention programmes drawing on the contribution of more sectors. Community involvement.
Approach: Application of strategy health for all and health promotion principles.
Lack of strategic links between activities and sectors.

Stage 4: *Focus*: The policy jump. Health explicitly on policy agenda. Inequalities begin to be addressed. City health strategies and plans based on limited inter-sectoral input.
Approach: Emphasis on: policy, health determinants, the needs of vulnerable and socially disadvantaged groups, partnerships for health.

Stage 5: *Focus*: The development of integrated health policies and plans with broad inter-sectoral input.
Approach: Health and sustainable development become core values in city policies and long term plans. Emphasis on accountability, inequalities, health determinants and the positive aspects of health.

Source: Tsouros 1998

WHO drawing on the expertise and experience of its academic and city partners developed and provided the network with guidance and tools to support the implementation process (e.g. Wilkinson and Marmot 1998; WHO 2001; Barton and Tsourou 2000; WHO 1997; WHO 2002; Danish National Institute of Public Health 2001). Last but not least the Phase III evaluation is focused on the following themes: partnerships for health; action for equity and social determinants of health; community participation; city health development planning; links to other initiatives; impact on structures and processes; and the overall impact of Healthy Cities. The results of the evaluation will be presented at the International Healthy Cities Conference in Belfast in October 2003.

References

Barton, H. and Tsourou, C. (2000) *Healthy Urban Planning*. London and New York: Spon Press, 184.

Danish National Institute of Public Health (2001) *Analysis of Baseline Healthy Cities Indicators*. Copenhagen: WHO, 50.

Draper, R. *et al.* (1993) *WHO Healthy Cities Project: Review of the First Five Years (1987–1992): a Working Tool and a Reference Framework for Evaluating the Project*. Copenhagen: WHO Regional Office for Europe, 137.

Tsouros, A. (1998) Urban health and healthy cities: WHO's plans for the future. *Eurohealth*, 4(2), Spring.

World Health Organisation (WHO) (1997) *City Planning for Health and Sustainable Development*. European Sustainable Development and Health Series: 2, Copenhagen: WHO European Commission (DG Environment), 106.

WHO (2001) *A Working Tool on City Health Development Planning (Concept, Process, Structure and Content)*. Copenhagen: WHO, 24.

WHO (2002) *Community Participation in Local Health and Sustainable Development*. European Sustainable Development and Health Series: 4, Copenhagen: WHO European Commission (DG Environment), 94.

WHO/Centre for Urban Health (1997) *WHO Healthy Cities Project: Phase III: 1998–2002 – the Requirements and the Designation Process for WHO Project Cities*. Copenhagen: WHO Regional Office for Europe.

WHO Healthy Cities Project Office (1993) *Setting Standards for WHO Project Cities: the Requirements and the Designation Process for WHO Project Cities. WHO Healthy Cities Project Phase II (1993–1997)*. Copenhagen: WHO Regional Office for Europe.

Wilkinson, R. and Marmot, M. (1998) *Social Determinants of Health: The Solid Facts*. Copenhagen: WHO Regional Office for Europe/Centre for Urban Health.

For further information on the European Healthy Cities Programme:
<www.euro.who.int/ healthy-cities>

Chapter 3

Healthy Cities Project in the Western Pacific

Hisashi Ogawa

URBAN HEALTH PROBLEMS

Urbanisation

As was stressed in such United Nations conferences as the Earth Summit in Rio de Janeiro in 1992, the Population Summit in Cairo in 1995, and the Habitat II City Summit in Istanbul in 1996, the rapid growth of urban populations has become a worldwide concern. The global population has increased from 2.5 billion in 1950 to 3.7 billion in 1970 and 6 billion in the year 2000 (United Nations 2000). The percentage of urban population has also increased over the last 50 years. In 1950, only 30 per cent of total population lived in urban settings, but in 1995 some 2.6 billion people lived in cities and towns. This represents 45 per cent of total world population. Of the 2.6 billion urban dwellers, about two-thirds, or 1.6 billion people, live in developing countries. Out of this 1.6 billion urban population, 600 million people (or 30 per cent) live in a severe life-threatening environment.

In the Western Pacific Region, the total population grew from 736 million in 1950, to 1.09 billion in 1970 and to 1.6 billion in 1995. The urban population was only 17 per cent of the total population in 1950, but grew to 25 per cent in 1970 and 37 per cent in 1995. It is estimated that by the year 2020 more than half of the total population in the Western Pacific Region will live in urban areas.

Economic and industrial development usually accelerates the urbanisation process. Rapid economic growth creates various opportunities for employment, education, cultural experiences and services. These opportunities attract people to cities. In turn, the concentration of people in cities brings together a range of skills and new ideas, leading to improvements in the economic performance of the cities. As a result, the urban population increases further. Population growth in a city is therefore often regarded as a positive development. However, the benefits and problems of urbanisation are not equally shared by city dwellers. Urban growth has affected different groups of people in the city in different ways.

Urban health problems and challenges

Urban growth in developing countries has brought about a complex situation with respect to health service delivery. Health care facilities and services are concentrated in cities, but their quality and accessibility vary greatly from one district to another and from one income group to another. Low-income groups usually have less access to better quality health services than their high-income counterparts. As a result, health indicators, such as infant mortality rates, of low-income groups are often much worse than those of wealthier groups. For example, in Metro Manila, the Philippines, the infant mortality rate among low-income groups is almost three times higher than that of their high-income counterparts.

In urban areas the poor are exposed to various health hazards. Insufficient and inadequate housing and urban infrastructure lead to unhygienic conditions. Many people, even in industrialised countries, are unable to find a home at all. An insufficient and unsafe water supply is often a problem for poor communities, as are inadequate sewage disposal and poor drainage. There is often no garbage collection. Even in areas where garbage collection is provided, services are often irregular and unreliable. These unhygienic conditions allow infectious diseases such as tuberculosis, influenza, typhoid, cholera, and dengue fever to be transmitted easily within poorer communities and to other groups, including high-income populations, within the city. Inadequate housing and urban infrastructure is particularly acute in many cities of developing countries in the region, such as Cambodia, the Lao People's Democratic Republic, Mongolia, the Philippines and Viet Nam.

Many manufacturing enterprises, particularly small-scale or cottage industry, are located in cities of developing countries. The occupational environment of these factories is often unsafe and hazardous to workers' health. Poor layout of facilities and machines and increased use of potentially toxic chemicals cause accidental injuries and deaths to workers as well as acute or chronic conditions. In addition to their occupational health and safety problems, these factories cause air, water and noise pollution.

Air pollution is becoming a major problem in many large cities in the region. The main sources of air pollution are the energy, transportation and industrial sectors. In northern China and Mongolia air pollutants from coal-fired power plants and the burning of coal for domestic cooking and heating cause particular problems. Motor vehicle emissions, such as particulate matter from diesel-engine vehicles and lead from leaded gasoline, are a major health hazard in cities like Manila. In the Klang Valley, which includes Kuala Lumpur, the majority of the particulate matter emissions are not from vehicular emissions, but from industrial sources, including power plants. The balance differs greatly from city to city and each city must take appropriate measures to deal with its own pollution problem.

Increased traffic in urban areas also causes noise pollution and road accidents. Some cities, such as Kuala Lumpur and Manila, have introduced systems to limit the traffic of large vehicles to certain hours of the day. The transition to the market economy in Cambodia, the Lao People's Democratic Republic and Viet Nam has led to an enormous increase in the number of motorcycles and a consequent growth in injuries and deaths from road accidents.

In addition to these changes in the physical environment, urban dwellers in the region have experienced considerable changes in their social environments. Urban violence, crime, and substance and sexual abuse, often a symptom of stress, have increased significantly in recent years.

The different health concerns of the urban rich and the urban poor are strikingly evident in the field of nutrition. While many of the urban poor suffer from nutritional deficiency, other city dwellers worry about obesity and unbalanced diets. The lack of physical exercise and insufficient sleep are common among busy office workers. Other health issues, such as smoking tobacco, affect rich and poor. Despite the efforts of various organisations, including the World Health Organisation (WHO), cigarette smoking and advertisements for cigarettes persist. Unhealthy lifestyles are a major cause of non-communicable diseases among urban dwellers.

The list of challenges posed by urbanisation is therefore a long one, ranging from the need to improve the living environment, in particular the supply of sufficient and safe drinking water, to urban inequities, traffic and unhealthy behaviour patterns.

Approaches to solving urban health problems

How are we to solve this long list of complex problems? Most of all, we need a change of attitude. In the past, government departments, international organisations and individuals have been too focused on their own interests. Government ministries pursued their own agendas, paying little regard to the interests of the nation as a whole. Likewise, international organisations were also too concerned with their own mandates.

It is obvious that many of the determinants of health in urban areas are not under the direct control of the health services. This is particularly true for urban problems associated with the living environment. The health sector must therefore work with the housing sector to improve the safety and conditions of houses, with the transport sector to control air and noise pollution and traffic accidents, with industry to implement programmes of occupational health and safety, and so on. One clear lesson from the urbanisation of the region is that health professionals need to learn to work more effectively with professionals of other sectors.

'Health' needs to be everyone's business, not just that of the health professionals. We must remove the barriers that separate us. Health is the responsibility of individuals, community, government and private companies. Attitudes and lifestyles must also be changed, and healthy living needs to be promoted.

The Healthy Cities approach generates intersectoral action and community participation in identifying and solving priority health problems in urban areas by addressing the physical and social health determinants. In countries of the Western Pacific Region, about 180 cities are currently implementing Healthy Cities projects. Some of these countries are economically less developed, with a lack of basic infrastructure to support safe and healthy urban living. In other countries the basic urban infrastructure is more or less in place, but lifestyle-related ill health is a growing problem. Urban development varies from city to city, and therefore there is a need for each city to identify its own priority health problems and develop and implement its own solutions. The following section outlines how the Healthy Cities programme in the Western Pacific Region has been developed over the years.

OVERVIEW OF HEALTHY CITIES IN THE WESTERN PACIFIC

Since the late 1980s when Australia, Japan and New Zealand embarked on their Healthy Cities projects, several more countries in the Western Pacific Region have joined the Healthy Cities movement. These countries include Cambodia, China, Lao People's Democratic Republic, Malaysia, Mongolia, Republic of Korea, the Philippines, and Viet Nam. Countries like Fiji and Papua New Guinea consider joining the movement. Currently about 180 Healthy Cities projects are implemented in the region. These projects share some common features in developing and implementing Healthy Cities projects (e.g. intersectoral collaboration and community participation). However, they also display a diversity of priority health issues that they address, reflecting the different states of economic development, physical environments, political/administrative systems, and social and cultural norms of the cities.

Countries in the Western Pacific Region promote the healthy settings approach through other settings (e.g. islands, schools, workplaces, marketplaces, villages/communities, hospitals, etc.). Healthy Islands initiatives have been developed, following the Meeting of the Ministers of Health in the Pacific in Fiji in 1995. Almost all countries in the region have initiated health-promoting schools projects. Healthy workplaces have been initiated in several countries and regional guidelines have been developed. Similarly, healthy marketplaces, healthy hospitals and healthy villages/communities projects have been initiated in some countries. The experiences of these initiatives were reviewed at the WHO Meeting on Health Protection and Health Promotion: Harmonizing Our Responses to the Challenges of the 21st Century, in August 1999. The meeting also recommended that the integration of these healthy settings into Healthy Cities projects should be promoted.

Since 1994, WHO has:

- convened technical review workshops on Healthy Cities (Johor Bahru in 1995; Beijing in 1996; Malacca in 1999; and Johor Bahru in 2001);
- documented the experiences in developing Healthy Cities projects;
- worked with training/education institutions to offer training courses on Healthy Cities (four-week course by the National Institute of Public Administration in Malaysia with financial support of the Japan International

Cooperation Agency; one-week course by the Flinders University in South Australia; and one-week and two-week courses by the Tokyo Medical and Dental University in Japan);

• published regional guidelines for developing a Healthy Cities project in June 2000;

• developed and maintained a regional database on Healthy Cities projects and made it available on WHO website;

• formulated with member states a regional action plan for 2000–03 at the regional workshop in Malacca in October 1999.

In recent years, the focus of WHO activities has been shifted to the development of practical evaluation methodologies for Healthy Cities projects and collaboration with member states in implementing the regional action plan. In October 2001, WHO convened another regional workshop to review and evaluate the progress made in implementing the regional action plan; to review case studies on evaluation methodologies for Healthy Cities projects; and to discuss future directions in promoting the Healthy Cities approach.

The following sections illustrate details of the development of Healthy Cities in the Western Pacific, the framework for developing a regional network, and findings of the recent regional workshops.

DEVELOPMENT OF HEALTHY CITIES IN THE WESTERN PACIFIC

In the beginning

In the late 1980s to early 1990s, a number of Healthy City projects were initiated in industrialised countries mainly in Europe and North America. In the Western Pacific Region, Australia, Japan and New Zealand joined this movement. The Australian pilot project was implemented in Noarlunga, Canberra and Illawarra from 1987 to 1990 (Whelan *et al.* 1992). Tokyo started to put the idea into practice in the late 1980s, and the Tokyo Metropolitan Government launched a Healthy Cities project in 1991 with the establishment of Tokyo Citizens Council for Health Promotion (Nakamura and Takano 1992). The Japanese Ministry of Health and Welfare also launched a nationwide programme, called Health Culture Cities, in 1993. In New Zealand the concept of Healthy Cities was used in Manakau to develop the first Healthy Communities project in 1988 (Randle and Hutt 1997).

During the same period, the WHO Regional Office for the Western Pacific began a series of consultative meetings on urban health issues with experts from its member states. The intention was to address not just urban health issues in industrialised countries, but also those in developing countries in the region that were facing more formidable challenges in protecting and enhancing health of urban dwellers. This coincided with discussions at the World Health Assembly in

May 1991 that produced a resolution agreeing on the need for developing pro-
grammes to prevent and control the adverse health effects of rapidly growing
urban areas (WHO 1991). In 1991 alone, the WHO Regional Office for the
Western Pacific convened four regional meetings (the Working Group on
Integration of Environmental Health into Planning for Urban Development,
February 1991, Kuala Lumpur; the Working Group on Urban Health
Development, September 1991, Osaka; the Western Pacific Advisory Committee
on Health Research, Subcommittee on Health Promotion, October 1991, Manila;
and the Consultative Group on Health and Environment, November 1991,
Manila) that addressed urban heath issues, among other things.

The results of these regional meetings were summarised in a document entitled
Technical Discussions on a Healthy Urban Environment, which was the subject of
a technical discussion conducted in conjunction with the forty-third session of the
Regional Committee for the Western Pacific, held in Hong Kong in September
1992 (WHO 1992). The Regional Committee endorsed this WHO initiative to
promote urban health development activities in the region.

Initiating Healthy Cities projects in developing countries

Following the endorsement of the Regional Committee, the WHO Regional
Office for the Western Pacific initiated city-specific urban health development
activities in selected developing countries in the region. In August 1993, WHO
convened a Bi-regional Meeting on Urban Health Development in Manila, involving participants from selected cities in the WHO South-East and Western Pacific
Regions (WHO 1993). The participants discussed the promotion of urban health
development programmes in their cities, and prepared project proposals for
resolving specific urban health issues.

Building on the outcome of the Bi-regional Meeting, towards the end of 1993
WHO developed a more broadly-scoped project proposal designed to involve
selected cities as model cases and the Ministry of Health as a national focal point
to coordinate and facilitate various Healthy Cities-type activities. This generic
proposal was discussed with the governments of China, Malaysia and Viet Nam,
and more country-specific proposals were developed and endorsed by the respective governments in early 1994. The Healthy Urban China project and the Healthy
Urban Malaysia project commenced in the third quarter of 1994, as well as the
project in Viet Nam which focused on the integration of health and environment
considerations into planning for sustainable development.

Expanding the Healthy Cities movement

In 1995, the WHO Western Pacific Regional Office and the United Nations
Development Programme (UNDP)/World Bank/United Nations Centre for
Human Settlements (UNCHS) Urban Management Programme Regional Office
for Asia and the Pacific conducted a regional workshop on urban health and environmental management. At the workshop, experiences in implementing Healthy

Cities projects in China, Malaysia and Viet Nam were presented and shared with participants from other countries in Asia and the Pacific.

From 1996, Cambodia, the Lao People's Democratic Republic, Mongolia and the Republic of Korea have initiated Healthy Cities projects, while the Philippines initiated three Healthy Cities projects in Metro Manila, and Fiji and Papua New Guinea joined to initiate Healthy Cities activities in 1999.

In 1997, WHO designated the Department of Public Health and Environmental Science of Tokyo Medical and Dental University as the WHO Collaborating Centre for Healthy Cities and Urban Policy to strengthen the Healthy Cities work in the region.

Since 1997, the learning and exchanging of information on Healthy Cities has been promoted by organising study tours and short courses. The study tours have been undertaken for Healthy Cities practitioners in Cambodia, China, the Lao People's Democratic Republic, Mongolia, the Philippines and Viet Nam to visit Australia, Japan and Malaysia, and for Malaysian practitioners to visit Australia and Japan. In 1997, a short course on environmental management for health in urban areas was conducted at the WHO Collaborating Centre in Environmental Health in the University of Western Sydney at Hawkesbury. Since 1993, a one-week course on Healthy Cities and Communities has been offered at the Flinders University of South Australia, and attended by participants from developing countries in the region. The National Institute of Public Administration, Malaysia (INTAN) with funding from the Japan International Cooperation Agency (JICA) and in cooperation with the WHO Western Pacific Regional Office has offered the INTAN/JICA/WHO international course on the promotion of healthy environ-ment in urban areas (Healthy Cities programme) since 1999. The WHO Collaborating Centre at the Tokyo Medical and Dental University has also offered two short courses (one week and two weeks) on Healthy Cities since 2001. WHO has supported these courses which have been attended by participants from devel-oping countries in the region.

WHO has also facilitated the learning and sharing of experiences by organis-ing regional meetings. In October 1996, the first regional consultation on Healthy Cities was held in Beijing, China, and the early efforts of Healthy Cities projects in the region were presented (WHO 1997a). WHO has organised two more regional workshops on Healthy Cities: one in Malacca, Malaysia in October 1999 and the other in Johor Bahru, Malaysia in October 2001. The outcomes of these regional workshops will be elaborated on later in this chapter.

As a result of the Malacca workshop, regional guidelines for developing a Healthy Cities project (WHO 2000a) and a regional action plan on Healthy Cities for 2000–03 (see Box 3.1 on page 28) were prepared. WHO has also published case studies on selected Healthy Cities projects and a regional Healthy Cities projects database. All these documents are made available on the WHO website (<www.wpro.who.int>), to facilitate dissemination and sharing of information and experiences.

Box 3.1.   Regional action plan on Healthy Cities for 2000–03

To strengthen capacity in implementation of Healthy Cities projects

National action

1. An appropriate structure should be established or designated to coordinate Healthy Cities actions within countries. This structure should vary according to the particular needs of the country. The structure would maximize collaboration between Healthy Cities projects within countries and become a focal point for WHO liaison and liaison with Healthy Cities projects in other countries.
2. The national coordinating structure should develop national guidelines that are based on the WHO Western Pacific Regional Office's regional guidelines for Healthy Cities.
3. The national Healthy Cities coordinating structure should provide technical support, including training; encourage networking and information exchange between cities through meetings, newsletters, Internet, workshops, study visits; assist with building awareness about the benefits of the Healthy Cities approach; encourage and support monitoring and evaluation of Healthy Cities projects; work with universities to develop appropriate research methodologies, including participatory research for Healthy Cities; and maintain an effective database of Healthy Cities projects within the countries.
4. The national Healthy Cities coordinating structure should provide seed funding to kick start projects, and to encourage other agencies to provide resources for local Healthy Cities projects and to integrate their activities within Healthy Cities projects.
5. The national Healthy Cities coordinating structure should prepare an annual report on the progress in implementing Healthy Cities projects within the country and present this to the WHO Western Pacific Regional Office.
6. The national Healthy Cities coordinating structure should advocate to national and provincial governments and relevant national and international partner organizations, including WHO, for the establishment of policies that promote the Healthy Cities approach.

International community

1. Training and professional development opportunities should be provided for coordinators and staff of Healthy Cities projects to develop skills in:
   - leadership and management, including working across sectors and with communities
   - securing political commitment
   - implementation and sustainability of the projects
   - evaluation and research methodologies.
2. Information sharing and networking between national and city projects should be facilitated by meetings, workshops, newsletters, Internet, country visits and a regional database.
3. Research and evaluation projects should be supported to establish evaluation methodologies and indicators to demonstrate the benefits that accrue from Healthy Cities projects.
4. Awareness of the Healthy Cities concept should be promoted among international development agencies to encourage them to fund Healthy Cities initiatives.
5. Regional guidelines should be produced and revised periodically.
6. A global Healthy Cities summit should be organized every three years.

To develop mechanisms for advocacy, communication and networking

National action

1. A national network of Healthy Cities projects should be created using appropriate communication technology in the country.
2. Opportunities should be created for direct exchange between Healthy Cities projects, including study tours, twinning programs and national meetings.
3. A database on Healthy Cities projects at national level should be established.
4. The city health profiles of Healthy Cities projects should be publicized to raise awareness about the health and environmental situation of the cities and develop more effective intersectoral collaboration and planning.

International community

1. An international information network should be developed to link persons and organizations involved in Healthy Cities programs, in form of Internet facility, website, mailing list, etc.
2. Opportunities should be created for direct exchanges between Healthy Cities projects, including study tours, twinning programs, regional meetings, etc.
3. A database on models of good practices should be created and updated regularly.
4. The following channels of communication may be used to enhance the communication among Healthy Cities:
    – newsletters
    – documentation of annual reports.

To set up systems that ensure the sustainability of projects and programs

National action

1. The Healthy City Plan should be integrated into long-term national planning and should have links with other development plans such as urban development, tourism, housing and agriculture.
2. The national coordinating structure should liaise with all relevant Ministries and departments at the national level in supporting Healthy Cities projects. The national coordinating structures should support the state/provincial governments to monitor and evaluate the activities at the state/provincial level.

    Non-government organizations and the private sector should be encouraged to participate in Healthy Cities projects at all levels. This is to obtain sponsorships from the private sector and develop local projects that are revenue generating.
3. The documentation from local city projects should be shared to improve awareness of Healthy Cities projects among leaders and practitioners.
4. The national coordinating structure should emphasize local ownership and show that the project is beneficial to the local community.
5. Countries should consider developing legislation to allocate part of benefits accrued to urban development activities to Healthy Cities projects.

International community

1. The international community should undertake research on Healthy Cities projects and should promote and support collaboration with countries in terms of developing effective policy instruments, quantifying benefits and documenting standards for enforcement. There should be strong emphasis on monitoring and evaluation.
2. There should be a system of disseminating guidelines produced by WHO and other international partner agencies to countries.
3. Regional proposals for sustainable financing of Healthy Cities projects should be developed. A number of countries could come together and develop a regional proposal to support Healthy Cities projects.
4. Many international agencies (e.g. UNDP, UNCHS, World Bank, etc.) are involved in urban developments and should play a more active role in Healthy Cities.

Source: WHO 2000b

WHO has participated in Healthy Cities conferences organised by other organisations. WHO collaborated with CityNet (a network of local governments in Asia and the Pacific) in providing a session on Healthy Cities during their meeting. WHO co-sponsored two international conferences on Healthy Cities organised in Tokyo and Canberra in 2000, and participated in the first Association of South East Asian Nations (ASEAN) conference on Healthy Cities in 2002.

Developing related healthy settings

While Healthy Cities activities were being developed, other 'healthy settings' activities were developed.

The Ministerial Conference on Health for the Pacific Islands, held in Fiji in March 1995, adopted 'Healthy Islands' as the approach to building healthy populations and communities in the Pacific region and produced the Yanuca Island Declaration on Health in the Pacific in the twenty-first Century (WHO 1995). The ministers revisited the Yanuca Island Declaration and re-affirmed their commitment to this approach at their meeting in Rarotonga, Cook Islands in 1997 (WHO 1997b). The progress of developing and implementing Healthy Islands initiatives was reviewed at the ministers' meeting in Palau in 1999, and the ministers endorsed the further expansion of this regional initiative (WHO 1999a). The ministers' meeting in Madang, Papua New Guinea in 2001 endorsed a regional action plan on Healthy Islands for 2001–05 (WHO 2001a). Regional guidelines on Healthy Islands were published in 2002 (WHO 2002).

Since the mid-1990s, 'elemental healthy settings' (e.g. schools, workplaces, hospitals, marketplaces, villages/communities) projects have been developed and implemented in member states. Almost all countries in the Western Pacific Region implement health-promoting schools, while some countries are developing projects on other elemental healthy settings mostly as pilot projects. Since 1997, the integration of elemental healthy settings in Healthy Cities and Healthy Islands projects has been promoted in the region. To support these activities, WHO has produced regional guidelines on healthy workplaces and health-promoting schools, and is preparing regional guidelines on healthy marketplaces.

The WHO Meeting on Health Protection and Health Promotion: Harmonizing Our Responses to the Challenges of the 21st Century was convened in August 1999. The meeting reviewed various healthy settings initiatives in the region and developed a regional action plan for Healthy Settings (WHO 1999b).

FRAMEWORK FOR DEVELOPING A REGIONAL NETWORK ON HEALTHY CITIES PROJECTS

Roles of national government and WHO

A Healthy Cities project is successful and sustainable only when people and the local government make a commitment to the improvement of their health and quality of life and mobilise their own resources and apply their innovative ideas to develop and implement the project. It is, therefore, essential that the initiative of developing a Healthy Cities project must come from the city itself.

The national government also plays an important role in the development of Healthy Cities projects. Their role is to support the development and implementation of these projects by:

- providing useful information, guidelines/guidance and technical advisory services (and to a limited extent, financial support in seed money) to cities interested in developing Healthy Cities projects;
- helping the city to evaluate and monitor the progress and effectiveness of the project implementation;
- facilitating the exchange of experiences (e.g. through national conferences) among the cities participating in the Healthy Cities programme in the country; and
- liaising with WHO to implement various inter-country activities (e.g. regional workshops/seminars; study tours; technical consultancy services; etc.).

In order to provide these supporting functions, the national government should establish a national intersectoral coordination body (e.g. task force, committee, etc.), with its coordinator, for the Healthy Cities programme. Such a coordination body should involve relevant government agencies (e.g. agencies responsible for health, the environment, local governments, urban planning, education, labour, commerce, industry, etc.); non-government organisations; and academia. It should also develop a national action plan for the Healthy Cities programme, and secure budget to implement it.

WHO's role is to facilitate the development of Healthy Cities projects and implement inter-country activities in collaboration with interested parties (e.g. other international partner agencies, non-government organisations, WHO Collaborating Centres, etc.). WHO also supports Healthy City projects directly or indirectly through the national government, by providing information, technical advisory services and limited seed money for applied studies on innovative approaches and local initiatives. In collaboration with countries in the region, WHO develops a regional action plan to facilitate the networking of Healthy Cities projects.

Mechanism for networking and supporting Healthy Cities projects

The structure of networking and supporting Healthy Cities projects is shown in Figure 3.1. The national coordinator is usually located in a section of the ministry of health in the country. However, in some countries there is no formally designated national coordinator, and communication is made directly from the local project coordinator to WHO. When more than one such project is implemented, it

Fig. 3.1.   Organisational structure of networking and supporting Healthy Cities projects in the Western Pacific Region

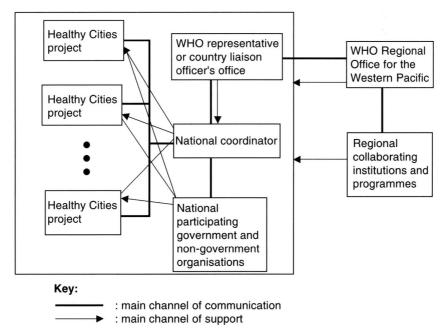

Key:

————— : main channel of communication
————▶   : main channel of support

is desirable to have a designated national coordinator in the country. Also, the national coordinator could be a government agency other than the ministry of health. A non-government organisation could be a national coordinator. However, the mobilisation of various resources for sustainable project implementation would usually be easier with a government agency than a non-government body, particularly in developing countries.

WHO representatives and country liaison officers in countries also play an important role in the implementation of Healthy Cities activities. They provide direct advice to the national coordinator and project cities on general aspects of Healthy Cities projects, and serve as a key link for communication with, and support from, the WHO Regional Office for the Western Pacific.

In addition to these institutions already mentioned, Figure 3.1 depicts other organisations which could provide valuable functions for networking and supporting Healthy Cities projects. At the national level, they include relevant government agencies and non-government organisations. At the regional level, WHO Collaborating Centres and universities actively involved in urban health issues provide their expertise. Programmes implemented by other international partner agencies and regional non-government organisations can cooperate with WHO in networking and supporting Healthy Cities projects. Such programmes and organisations include the United Nations Economic and Social Commission for Asia and the Pacific (ESCAP); UNDP/World Bank/UNCHS Urban Management Programme for Asia and Pacific; The Urban Governance Initiative (TUGI); CityNet; United Nations Environment Programme International Environmental Technology Centre (UNEP/IETC); JICA; WHO Centre for Health Development (WCK); etc.

MAIN OUTCOMES OF RECENT WHO REGIONAL WORKSHOPS

The current status of development of Healthy Cities programmes in the Western Pacific Region is best summarised in the outcomes of two recent regional workshops organised by WHO. As mentioned earlier in this chapter, the main findings of these regional workshops are summarised below.

The workshop in Malacca, Malaysia in October 1999 (WHO 2000b) concluded the following.

1. The Healthy Cities concept and approach have been generally accepted among cities and countries in the Western Pacific Region, especially within the health sector and local governments. The number of Healthy Cities projects in the region is growing. However, the stages of development of Healthy Cities initiatives vary from country to country and also within cities in the same country. This variation depends, to some extent, on the stage of socio-economic development of the country of concern. Because of this difference, the sharing of experiences among cities implementing Healthy Cities projects

in the region provides an excellent learning opportunity for them to strengthen their programmes.

2. The priority areas of concern, especially among developing countries, include basic sanitation, safe water supply, proper sewerage disposal, safe food and better living conditions. More developed countries noted social and lifestyle-related issues and industrial pollution as their priorities. Some suggested items for a city health profile and indicators for developing a Healthy Cities project are given in Box 3.2.

Box 3.2.   Suggested items for a city health profile and indicators for developing a Healthy Cities project

Topic	*Indicators*	
Demography and epidemiology	• Total population	• Disabilities
	• Age and sex breakdown	• Suicide rates/ occupational injury
	• Birth rate	• Perceptions of health and well-being
	• Fertility rate	
	• Death rate	• Individual risk factors
	• Morbidity rate	• Immunization rate
	• Communicable diseases	• Nutrition
		• Alcohol and drugs
	• Non-communicable disease	• Smoking
		• Exercise
	• Injuries/accidents	• Screening rates (cancer)
	• Crime	
City background	• History	• Climate
	• Culture	• Topography
Physical environment	• Environmental quality	• Soil
	• Air	• Scenery
	• Water	• Percentage green space/parks
	• Noise	
Living environment	• Access to safe drinking water	• Insects and rodent control
	• Adequacy of housing facility	• Sewage treatment
		• Waste treatment
	• Amount of living space	• Coverage of solid waste collection
	• Rates of homelessness	• Recycling
		• Food hygiene

Urban infrastructure	• Description of urban planning/zoning system • Main mode of transport • Availability of public transport • Availability of communication and information technology • Use of public media
Organizations and services	• Description of administrative structure of departments, districts and communities and local government • Description and assessment of the effectiveness of existing intersectoral coordinating mechanisms • Description of availability of: hospitals; community health facilities (maternal/child, disability, aged care); schools; community centres; sporting facilities; environmental health services (food inspector, standard of monitoring/enforcement)
Economic	• Assessment of impact of economy on health (main industries/business, health of economy, level of development)
Social	• Sources of social stress • Description of social support mechanisms/ networks (family/household, community, cultural, gender relations)
Legislation and regulations	• Disease prevention and control • Hospitals, schools, workplaces, markets, etc. • Food hygiene, building, housing • Drinking water, waste management • Air, water, noise, soil, etc.

3. There is a growing concern among the ongoing Healthy Cities projects to secure the sustainability of Healthy Cities projects. The evaluation of the effectiveness of Healthy Cities projects is also considered crucial to project sustainability.

4. WHO will maintain the regional database on Healthy Cities projects with only active projects included in the database. The project already on the database will submit to WHO a yearly report to show that it is actively implemented, and all new entries to the database will include the evidence that all criteria for a Healthy Cities project are met.

5. The regional action plan on Healthy Cities for 2000–03 consists of actions that should be taken by both countries and international community, including WHO.
6. It is recognised that variability exists in the stage of development of Healthy Cities programmes among countries and also specific needs are different from country to country. Therefore, it is recommended that countries should use the structure of the regional action plan to develop their own national action plans.

After the 1999 workshop in Malacca, Malaysia, the focus of WHO activities has been shifted to the development of practical evaluation methodologies for Healthy Cities projects and collaboration with member states in implementing the regional action plan.

In October 2001, WHO convened a regional workshop in Johor Bahru, Malaysia (WHO 2001b) to review and evaluate the progress made in implementing the regional action plan; to review case studies on evaluation methodologies for Healthy Cities projects; and to discuss future directions in promoting the Healthy Cities approach.

Reports from countries at the workshop revealed the following.

1. Several countries demonstrated a good progress in implementing the 2000–03 regional action plan. They have strengthened capacity in implementation of Healthy Cities projects in important areas including: developing a national coordinating structure, preparing national plans and guidelines which provide technical support to the cities, and advocacy to national and provincial governments. Also countries have developed mechanisms for advocacy, communication and networking as part of a national network and vehicle for direct exchange.
2. Concerning the setting up of systems that ensure the sustainability of projects and programmes (one of the items in the regional action plan), most countries have been preparing for implementation, focusing on the establishment of appropriate evaluation methodologies for Healthy Cities activities.
3. Twenty-three cities reported on the significant progress made towards implementing the Healthy Cities approach. A wide variety of activities were reported covering improvement of physical infrastructure, protection and enhancement of the natural environment and social, cultural and economic strengthening activities.
4. Success factors identified from the presentations included: local political and administrative support, effective planning processes, committed leadership, meaningful community involvement and the use of a variety of settings for implementation.
5. Sustainability and strengthening of Healthy Cities in the future will depend on improved evaluation and monitoring processes, information dissemination, increased community involvement, broadening the range of activities

Healthy Cities covers, harnessing the power of the combination of top down and bottom up action to solve health problems, and ensuring the initial momentum is maintained.

With respect to evaluation methodologies for Healthy Cities, the workshop concluded the following.

1. Each evaluation programme should be adapted to national cultures. It should act as a means of involving the community in Healthy Cities projects. The results of evaluation should continuously feed back to the design and implementation of projects.
2. Evaluation designs should adopt ecological, qualitative, and quasi-experimental methods and thus expand the repertoire beyond epidemiological approaches and standards (such as randomised trials) that are more appropriate for clinical interventions.
3. Quality of life in cities has many dimensions. Sets of indicators for evaluation of Healthy Cities projects should reflect this. They should not be restricted to narrow, mono-disciplinary approaches that do not account for the richness and the diversity of life in each setting.
4. Further development of evaluation methods should be promoted through the publication of common terminology, the dissemination of models of good practice, and the creation of opportunities for skill development.

Some constraints to the effective implementation of Healthy Cities projects have been recently observed. There have been changes in city leadership (mayors) and national coordinators in some countries, which sometimes temporarily halted the project implementation and required briefing, awareness raising and training of these people in the Healthy Cities concept and approach. Another area of concern was insufficient local initiative and motivation which always required external input to implement activities. Finally, the involvement of the private sector in Healthy Cities activities has still been minimal in the region, and needs to be promoted further.

FUTURE PRIORITIES

The priority areas that require strengthening for further promotion of the Healthy Cities approach include:

*   sustaining the momentum created;
*   going beyond the health sector;
*   involving the community and private sector;
*   reporting and documentation;
*   strengthening national coordination;

- evaluating projects;
- developing and maintaining databases; and
- disseminating information on Healthy Cities programmes and activities at local, national and international levels.

In order to address these areas, future activities should focus on:

- training and awareness raising of many different stakeholders (government and non-government organisations, profit and non-profit organisations and the community) through workshops, seminars, study visits and other infor-mation dissemination mechanisms;
- their involvement in planning, implementation and evaluation of Healthy Cities projects;
- strengthening documentation and reporting of project implementation and use of websites to disseminate the information; and
- development of national guidelines and capacity to support local initiatives.

References

Nakamura, K. and Takano, T. (1992) Image diagnosis of health in cities: Tokyo Healthy City. In Takano, T., Ishidate, K. and Nagasaki M. (eds) *Formulation and Development of a Research Base for Healthy Cities*. Tokyo: Kyoiku Syoseki, 50–67.

Randle, N. and Hutt, M. (1997) Healthy Cities: A Report for Midland Regional Health Authority (unpublished report).

United Nations (UN) (2000) *World Population Prospects – the 2000 Revision*. (All popula-tion figures on this page are taken from this source), New York: UN.

Whelan, A., Mohr, R. and Short, S. (1992) *Waving or Drowning?: Evaluation of the National Secretariat*. Healthy Cities Australia, Final Report.

World Health Organisation (WHO) (1991) *World Health Assembly Resolution WHA44.27 on Urban Health Development*. Geneva: WHO.

WHO (1992) *Technical Discussions on a Healthy Urban Environment*. Background Document. WPR/RC43/Technical Discussions/2. Manila: WHO.

WHO (1993) *Report on Bi-regional Meeting on Urban Health Development*. Manila: WHO.

WHO (1995) *Yanuca Island Declaration*. WHO/HRH/95.4. Manila: WHO.

WHO (1997a) *Report on Regional Consultation on Healthy Cities*. Manila: WHO.

WHO (1997b) *The Rarotonga Agreement: Towards Healthy Islands*. WHO/HRH/DHI/97.1. Manila: WHO.

WHO (1999a) *The Palau Action Statement: On Healthy Islands*. WPR/HRH/DHI/99.1. Manila: WHO.

WHO (1999b) *Report on Meeting on Health Protection and Health Promotion: Harmonizing Our Responses to the Challenges of the 21st Century*. Manila: WHO.

WHO (2000a) *Regional Guidelines for Developing a Healthy Cities Project*. Healthy Settings Documents Series No. 2. Manila: WHO.

WHO (2000b) *Report on Workshop on Healthy Cities: Preparing for the 21st Century*. Manila: WHO.

WHO (2001a) *Madang Commitment Towards Healthy Islands.* WPR/ECP/DPM/2001. Manila: WHO.

WHO (2001b) *Report on Workshop on Healthy Cities: Evaluation and Future Directions.* Manila: WHO.

WHO (2002) *The Vision of Healthy Islands for the 21st Century: Regional Implementation Guidelines.* Manila: WHO.

Chapter 4

Health and sustainability gains from urban regeneration and development

Colin Fudge

INTRODUCTION

In addressing the relationship between urban development and social gains through the use of town planning systems within market economies one is reminded of the origins and evolution of town and country planning. In many countries, and certainly in the UK, town and country planning as a task of government has developed from public health and housing policies. The nineteenth-century increase in population and the then growth in towns led to public health problems which demanded a new role for government and new mechanisms of intervention in the market and with private property rights in the interest of social well-being.

Social reformers at that time noted that despite the advances to achieve social results through town planning the physical impact on British towns was somewhat depressing. In the words of Unwin:

> Much good work has been done. In the ample supply of pure water, in the drainage and removal of waste matter, in the paving, lighting and cleansing of streets, and in many other such ways, probably our towns are as well served as, or even better than, those elsewhere. Moreover, by means of our much abused bye-laws, the worst excesses of overcrowding have been restrained; a certain minimum standard of air-space, light and ventilation has been secured; while in the more modern parts of towns, a fairly high degree of sanitation, of immunity from fire, and general stability of construction have been maintained, the importance of which can hardly be exaggerated. We have, indeed, in all these matters laid a good foundation and have secured many of the necessary elements for a healthy condition of life: and yet the remarkable fact remains that there are growing up around our big towns vast districts, under these very bye-laws, which for dreariness and sheer ugliness it is difficult to match anywhere, and compared with which many of the old unhealthy slums are, from the point of view of picturesqueness and beauty, infinitely more attractive.
>
> (Unwin 1909, in Cullingworth and Nadin 2001)

It was on this point that public health concerns and architecture and urban design met. The experiments in 'utopian' communities in the UK at Saltaire (1853), Bournville (1878), Port Sunlight (1887) and elsewhere provided living experiments on how to combine these elements albeit within the context of 'benevolent paternalism'. Ebenezer Howard and the Garden City Movement and the American Regional Planning Association added their voices to the thinking of the times (and indeed the sustainability thinking of today). In addition, many similar concerns and new ways of approaching town design for social result were emerging in Scandinavia and other parts of the world.

Since this period of creative ideas we have a century of histories of town planning in different countries that have involved rafts of government legislation, changing institutional frameworks, tensions between flexibility and certainty, varying ideological positions on how to intervene in the market, tensions over the concerns of rural and urban areas, arguments over the appropriate spatial envelope for planning, comprehensiveness versus sectoral approaches, questions over who should be included in the planning process and arguments over the scope of planning, social engineering and physical determinism.

In some ways these issues will always be with us; however it is not the purpose of this chapter either to provide a detailed history of planning or to set out to resolve these tensions. This brief glimpse at the origins of town planning is to remind ourselves that in one sense we have been here before and can perhaps learn from our experience. The most significant difference today is that the scale of urbanisation in the world at the beginning of the twenty-first century and the rate of expansion over the next 30 years (see Figures 4.1, 4.2 and 4.3) focuses our attention more firmly on the future of towns and cities and their impact for their local populations and on global environmental, economic, social and health concerns.

Fig. 4.1.   Percentage of population living in urban areas in 1996 and 2030

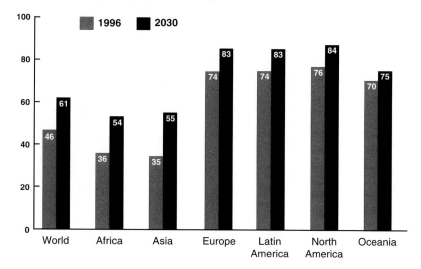

Fig. 4.2. World's urban agglomerations with populations of 10 million or more inhabitants in 1970, 1996 and 2015

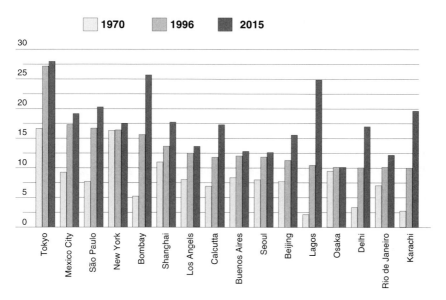

Fig. 4.3. World's urban agglomerations with populations of 10 million or more inhabitants: 1950 to 2015

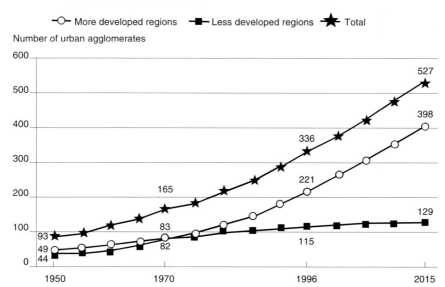

Source of figures 4.1–4.3: Population Division, United Nations (UN 1996, 1998)

This chapter focuses on urban development and urban regeneration processes, outputs and outcomes. It critically explores different governmental approaches to achieve health and sustainability gains from urban development. The chapter is divided into three parts.

1. The sustainable development policy aspiration in local and global contexts.
2. Policy approaches to achieve health and sustainability gains through urban regeneration and development.
3. Challenges for the twenty-first century: implications for practice and research.

THE SUSTAINABLE DEVELOPMENT POLICY ASPIRATION AS LOCAL AND GLOBAL CONTEXTS

One of the major influences on governments has been the sustainable development aspiration of contemporary public policy at different levels of government – locally, regionally, nationally, in large international blocks such as the European Union (EU) and through international commitments and agreements.

This needs to be understood within the equally compelling development of globalisation, global markets and global competition between countries and indeed cities themselves. Nevertheless it is useful to rehearse the principles and ideas that have emerged over the last 20 years in relation to achieving sustainable futures.

Guiding principles

What then are the guiding principles of sustainability around which a common agenda for action may be formulated? The UK Round Table on Sustainable Development, for example, has defined the following as essential:

- *the precautionary principle*: where there are threats of serious or irreversible damage to the environment, the lack of full scientific certainty should not be used as a reason to delay taking cost-effective action to prevent or minimise such damage;
- *the integration principle*: environmental requirements must be integrated into the definition and implementation of all areas of policy-making;
- *the 'polluter pays' principle*: the costs of preventing or cleaning up pollution and wastes should be borne by those responsible for causing it and not by society at large (i.e. the external costs of production should be internalised);
- *the preventative principle*: society should avoid incurring the costs of development activities which seriously damage natural or physical capital; and
- *the participative principle*: widespread and informed public participation in decision-making is an essential prerequisite for development which may be sustainable.

Although there is a range of positions in different sectors and interest groups, a list around which practical discussion towards urban and regional action might take place includes:

- *environmental limits to growth*, as framed in the concept of 'carrying capacity' within which all forms of development and management must be contained;
- *demand management*, through which new patterns of production and lifestyle/consumption may be achieved;
- *environmental efficiency*, where maximum economic benefit is extracted from each unit of resource used;
- *welfare efficiency*, where maximum human benefit is extracted from each unit of economic activity; and
- *equity*, where the interests of the poor and of future generations are implicit in all considerations of policy and practice (intra- and inter-generational equity).

The problems with both conceptualising sustainable development and applying the principles derive from the requirement to bridge the very different paradigms of the so-called 'hard' disciplines associated with the environmental sciences, and those of management and social sciences. The extent to which different elements of the 'capital' of sustainability may be substitutable, e.g. whether an increase in human knowledge can compensate for resource losses, is also, by definition, unknown (see e.g. Pearce *et al.* 1990). The concept of 'carrying capacity' seems to offer the possibility of setting objective limits upon the use of both natural and man-made resources (see e.g. House of Lords 1995). However, this concept too is interpreted differently by various users to reflect their own perceptions of value (see e.g. O'Neill 1996). Moreover, issues such as democratic probity have yet to be addressed at all (the majority may choose not to pay the price for sustainability policies and practice). Tensions arise from the potential breadth and scope of sustainable development, both spatially (from global to local) and temporally (from 'as soon as possible' to the very long term). Relevant policy areas include environment, transport, land use planning and practice, health, technology and business practice, as well as the frameworks for trade; and the instruments which might be brought to bear thus range from legislation and market regulation to systems management and community action. There are problems of definition, measurement, attribution of value, and the use of indicators (e.g. LGMB 1995; Countryside Commission 1995; HMSO 1996). Work continues into green accounting (e.g. Organisation for Economic Cooperation and Development – OECD 1999; Green Alliance 1997) and, particularly through alternatives to gross national product (GNP) as measures of national well-being. However, it may be argued that the growth paradigm and the strength of business interests to a large extent still prevail. There is a dominant central commitment to international competitiveness which tends to militate against business and capital engaging with more environmentally and socially beneficial forms of production and management (Welford 1995).

Globalisation, fostered by technological, informational and managerial change, proceeds apace; eco-efficiency may be superimposed but would require concerted international effort, of which there is inconclusive evidence (Fussler and James 1996). Localisation, on the other hand, which underpins sustainability thinking in many countries, emphasises place, community and individual. The question which then arises is how urban and regional actors may most usefully resolve these dilemmas to make progress at the urban and regional level.

Towards urban and regional sustainable development
Given the fundamental principles of sustainable development outlined above, what are the elements upon which sustainability within cities and regions may be built? Arguably, they include:

- 'standard' elements which relate to environmental conservation and protection and to equity and futurity;
- elements which relate to the diversification of the urban and regional economy as a 'defence against adversity';
- the concept of urban and regional self-sufficiency, where the intention is to minimise environmentally and economically wasteful resource inputs and transfers; and
- the concept of territorial integration, taking a holistic approach to differing spatial interests e.g. central city *and* edge city *and* rural hinterlands.

European influence
Since the late 1980s (Brundtland 1997), the EU has sought to consolidate its actions for environmental protection, and to reorientate environment policy to promote the objectives of sustainable development.

Integration of urban issues has been pursued extensively since the publication of the Green Paper on the Urban Environment (Commission of the European Communities [CEC] 1990). The Expert Group on the Urban Environment was established in 1991, and its work on sustainable development published in European Sustainable Cities (CEC 1994, 1996). The European Sustainable Towns and Cities Campaign, launched in Aalborg in 1994, now includes over 2000 local authorities as well as the major European local authority networks, Eurocities, the United Towns Organisation (UTO), the Council of European Municipalities and Regions (CEMR), the International Council for Local Environmental Initiatives (ICLEI) and the World Health Organisation (WHO)'s Healthy Cities programme (1994). The two 'urban communications' (CEC 1997 and 1998) have contributed to the 'urban policy' debate culminating in the European Urban Forum in Vienna. The positive response to the Urban Forum continues to demand considerable energy and activity at the European Commission level to meet the raised expectations of the urban communities across Europe and in the accession countries. DG Environment, the environmental part of the European Commission, the EU Urban

Environment Expert Group and member state governments are taking part of the agenda (urban environment) forward with a new work programme and more focused expert group (see Figure 4.4).

In addition new working groups are taking forward work on the urban thematic strategy which is part of the Sixth Environmental Action Plan.

Various targeted funding programmes encourage both research and development and action on the ground. The EU Fifth Framework Programme for Research and Technological Development has funded innovative trans-European research and demonstration programmes into aspects of sustainability including competitive and sustainable growth, sustainable mobility and inter-modality, and improving the quality of life and the management of living resources as well as preserving the ecosystem. In addition a range of structural funding programmes for disadvantaged regions in Europe now include requirements to meet sustainability criteria.

The key messages which have come from attempts in Europe to influence policy and practice at the urban and regional level include the following.

- *Balancing progress* In the longer term, meeting the challenge of sustainability requires major changes in attitudes in society and in the operation of economies. However, in the short term, much can be achieved through practical incremental steps to reduce non-sustainability as much as to achieve sustainability. These steps include realigning existing policies and mechanisms, and identifying a strong set of principles and related indicators on which environmentally-sound action may be based.
- *Integrating policy* Integration must be sought horizontally between sectors, to stimulate synergistic effects of all dimensions of sustainability, and vertically between policy levels, to achieve greater coherence of policy and actions within cities and regions and to avoid contradictions across levels.

Fig. 4.4.   Work programme of the current EU Expert Group on the Urban Environment

Towards a local sustainability profile ⟶ Chair of Working Group
European common indicators   Nedialka Sougareva
French Ministry of the Environment

Sustainable land use ⟶ Chair of Working Group
Michael Bach
UK Department of Environment, Transport and the Regions

Implementation of environmental legislation ⟶ Chair of Working Group
Italian Ministry

Urban design for sustainability ⟶ Chair of Working Group
Gabriele Langschwert
Austrian Environment Ministry

- *Closing resource cycles* Ecosystems thinking emphasises the region as a complex system characterised by flows of energy, nutrients, materials and other resources which include finance and human resources. Working towards closing cycles by integrating flows and minimising waste will promote sustainability at the urban and regional level. The notion of ecological footprinting may assist the process (Rees 1998).
- *Designing for sustainability* There is a growing need for transforming the design of buildings and products to a sustainable future incorporating the principles of sustainability. Similarly the planning and urban design of parts of the whole of cities requires new approaches whether it be new buildings, conservation, the renewal and creation of public space or the retrofitting of areas both within and on the periphery of cities.
- *Management, governance and capacity-building* Sustainable urban and/or regional management will require a range of tools addressing environmental, social and economic concerns to assist integration of policy and practice. Also required will be a reconsideration of the processes and practices of governance, including the institutional arrangements and capacities of different levels of government and agencies, and the roles and operation of partnerships between public and private sectors, NGOs and citizens. Learning from Agenda 21 processes is crucial to future forms of governance (CEC 1996).

From experience in Europe it is suggested that increasingly the relationships between urban and regional environments and economies will be of over-riding importance. Themes for exploration and development in relation to this identified by Roberts (1995) include:

- the roles of environmental auditing and assessment;
- the development of green accounting;
- the availability of environmental funds;
- the development of environmental regulation;
- urban and regional opportunities arising from green packaging and product design;
- the urban and regional importance of green credentials;
- urban and regional relationships between citizens–consumers–companies;
- the avoidance of pollution and environmental degradation; and
- obligations towards pollution control and management.

These themes have been taken up in the Sustainable Futures Charter of Business and Municipality (City of Bremen 1997) and through the Bremen Initiative and are becoming internalised within some larger firms and companies. This internal resolution of the tensions between economic pressures and environmental and health values needs to be encouraged through complementary behaviour at all levels of government, including the urban and regional level. A range of new management tools is also being developed, refined and implemented on varying scales, including:

- tools for formulating, integrating and implementing local environmental policies (e.g. environmental charters, strategies, management systems, strategic and impact assessments);
- tools for collaboration and partnership (e.g. round tables, forums and networks, citizens' juries, focus groups, Global Action Plan activities, green commuter plans);
- tools for quantifying sustainability (e.g. checklists, targets, measures and indicators); and
- tools for greening the market (e.g. local environmental levies, utility regulation, environmental and social criteria in purchasing and tendering).

However, smaller and medium sized businesses, which often make up large parts of national economies, remain largely unengaged with the sustainability agenda; the potential synergies between urban and regional economies, health and environment need identification, attention and development.

In the keynote address for the European Sustainable Cities and Towns Conference in Hannover (February 2000) the author concluded that whilst the worlds of government and practice had a fairly well developed knowledge and understanding of the policy and technical changes that are needed for more sustainable futures, the progress is too slow in relation to the evidence that has emerged from European, WHO and United Nations (UN) indicators (European Environment Agency 1999; UN Global Outlook 2000, 1999; WHO 1999). In addition the Swedish Research Councils are increasingly concerned with the non-implementation of policies of international, business and local levels to global climate change (Fudge and Rowe 2000, 2001).

Given these concerns there remains nevertheless an impressive transformation of practice through innovative policies at the local authority level across Europe and a growing range of research programmes both of which indicate that sustainability including health is slowly becoming more integrated into the mainstream agenda of government policy (Fudge and Rowe 1997).

Let us now turn to the more detailed analysis of how health and sustainability gains can be achieved through urban regeneration and development.

POLICY APPROACHES TO ACHIEVE HEALTH AND SUSTAINABILITY GAINS THROUGH URBAN REGENERATION AND DEVELOPMENT

The confusion over just what is the appropriate policy for attempting to achieve health and sustainability gains from urban development conceals different perceptions, ideological positions and indeed professional values as to the rationales or justifications for intervening in land, property and local markets. To ensure that proposals for urban development can be implemented, deal positively with externalities, involve stakeholders and citizens within the process and create positive 'win-win' outcomes, consideration needs to be given to the policy vehicles that may provide support for these kinds of outcomes as opposed to processes of urban change that are seen by commentators as too narrowly defined. On examination of the literature, and drawing on my own theoretical and practice experience, it is suggested that we need to consider three broad policy approaches.

1.   Utilising the town planning system through forms of 'planning agreements'.
2.   National policy and taxation.
3.   Innovative approaches to urban regeneration and urban development.

In examining these three categories we need to first explore what underpins these policy approaches, and second, to recognise that they are not mutually exclusive but can be reinforcing or contradictory. In contemporary UK government 'policy speak' we may need to find out how we can achieve 'joined-up policy', 'joined-up working' and 'joined-up governance' (DETR 1999a).

Utilising the town planning system through forms of 'planning agreements'

The challenge for policy-makers concerned with planning has been to provide a framework which encourages practices that allow efficient development whilst ensuring that adverse social, health and environmental costs are limited. A practice has emerged that creates separate legal obligations alongside planning permissions. The use of planning agreements to create development obligations has attracted some controversy. For some 'planning gain' is a legitimate contribution from developers, for others it is an unconstitutional tax and a form of negotiated bribery. In this controversy, there is both an issue concerning the proper 'mechanism' to create an obligation and the 'substantive' question of what can be required.

Implementation of planned development

In this rationale, the plan provides a clear framework justifying a development. Within such a framework, agreements may be used to address management problems with respect to development, or developers themselves may be encouraged to contribute to the provision of planned infrastructure to enable their development schemes to proceed. Examples include: permissible transport routes to and from a quarry; the payment for a new road junction to be constructed; agreement to provide public toilets, public car parking and a day nursery; and a percentage (10 per cent) of affordable housing within a private sector housing development.

Dealing with externalities or adverse impacts of development

This rationale involves understanding and defining the impacts of development including, for example, social and health costs. In contrast to the first rationale, it is not so much concerned with making the development work in its own terms as with attempting to accommodate the development and its impact over a wider area and community. It operates by identifying the wider impacts of each project rather than by the detailed framework of a development plan, though the principles and criteria for alleviation and compensation may be set out in the plan. This approach lends itself to negotiation. Through the stretching of the link between development and any social costs created, it can be used to justify/legitimate a wide range of community benefits which could be achieved through negotiation with the developer. (For a wider discussion of social town planning see Greed 1999.)

Local development charge or betterment

In the third rationale the developer is seen as having a duty to return some of the financial profit from the development to the community. This mechanism can be provided through national policy often administered at the local level or through local development charges. This approach has been attempted in the UK under Labour governments since 1945 and has been evaluated through research.

In contrast to the third rationale, the first and second rationales both establish reasons for refusing the proposed development on the grounds that without the obligation the development is unacceptable in planning terms. The important difference between the first two rationales lies in the relationship which is required between the development and the obligation. With the first rationale, the focus is on making the proposed development fit in with a scheme already envisaged. This tends to require a direct and tight relationship between the development and the obligation. In the second rationale the emphasis is on the relationship between the development and its impact.

In the United States the courts have developed a 'rational nexus test' under which the obligation must directly and proportionately solve the planning problems which would otherwise be caused by the development. This needs to be contrasted with a rival 'reasonable relationship test' which would allow a balancing of the problems caused by the development with the benefits produced by the obligation. These US tests are, respectively, similar to those in the English courts, respectively the 'clear and direct nexus test' and the 'fair and reasonable test'. The main point being developed here is the influence and involvement of the courts and legal definition and how much this influences the scope that an obligation may have.

However, there has also been an argument for the use of agreements to negotiate a contribution from developers to social and community development, i.e. rationale 3. This argument has gathered force in the face of repeated failures of schemes (e.g. in the UK) designed to capture the betterment produced by the public sector's efforts in planning and infrastructure provision as a charge on developers' profits (see Cullingworth and Nadin 2001 for a history).

National policy and taxation

The second major policy mechanism is through national taxation. For example, there has been considerable debate in the EU over the introduction across the 15 member states of a tax on fuels (Carbon Tax) as a direct influence on emissions, as an encouragement to switch away from fossil fuels to combat global climate change and to improve health and environment outcomes. Similarly at national levels, governments have often used VAT or purchase taxation to attempt to achieve wider social objectives, for example reducing taxation on energy conservation materials and processes. This policy area lists a number of these types of taxation and the broader point of general versus specific taxes.

- General versus specific taxation (hypothecation) – for example the recent policy decisions in the UK on road pricing and the 'taxation' being admissible to offset the infrastructure costs of new forms of public transport such as a tram system.
- Betterment taxation in the example of the Community Land Act and Development Land Tax in the UK under successive Labour governments.
- Greenfield taxation as a means of encouraging development on previously used land – brownfield land (see EU Urban Environment Expert Group report on Sustainable Land Use 2001).
- Carbon tax – see for example Denmark and attempts by the EU.
- Land Fill Tax (1998) UK – a tax whereby local environmental schemes could benefit from the payments received from Land Fill Tax.
- VAT (or no VAT) on different forms of development – for example the debate in reaction to VAT on the conservation of historic buildings.
- Percent for Art (US/UK) and then on to ideas of percent for Design; percent for Sustainability; percent for Health. This involves a percentage of the project cost that is receiving planning permission being used for, for example, public art.

Innovative approaches to urban regeneration and urban development

The shift towards a more comprehensive interpretation of the planning, development and regeneration process incorporating issues of finance, management, partnership and participation as well as social, health, environment and economic issues is becoming more established in the UK and elsewhere. It is in the nature of an integrated development or regeneration policy to establish the widest cross programme linkage between differing aspects of any particular problem facing urban and indeed rural communities. These more innovative approaches tend to involve partnerships between public and private sectors; new ways of working with communities; the involvement of NGOs; devolution to communities so that they develop their own initiatives and a very different set of roles for government and indeed for public servants and professionals. This third policy strand lists regeneration in the UK; regeneration and health; and a comparison of initiatives in the UK and the USA.

- Regeneration in the UK.
  The policy history, funding regimes, innovative approaches and moves towards sustainable regeneration are set out in *Sustainable Regeneration* (Department of Environment Transport and Regions – DETR 1998).
- Regeneration policies – the health connection (see Kings Fund 1999).
  More recently those involved in regeneration with their communities have attempted to find ways of meeting health objectives through regeneration processes and neighbourhood renewal.
- US–UK experience compared.
  This involves an examination of the US approach including the use of public-private partnerships, community initiatives, city visioning, development trusts, urban regeneration agencies and the Local Initiatives Support Corporation (LISC).

CHALLENGES FOR THE TWENTY-FIRST CENTURY – IMPLICATIONS FOR PRACTICE AND RESEARCH

In the new millennium, unprecedented growth in urban living gives rise to problems of persistently high unemployment rates, concerns about the future economy of cities, social exclusion, crime, the preservation of our natural and built environments, the quality of life, pressures on natural resources and negative impacts on health. However, an alternative current debate is about the potential, opportunities and possibilities of a new 'urban renaissance' as strongly advocated in the UK by the Rogers Report (DETR 1999b).

In addition, whilst these problems and opportunities are faced in some measure in all cities, there is an increasing discrepancy between the scale of problems in developed and developing countries, even though cities are increasingly inter-related in global economic and environmental systems.

Challenges for practice and research
In facing these challenges, a range of broad actions have been suggested. These include:

- the urgent implementation of modern infrastructure for environmental and health protection, providing access to basic life support systems;
- the challenging and adjustment of urban production and consumption patterns to the needs of resource protection. This requires more attention to strategies for recycling and product responsibility of manufacturers; the management of energy consumption; changes in behaviour patterns related to

mobility and lifestyle; and environment and health concerns incorporated into economic decision-making;
- the design of new cities and crucially the restructuring of existing cities for sustainability, particularly through urban regeneration;
- the planning and design of regional relationships between towns and cities and rural hinterlands for sustainability (including operationalising the notion of ecological footprints);
- the development of a capacity to lead, manage and govern in new ways in cities to contribute to global sustainability.

In addition, different concepts and models have been discussed that aid analysis and policy development. These focus on the inter-relationship between economic, environmental, health, social, energy and cultural concerns and the significance of integrated and holistic approaches at all levels of government. They also encourage new ways of working involving partnerships, community empowerment and innovations in governance.

At the follow-up to the European Urban Forum held in Helsinki (2000) a number of questions and issues were posed by the author that provide an agenda for practice and research. These broad issues include the following.

Global from the local
- How do we get towns and cities at their local levels to make their contributions to global concerns such as climate more explicit?
- Similarly, how do you convey to urban citizens their global responsibilities in relation to their local activities and ways of life?
- The move towards the cancellation by the 98 countries of debt repayments in relation to the poorest 40–50 countries in the world is seen as a step towards positive redistribution. What other steps are needed to start to address in global terms the changes to lifestyle and economy by the rich countries in relation to those that are poorer?
- How does the city locality face up to the demands and implications of global economy and global competition? Where loyalty to locality may be of a low priority for global business?
- Similarly, how do cities 'scale up' to face global players? What further role is there for organisations like Eurocities, the European Commission, WHO?

Urban, rural and regional
- Do we need to reframe the notion of urban to include the urban-rural interdependency and relationship? This would emphasise ideas about ecological footprints, the reach of urban economies and notions of the sustainable city region (Rees 1992, 1998).
- In thinking about these questions many more come to mind, particularly about the concepts of ecosystems, ecological footprints and the principles

and use of ecological models. In addition there are a number of further questions concerning:

- 'ecological modernisation'
- informal versus formal working practices
- integration within a structure of sectors
- education and training for urban professionals
- the 'social' component of sustainability
- the relationship between public, private and community partners.

Planning, development and land

- Developing new sustainable settlements seems relatively straightforward – how do we adapt/retrofit existing urban areas for sustainability?
- Similarly developing small scale, local initiatives seems relatively straightforward (and there are numerous examples) – how do we scale up?
- Land use change is a slow process and too narrowly conceived – do land use and spatial planning systems need to be reconceptualised?

In practical terms, how do we:

- rethink the use of land as a resource? In doing this we may wish to reconsider notions of betterment, land taxation and ownership in relation to planning systems;
- define and measure carrying capacity?
- develop sustainability appraisal? Including how do we define and value 'quality of life'?
- use the planning system to achieve 'sustainability gain' or 'health gain'?

Organisational change for sustainability

- How far is the sustainability agenda driving organisational change?
  or
- How far are other agendas 'limiting' the organisational requirements to achieve sustainable futures?
- Are there 'ideal' organisational arrangements for tackling sustainability?
- What or who are the organisational barriers to sustainability?

General

- Do 'natural environment' and biodiversity issues need to be brought back onto the urban agenda? This implies that they have slipped down or off the urban agenda.
- Some cities, for example, have been exploring the development of local food production and/or influencing supermarkets to change their policies to more organic and 'local' food sourcing. What changes are necessary to encourage this on a larger scale?

- Clearly cities have influence on their own and enormous influence collectively to start to shift the market towards products that are sourced and designed for sustainable futures. Have we done enough 'locally', nationally and internationally to achieve more through sustainably sound procurement measures?
- Sustainable regeneration involving environmental, social, community, health and cultural concerns as well as economic is a developing pattern in some cities. What do we need to change to ensure that this becomes a more comprehensive and coherent policy?
- How do we move from 'demonstration' projects and programmes to mainstream?
- One of the most common issues facing most towns and cities is that of mobility and accessibility and the impact of the car in particular. Are we moving fast enough and with adequate resourcing to bring about large enough changes and gains on this issue?
- There is much written about the information age we are now inhabiting. What are the range of scenarios and implications for urban areas and the allocation and distribution of land uses in regions as a result of this phenomenon?

Against the global background of rapidly increasing urbanisation over the next 25 years we have examined the sustainable development policy aspirations and the crucial importance within this broad context of the healthy cities movement. Policy approaches to achieve health and sustainability gains have been explored in three ways: through adapting town planning systems; introducing socially beneficial policies and taxes at national government levels and through innovative approaches to urban development and regeneration. Finally we have looked at the implications for practice and research by raising a series of questions and issues that have emerged over the last five years. We have noted with some considerable concern the findings of the European Environment Agency (Eurobarometer 1999), the UN (Global Outlook 1999, 2000), and WHO (1999) all of whom report that, despite the considerable advances in practice, health and environment indicators show a worsening situation globally. This implies that through practice and research, governments at all levels, the private sector and NGOs need to strengthen their resolve and actions if the global environment conference in 2002 Rio plus 10 is able in due course to report positively in relation to actions rather than words.

Acknowledgements

I would like to acknowledge the assistance of my colleagues in the Faculty in Bristol and the work over the last ten years in the EU from the Expert Group on the Urban Environment, the European Campaign for Sustainable Cities and Towns, WHO, Eurocities and the International Council for Local Environmental Initiatives.

References

Bergrund, L. (1994) *Eco-balancing: a Göteborg example.* In Agenda 21, Report to the Manchester Conference.

City of Bremen (1997) *Business and Municipality: New Partnerships for the 21st Century.* (The Bremen Charter). Proceedings, International Conference, 13–15 March. City of Bremen, Germany.

Commission of the European Communities (CEC) (1990) *Green Paper on the Urban Environment.* COM(90) 218 CEC, Luxembourg: OOPEC.

CEC (1994) *European Sustainable Cities.* Part One, Luxembourg: OOPEC.

CEC (1996) *European Sustainable Cities.* Luxembourg: OOPEC.

CEC (1997) *Towards an Urban Agenda in the European Union.* Communication COM (97) 197 Final, Luxembourg: OOPEC.

CEC (1998) *Sustainable Urban Development in the European Union: A Framework for Action.* Communication COM (98) 605 Final, Luxembourg: OOPEC.

CEC (1999) *State of Europe's Environment – the Eurobarometer*, European Environment Agency, Copenhagen.

CEC (2000) *The European Urban Audit.* Luxembourg: OOPEC.

Countryside Commission (1995) *State of the Countryside – Environmental Indicators.* Cheltenham: Countryside Commission.

Cullingworth, B. and Nadin, V. (2001) *Town and Country Planning in Britain.* London: Unwin.

Department of Environment Transport and Regions (DETR) (1998) *Sustainable Regeneration – Good Practice Guide.* London: HMSO.

DETR (1999a) *Cross-cutting Issues Affecting Local Government.* London: HMSO.

DETR (1999b) *Towards an Urban Renaissance.* London: HMSO.

European Sustainable Cities and Towns Campaign (1994) *Charter of European Cities and Towns Towards Sustainability (the Aalborg Charter).* Brussels.

European Urban Environment Expert Group (2001), Sustainable Land Use Report, Brussels, DG Environment.

Fudge, C. (1995) *International Healthy and Ecological Cities Congress: Our City, Our Future.* Rapporteur's Report, Copenhagen: WHO.

Fudge, C. and Rowe, J. (1997) *Urban Environment and Sustainability: Developing the Agenda for Socio-Economic Environmental Research.* Research Report for DG XII, UWE, Bristol.

Fudge, C. and Rowe, J. (2000) *Implementing Sustainable Futures in Sweden.* Stockholm: BFR.

Fudge, C. and Rowe, J. (2001) Ecological Modernisation as a framework for sustainable development: a case study in Sweden. *Environment and Planning* A, 33: 1527–46.

Fussler, C. and James, P. (1996) *Driving Eco-Innovation: A Breakthrough Discipline for Innovation and Sustainability.* London: Pitman Publishing.

Greed, C. (1999) *Social Town Planning.* London: Routledge.

Green Alliance (1997) Making environmental decisions: cost benefit analysis, contingent valuation and alternatives. Proceedings of a Conference, Green Alliance/Centre for the Study of Environmental Change, January 1997. Green Alliance, 49 Wellington Street, London WC2E 7BN.

House of Lords (1995) *Report from the Select Committee on Sustainable Development.* Session 1994–95, June 1995. London: HMSO.

Local Government Management Board (1995) *Sustainability Indicators Research Project: Report of Phase One*. London: LGMB.

Organisation for Economic Cooperation and Development (OECD) (1999) *Better Governance for More Competitive and Liveable Cities*. Report of the OECD-Toronto Workshop. Paris: OECD.

O'Neill, J. (1996) Cost benefit analysis: rationality and the plurality of values. *The Ecologist*, 16 (3): 98–103.

Pearce, D., Barbier, E. and Markayanda, A. (1990) *Sustainable Development*. London: Earthscan.

Rees, W. (1992) Ecological footprints and appropriated carrying capacity: what urban economics leaves out. *Environment and Urbanisation,* 4: 121–30.

Rees, W. E. (1998) Is 'sustainable city' an oxymoron? *Local Environment,* October, Vol. 2, No. 3: 303–10.

Roberts, P. (1995) *Environmentally Sustainable Business: A Local and Regional Perspective*. London: Paul Chapman Publishing.

UN (1996) *World Urbanization Prospects Database – 1996 Revision*. Department of Economic and Social Affairs, Population Division, New York.

UN (1998) *World Population Estimates and Projections – 1998 Revision*. Department of Economic and Social Affairs, Population Division, New York.

UN (1999) *Global Outlook*, UNEP Annual Report, New York.

UN (2000) *Global Outlook*, UNEP Annual Report, New York.

Welford, R. (1995) *Environmental Strategy and Sustainable Development: the Corporate Challenge for the Twenty-First Century*. London: Routledge.

World Commission on Environment and Development (1987) *Our Common Future (The Brundtland Report)*. Oxford: Oxford University Press.

Chapter 5

Analysis of health determinants for Healthy Cities programmes

Health profiles and indicators

June Crown

BACKGROUND

The World Health Organisation (WHO)'s Healthy Cities Project began in 1986. It was rooted in the 'Health for All' strategy (WHO Regional Office for Europe 1985) and was established in recognition of the changing patterns of life in all parts of the world in the late twentieth century. Increasing proportions of the population are now living in urban environments, many of which are detrimental to health. It is unusual for these migrations to towns and cities to be planned, so important infrastructure requirements and determinants of health such as housing, sanitation, employment and pollution lag behind population growth.

Eleven cities joined the project at the outset. They were selected for their interest in a broad approach to public health and their willingness to commit time, energy and resources to the work. In each city, civic leaders, health professionals and citizens came together to define the health problems and needs of the city, and to devise plans to secure improvements.

Each city was expected to recognise the importance of a sustainable environment, supportive social networks, a vital economy and the provision of reliable basic services to meet the needs of citizens. There was encouragement to re-orientate health services towards a focus on primary health care.

It was obvious at the start that it was necessary to develop ways of measuring the 'health' in Healthy Cities. Cities needed to have objective methods to define the current levels of health in the community and to assess the factors which influence health status. Cities wanted to set targets for improvements and to have ways of marking their progress towards the achievement of those targets. The traditional measures of 'health', such as mortality and morbidity rates were inadequate for these purposes.

The early work on city profiles and indicators arose from these needs. It has continued and developed throughout the life of the project. Efforts have been made to find measures which can be useful as a basis for comparisons between cities and for the identification of trends over time. This has meant finding approaches which are clearly and precisely defined, culturally sensitive and capable of accurately identifying changes in relatively small populations or districts.

The topics covered must include environmental, socio-economic and organisational matters as well as the traditional health measures and should also give insights into trends and sustainability.

MEASURING THE HEALTH OF A CITY

It is difficult to define, describe and measure the 'health' of a city. The health of citizens needs to take into account physical, psychological, emotional and spiritual health. The measures which are available to us for even the most objective of these, physical health, are relatively crude for what is a sophisticated concept.

Many factors interact to affect the health of citizens. They can be grouped into four main categories (see Figure 5.1).

- **Health promotion**
  At the level of the individual, health promotion programmes can provide knowledge about health and its determinants that can enable people to make informed decisions about lifestyles. Good access to education, especially for women, whose activities have such a major impact on the health and welfare of their families, is an essential requirement for the promotion of health and the prevention of disease.
  One set of measures for a healthy city must therefore be the levels of adherence to healthy lifestyles, as assessed by tobacco and alcohol consumption, diet, participation in physical exercise, misuse of drugs and safe sexual practices.
- **Health services**
  Health services are significant contributors to the health of the population. However, it is important to recognise that the greatest impact of health services on health status comes not from the high profile diagnostic and treatment services but from the other parts of the therapeutic range. Preventive health services such as vaccination and immunisation, family planning and some screening programmes have saved far more lives than surgery. Excellent rehabilitation services play a vital role in reducing disability and handicap.

Fig. 5.1.   A model for health improvement

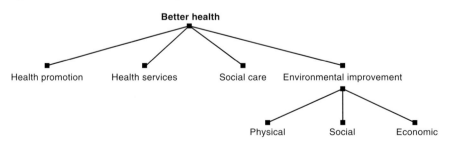

- **Social care**

  Social care is similarly a major factor in the well-being of citizens. Support which enables people to remain at home rather than in some form of residential care maintains social inclusion, reduces discrimination and stigma and promotes inter-generational solidarity and respect. All these factors influence health.

- **Environmental factors**

  However, it is the broad environmental factors which are the main determinants of the health of a community.

  The *physical* environment includes the traditional areas of public health concern – clean water, adequate sanitation and unpolluted air. Although these are sometimes taken for granted in developed countries, there are many examples of the speed with which problems can arise if we lower our guard. It also covers the important areas of urban design, housing and transport.

  The *social* environment has a similar impact on mental and emotional well-being and includes problems such as the fear of crime and domestic violence as well as measures of community involvement and of participation in education at all ages.

  The *economic* environment covers fundamental determinants of health such as poverty and levels of employment which have major effects on people's ability to access good food and decent housing.

These factors have all been studied for many years. More recently, attention has been concentrated on the relationships of inequality and health (Acheson 1999). Wide divergences between different groups in society are clearly related to health status, though the mechanisms are not yet fully understood. It is a challenge to Healthy Cities to bring the experience of disadvantaged citizens closer to that of the better off, in matters relating to health and the determinants of health.

THE CITY PROFILE

The WHO Healthy Cities Project Technical Working Group on City Health Profiles and Indicators has defined a city health profile as a report that 'identifies in writing and graphs health problems and their potential solutions in a specific city' (1995). This profile can then form the basis of city health plans that set out strategies and programmes of intervention to improve the health of citizens (WHO Healthy Cities Project Office 1996).

It is not only participants in the Healthy Cities programmes that prepare city profiles. They are an essential part of the planning and development of policies in any municipal authority. The profiles that are produced for Healthy Cities, however, are characterised by a clear central objective of describing the health of the population and the factors that affect it, with a view to developing comprehensive plans for improvement. The profile helps to identify areas across agencies where there is the potential for change. A well produced profile provides a framework for a broad health impact analysis of proposals that are put forward. It is therefore important that decisions about the production of a profile are made not just by officials of the lead agency, but, wherever possible, by a small group representing as many as practicable of the interested parties or stakeholders. This gives the opportunity to assemble information from a variety of sources. The process of producing the profile can, in itself, make a significant contribution to wide understanding of the city's health status and problems, and will often create a starting point for collaborative action.

Purpose

The first step in preparing a profile for a Healthy City is to decide precisely the purpose of the document. Although a descriptive document, the profile should always identify clearly the areas where change is needed. It can thus be a powerful agent in influencing decision-makers as they prepare plans and allocate resources.

Target audience

Clarity about the purpose of a city profile helps to identify the target audience to which it is addressed. In most cases, the authors wish to attract several different groups. Ideally the profile should be of interest to local politicians and decision-makers; to other public and private agencies whose activities affect health; to officials who will be responsible for the implementation of change; to the press who can play a major role in public education and in influencing opinion; to educators and academics; and, of major importance, to the population themselves. It is obviously impossible to meet all these needs in one document and many cities produce their profiles in several versions. A detailed and closely analysed account accompanied by statistical appendices may be necessary for officials and academics. The executive summary with clear and attractive graphics is often more suitable for politicians. A cheap and informative 'newspaper' version can be widely distributed to the citizens. Cities are increasingly using electronic and other media as well as the traditional paper versions of their profiles.

Content

The content of the profile will vary according to the nature of the city, the availability of information and the resources allocated to the task. Much of the data is normally available from routine sources but it is valuable to add to these, whenever possible, information on specific local issues, perhaps obtained through special surveys (Nakamura and Takano 1992). Data which is broken down by locality is particularly useful in helping citizens and decision-makers to identify with the issues. It also helps in highlighting inequalities across the city which enable service providers to target interventions.

A content review of city health profiles, carried out on behalf of the WHO's European Healthy Cities network, concentrated on the following headings, which were derived from guidance provided in *City Health Profiles – How to Report on Health in your City* (WHO Healthy Cities Project Technical Working Group 1995).

- Demography
- Health status
- Socio-economic conditions
- Environment
- Inequalities
- Infrastructure
- Public health policies and services
- Recommendations
- Presentation

The review found that the only areas comprehensively covered were demography, mortality and the environment. Many of the profiles had little or no information on lifestyles, inequalities or infrastructure. More worrying, few made recommendations, indicating that they missed an important chance to set a health agenda for their city in an influential way.

Frequency of production

It is often difficult to decide on the frequency of production of a city health profile. On the one hand, it may be argued that a regular, annual profile, well publicised, can be a powerful means of keeping health issues in the minds of public and politicians. On the other hand, it is usually the case that the measures that are used to describe health status are generally slow to change, so annual reports may be repetitive and thus lose the interest of the target audiences. Most cities find that the first profile is relatively easy to produce because all the data and information is new to this purpose and the staff undertaking the work are enthusiastic about the project. Some cities deal with the problems of repetition in subsequent editions by introducing a cycle of special topics, such as children, mental health or ethnic minority groups, which can be presented in depth on a less frequent basis.

Resources

In many cities, the desirable frequency, size and style of the city profile may not be attainable because of the limited resources available for its production. It is important that a budget (financial and human resources) is established and is subject to review for each edition, including assessment of the opportunity costs of producing the profile, compared with alternative investments in the city's health.

Evaluation

Finally, the city health profile should be subject to evaluation. This does not mean a complex, expensive and critical process. A perfectly satisfactory evaluation can be undertaken locally or even in house, though academic departments are often willing to help. At the very least, a process evaluation should be attempted, to find out whether the profile was seen or read by an adequate number of the various target groups. Any profile that is not noticed has no chance of influencing policy, plans or people! A useful approach, which is used by some cities, is to set out certain explicit targets, which are expected to be achieved by the time of the next publication. A review of progress towards those targets is then included in the next profile.

INDICATORS: INITIAL EFFORTS

The cities that formed the first phase of the WHO Healthy Cities Project decided at an early stage that they wanted to be able to demonstrate objectively the benefits of the project to the health and well-being of citizens. A framework of Healthy Cities indicators was proposed, which was formally confirmed at the annual conference in Stockholm in 1990. All cities in the project were expected to gather the necessary data and submit completed indicators questionnaires. This was a requirement for cities that wished to be included in the second phase of the project.

The questionnaire was developed from the work of a Multi-City Action Plan (MCAP) (Healthy Cities MCAP Indicators 1992) and was designed to reflect three key policy statements, which had been generated with the support of WHO and were widely accepted internationally. These were:

1. The Health for All Targets (WHO Regional Office for Europe 1985).
    The World Health Assembly (WHA) resolved in 1977 that 'the main social targets of governments and WHO in the coming decades should be the attainment by all citizens of the world by the year 2000 of a level of health that will permit them to lead a socially and economically productive life' (Resolution WHA 30, 43). The WHO European Region proposed 38 targets that formed the basis for the indicators questionnaire.
2. The Ottawa Charter, adapted to city level.
3. The 11 qualities that a Healthy City should strive to achieve (WHO Regional Office for Europe 1992):
    - clean, safe physical environment
    - stable and sustainable environment
    - supportive community
    - public participation
    - meeting of basic needs
    - access to a variety of activities
    - diverse and vital economy
    - respect for cultures and heritage

- supporting city structures
- universal access to public health and health care
- high health status.

The purpose of the exercise was not to gather vast quantities of data as a bureaucratic or academic activity. Rather, it was seen as a means of providing a tool for the cities themselves which would help in the production of comprehensive city profiles. It was hoped that it would generate interest locally in various aspects of city life and encourage the development of creative new ways of describing and quantifying them.

It was also expected that the indicators, if accurate, credible and well presented, could be a powerful force in generating political commitment and administrative action in implementing healthy public policies. The breadth of topics covered and the wide range of data sources required were also expected to generate a sense of 'ownership' for all the participating groups.

In the event, 47 cities submitted information on at least some of the 53 agreed indicators. Many lessons were learned from the analysis of the data, which was undertaken by the South East Institute of Public Health, in the United Kingdom (Doyle *et al*. 1996; Doyle *et al*. 1999; WHO Regional Office for Europe 1998).

The indicators which were used were grouped as follows:

- **Health**:
  - Mortality
  - Main causes of death
  - Low birth weight.
- **Health services**:
  - Infrastructure (self-help groups, support programmes, health education)
  - Output (immunisation rates)
  - Resources (doctors and nurses)
  - Access (financial – percentage of insurance cover; geographic distance to emergency services; individual – services available in foreign languages)
  - Public profile (communication to public, debates in local authority council).
- **Physical environment**:
  - Pollution (air, water, household waste, land)
  - Housing (living space, quality, provision for special groups, homelessness)
  - Urban design (green space, pedestrianisation, sports facilities)
  - Transport (public transport extent and range, cycle routes).
- **Economic environment**:
  - Employment (overall and for disabled people; levels of poverty).
- **Social environment**:
  - Education
  - Literacy
  - Social structures (family structures, abortion rates, children in care)
  - Social disruption (crime, use of emergency services).

- **Public services**:
  - Budget for health and social actions.

Many lessons were learned from this first attempt at systematic analysis of the Healthy Cities indicators.

From the point of view of the cities themselves, it was clear that the difficulties experienced in obtaining the data had been underestimated. Many submitted incomplete information, although it was obvious that a good deal of effort had been expended.

The epidemiologists were frustrated in their efforts to analyse the data because definitions of the indicators had been ambiguous, or had been interpreted in different ways by cities. For example, the indicator relating to the area of 'green spaces' in the city did not specify whether these were only public spaces or whether privately owned green spaces should be included. Some cities included significant areas of open space used as cemeteries, while others did not. In addition, there were problems in the analysis of the data, even when there were reasonably consistent interpretations of the definition. For example, the interpretation of abortion rates is complicated by the different legal status of abortion in different countries, the local cultural and religious attitudes and the availability and use of other forms of fertility control.

For many indicators, data was of poor quality or incomplete. It was not possible to assess the validity of the data. For example the recorded rates of suicide were high in Hungarian cities and low in Polish cities. This is likely to be related to religious attitudes to suicide, which will affect the registration of the cause of death. These figures do not necessarily therefore reflect genuinely significant differences in suicide rates. Similarly, some countries in Eastern Europe and the newly independent states reported no or extremely few deaths from HIV/AIDS. This is very unlikely to have been the case in 1993–4 when the data was collected.

It was concluded that future approaches to the study of indicators across the Healthy Cities movement should be accompanied by robust efforts to establish clear and unambiguous definitions that are agreed and understood by all participants. Ideally there should be pilot studies involving a range of cities, before major effort is put into data collection on a wide scale.

REVISED INDICATORS

The cities that had participated in the first review of indicators reported that there had been benefits from the exercise. In spite of the difficulties in gathering and interpreting the data, the process had strengthened inter-sectoral links in cities. In some places, all the Healthy City partners had not previously been aware of the full range of activities that were reported, so the overall profile of the project was raised.

It was therefore decided to develop a second set of indicators. The indicators which had previously proved satisfactory and from which reliable data had been obtained were retained, with minor modifications. Some were reworded to improve the clarity of the definitions. Some indicators were discarded because it was considered that they were not likely to produce useful information.

The revised set of indicators comprised 31 items instead of the previous 53. They consist of four groups:

- **Health**:
  - Mortality
  - Main causes of death
  - Low birth weight.
- **Health services**:
  - City health education programme
  - Immunisation rates
  - Inhabitants per primary health care practitioner
  - Inhabitants per nurse
  - Percentage of population covered by health insurance
  - Availability of services in foreign languages
  - Health debates in city council.
- **Environmental indicators**:
  - Air pollution
  - Water quality
  - Sewage treatment
  - Household waste collection
  - Household waste treatment
  - Green space
  - Derelict industrial sites
  - Sport and leisure facilities
  - Pedestrianisation
  - Cycle routes
  - Public transport access
  - Public transport range
  - Living space.
- **Socio-economic indicators**:
  - Percentage of population in inadequate housing
  - Homelessness
  - Unemployment
  - Poverty
  - Availability of child care
  - Mothers' age at time of birth
  - Abortion rate
  - Employment of disabled people.

The 39 cities which were designated as participants in phase III of the Healthy Cities Project (1998–2002) were asked to complete the new questionnaire. Thirty-six of them submitted responses. The material is being analysed by the Danish National Institute of Public Health, under the supervision of Dr. N. Rasmussen (Van Rockel 1999). The preliminary findings show that the problems experienced in the analysis of the first set of indicators have not all been solved. Some cities were not able to provide the full sets of data that were required. The definitions of indicators need still further clarification. There remain uncertainties about the validity of some of the responses. The interpretation of some of the questions is still difficult and unclear. For example, whether the number of sports facilities included private facilities, or meant only public ones.

Further modifications and improvements to the indicators will be developed and discussed with city representatives when the analysis of the current data is complete.

ANALYSIS OF INDICATORS

The statistical analysis of the indicators that have been developed so far has to take account of the deficiencies in the data that has been described above. The information obtained on some of the questions was of an entirely descriptive nature that was not suitable for statistical analysis. The first approach on the quantitative data was a simple descriptive analysis using frequencies and rates and presenting the information in histograms. Even this was not always straightforward because of uncertainties about the denominators in some cases. After inspection of the data, correlation and regression analysis were used to examine the relationships between indicators which appeared to merit more detailed study.

One of the aims of the first study of Healthy Cities indicators was to characterise the similarities and differences between cities. The material was therefore subjected to cluster analysis and principal components analysis on those sets of data which were complete or virtually complete. These statistical approaches will form the basis of the initial analysis of the revised indicators to see if they can provide information or insights which are valuable to cities.

USES OF INDICATORS

The Healthy Cities indicators have the potential to be used in many ways, by cities themselves. They also provide important source material for policy-makers and researchers. This value depends, however, on the development of robust measures that overcome the difficulties that have been encountered so far. They must be capable of being accurately recorded and validated and of being collected reasonably economically. In most cities this is likely to mean continued reliance on data which is either statutorily required or that is routinely recorded for management or other purposes. If the indicators are a by-product of operational activities, their accuracy is likely to be improved as is the completeness of data recording. It is unlikely that many cities will be able to afford, in either financial or human resource terms, large and sophisticated surveys. This may limit the possible uses of this material, though much can be done with innovative and imaginative data analysis.

A description of the city

The first use, which is of prime importance to cities and which justifies the efforts they put into data collection, is to provide a quantitative assessment of the health and health needs of the city, to be incorporated into the city profile. In most cases this has been achieved, at least in part.

However, the general picture that was revealed did not give many surprises in most places and did not reveal the existence of health experience and problems that were not already apparent to workers in the city. More extensive and reliable quantitative data will lead to improvements. The qualitative information provided a useful record of the activities being undertaken which were often not otherwise brought together.

Progress in the city

The collection of one set of indicators can only provide a snapshot of the city at a particular moment. The real interest within the city is in the impact of health improvement programmes over a period of time. This further use depends on regular data collection and standard definitions of the indicators that are retained over time. There is sometimes a tension between this need for consistency and the wish to introduce improvements and amendments to the data set in recognition of new knowledge or changing priorities within the city. It is useful to agree on a small number of key indicators that will be retained in the long term and are recognised by partners in the project as useful markers of the most important determinants of health. These should cover the main fields of health, health services, environment and socio-economic measures and can act as triggers for more detailed investigations when needed.

Inequality in the city

The importance of inequalities as determinants of health is well recognised. The collection of city-wide data does not usually provide the evidence that is needed to quantify the diversity of experience in the city. Broad-based evidence may only confirm everyday knowledge about the desirable and less desirable areas of the city. However, if it is imaginatively and thoughtfully planned and collected, it can give a rich picture of the lives of citizens which can help to identify problems and generate ideas for targeted programmes of action.

In many cities, some information about different geographic locations (electoral wards, parishes, postal districts) is already available. Registration processes may record deaths, births, unemployment and benefit entitlements. Local planning authorities may have detailed information on housing, transport and education. Sharing this information between agencies will often confirm the overlap of disadvantage across the city. The presentation of such data graphically, in maps and diagrams, can be extremely powerful.

However, it is not only geographic differences that should be represented in this way. Information is also needed about inequalities between socio-economic groups, which are very resistant to change and which have in recent years been increasing in many parts of the world.

Specific information about disadvantaged and under-served groups in the community is also of great value in quantifying their problems and generating support for possible solutions. The groups in question are often not readily identified from routinely collected data, so special surveys may be needed to extend the range of information available on specific indicators. The groups concerned include ethnic minorities, travellers, single parents, older people and homeless people, and will vary in different countries and different cultures.

Comparison with other cities

There has been considerable interest from participants in the Healthy Cities Project in looking at comparative data. The intention is to identify 'similar' cities and compare their health status and determinants of health. This could lead to the recognition of problems and sharing of approaches to tackling them. It could also expose 'natural experiments' when similar cities have taken different approaches to common problems, the analysis of which might provide evidence about the effectiveness of the interventions.

The work so far, however, has not been encouraging. Cluster analysis of the first set of indicators was hampered by the inadequacies of the data. Cities with similar statistical profiles had very different cultures, economies and priorities that reduced the usefulness of joint work on problem identification and solving.

Other approaches have been taken to the comparison and 'twinning' of cities. These have relied on the identification of characteristics with which citizens can identify rather than a somewhat artificial and imperfect statistical approach. Shared information about the population and health indicators can be developed in a way that is meaningful and related to joint perceptions of key problems and opportunities. Groups of cities that have been considered in this way are ports, Baltic cities and European capitals (though these are very variable in size, economy and geography). Comparisons of cities within countries are likely to be easier to plan and analyse, since they are more homogeneous in language, culture, economy and basic information systems. They are also, though, more likely to take similar approaches to the solution of problems, so the learning opportunities are fewer.

It must always be borne in mind, however, that Healthy Cities is not a competition. League tables, with assumptions of winners and losers, or of success and failure, would be wholly inappropriate to a project which has a strong ethos of collaboration and support. The complexities of cities and the difficulties of devising robust objective measurements of the most relevant parameters for health make such an approach unhelpful at the present time.

Justification of the Healthy Cities Project

The WHO has a legitimate interest in the progress of Healthy Cities since it has to justify to member states the investment in this programme at a time when resources are limited and demands are great. The use of indicators to demonstrate the progress of the cities involved could be valuable in this context. It will never be possible, however, to demonstrate cause and effect and the use of non-project cities as 'controls' is becoming ever more difficult as more and more cities which are not formally in the project adopt a Healthy Cities' approach to their planning and strategic development.

Indicators and targets

Targets for the improvement of public health are popular, though as yet there is little evidence of their success at the national level (Sondile 1996; Water and Herten 1996; Department of Health 1998). However, they do identify a direction of travel, give an indication of priorities and provide a measure for expected progress. The work on indicators should complement the setting of targets, since systematic and quantified measures are essential.

The use of targets in cities is common in developing specific health plans. They will always be peculiar to the individual city. It is likely that cities and countries will vary in their levels of target setting, from those where the target is merely a continuation of present trends to those where the targets are much more demanding. In any event, the indicators should provide valid measures, and a city's performance could be assessed by its record in the achievement of its pre-set targets. In most cases these will be interim or process targets rather than health outcome targets because of the long timescales that are involved. In some areas, such as vaccination, interventions may be rapidly followed by measurable health outcome (reduction in rates of communicable disease). More commonly, significant achievements, such as changing diet or smoking habits, take much longer to translate into reduced mortality from cancer or heart disease.

THE FUTURE OF INDICATORS

The work that has been undertaken so far in WHO and elsewhere on indicators has been valuable in several ways. It has shown the difficulties of developing measures that are clearly defined, universally understood, capable of easy and accurate collection and systematic analysis. It has demonstrated the problems of interpretation across different cultural, ethnic, political and economic groups. It has shown that, at present, it is extremely hard to compare or quantify the health of cities in a meaningful way.

In spite of this, many cities have produced documents that are accurate, well presented, lively and draw a picture of the city that is recognised by all the residents. These publications have often led to well supported programmes of intervention that have made real differences to the lives of those people who are most in need.

The Healthy Cities participants themselves are still keen to pursue the development of improved indicators that will help them chart their progress. In spite of concerns about the levels of resource needed to obtain the data, they perceive benefits in the process which has in many cases cemented relationships between agencies that often have little tradition of collaborative working.

The priorities for the future include a range of activities in which cities, health professionals and academics can work together. It is necessary to continue work on the definition of existing indicators. It would be helpful to agree on a minimum set of core measures that might be used by all cities, to be complemented by their own specific indicators that are sensitive to their local needs. The development of new analytic methods, especially those which assist in demonstrating differences in relatively small populations (localities) will help in quantifying inequalities within cities. Perhaps the most interesting and difficult challenges are in developing new indicators that can provide adequate measures of the factors that are now considered to be crucial for health improvement, such as sustainability and equity. This would allow the cities to demonstrate the contributions which they are making to the broader national agendas for health, such as Health 21 (WHO Regional Office for Europe 1999) which is a strategy endorsed by all WHO European Region member states.

Indicators and city plans

As the Healthy Cities approach extends, interest in genuine multi-sectoral planning increases. When successful, this process is exciting, inspiring and capable of making a real difference to life in the city but it is not something that takes root overnight, however enthusiastic the partners. It inevitably takes time for different groups of professionals to realise that they use the same words in different ways. Agreement on a few key indicators which will act as markers for the city can be useful but it is essential that they are fully explored and discussed, however straightforward and unambiguous they may seem. Time spent at an early stage in establishing a common vocabulary is never wasted. It ensures that the goals and values are clear and are accepted throughout the city. It also makes it less likely that the public will be confused by differences in the messages they receive from agencies that are supposedly working together (Price and Tsouros 1996; Nakamura and Takano 1996).

Analysis

Up till now, the analysis of city indicators has been undertaken using well established methods, largely because this is all the data would stand. It is now necessary to develop or adapt more sophisticated methods which will throw light on the more complex issues which cities wish to address. In particular, we need methods which can unravel some of the interactions between determinants of health, which may then lead to novel and innovative ideas for interventions. In addition, developments in the analysis of small area statistics will give more powerful evidence about inequalities. An interesting recent development has been the use of multi-level modelling (Duncan *et al*. 1996; Langford and Bentham 1996; Diez-Roux *et al*. 1997; Malstrom *et al*. 1999; Yen and Kaplan 1999) which suggests that geographic differences in health status are not due solely to the effects of age, gender and socio-economic factors but that there are also 'environmental' causes of local differences.

Sustainability

The importance of sustainable environmental and economic development has always been recognised as a vital characteristic of the Healthy City. There has been increasing emphasis on sustainability, internationally, nationally and locally in recent years (WHO Regional Office for Europe 1997). Indicators for sustainability therefore need to be further developed across the key health, environment and economic fields. Many measures which are already in use are adequate for this purpose provided they are integrated into the process of health or environmental impact analysis. Sustainability must also be checked by observing trends. A few robust indicators can also form the basis for audit programmes, which need not be complex, but are extremely useful in monitoring and refining city plans.

Equity

Reducing inequalities is crucial if health improvements are to be achieved (Kunst and Mackenbach 1995; Acheson 1999; Wilkinson and Marmot 1998, 1999; WHO Regional Office for Europe 1999). Although this has been recognised for many years and efforts have been made to tackle inequalities in many countries and cities, it is unfortunately the case that in many places the trend is towards increasing, rather than diminishing, differences between groups. If cities have to make choices about the indicators which they will develop, a high priority should be given to investing resources in those which measure inequalities, in whatever ways are considered most meaningful locally. At least then, quantified evidence will be available to guide decisions on future plans.

CONCLUSION

The work on profiles and indicators which has been coordinated by WHO in support of the Healthy Cities Project has been time consuming and resource intensive, both for the cities in gathering the data and for professionals and researchers who have been attempting to analyse it. Many lessons have been learned. Cities will continue to need proper, systematic information to assist them in the planning, implementation and monitoring of their programmes. The further development of indicators should make a useful contribution to this, provided that the statisticians and analysts work in close collaboration with the cities themselves. The objective must be to devise measures that are useful and meaningful locally, but which are also valid and capable of adequate statistical interpretation. This collaborative process will be encouraged and enhanced if cities make good use of the profiles and indicators which are produced. Documents which are 'interesting' but remain on the shelves of researchers, while they are filed or discarded by decision-makers, serve no useful purpose. Our work must lead the way to the identification of effective programmes and to the commitment to change. Profiles and indicators can only describe the cities. The whole intention and purpose of the Healthy Cities movement is to change the city in the direction of better health for all citizens.

References

Acheson, D. (1999) *Report of the Independent Inquiry into Inequalities in Health*. London: Department of Health.

Department of Health (1998) *The Health of the Nation – a Policy Assessed*. London: The Stationery Office.

Diez-Roux, A.V., Nieto, F. J., Muntaner, C. *et al.* (1997) Neighbourhood environments and coronary heart disease: a multilevel analysis. *American Journal of Epidemiology,* 146: 48–63.

Doyle, Y. G., Brunning, D., Cryer, P. C., Hedley, S. and Russell-Hodgson, C. (1996) *Healthy Cities Indicators: Analysis of Data from Across Europe*. Copenhagen: WHO Regional Office for Europe.

Doyle, Y. G., Tsouros, A. D., Cryer, P. C., Headley, S. and Russell-Hodgson, C. (1999) Practical lessons in using indicators of determinants of health across 47 European cities. *Health Promotion International,* 14: 289–99.

Duncan, C., Jones, K. and Moon, G. (1996) Health-related behaviour in context: a multi-level modelling approach. *Social Science and Medicine,* 42: 817–30.

Healthy Cities MCAP Indicators (1992) *Guide Note for the Healthy Cities Indicators*. Copenhagen: WHO Regional Office for Europe.

Kunst, A. E. and Mackenbach, J. P. (1995) *Measuring Socio-economist Inequalities in Health*. Copenhagen: WHO Regional Office for Europe.

Langford, I. H. and Bentham, G. (1996) Regional variations in mortality rates in England and Wales: an analysis using multi-level modelling. *Social Science and Medicine,* 42: 897–908.

Malstrom, M., Sundquist, J. and Johansson, S. E. (1999) Neighbourhood environment and self-reported health status: a multilevel analysis. *American Journal of Public Health,* 89: 1181–6.

Nakamura, K. and Takano, T. (1992) Image diagnosis of health in cities: Tokyo healthy cities. In Takano, T., Ishidate, K. and Nagasaki, M. (eds) *Formulation and Development of a Research Base for Healthy Cities.* Tokyo: Kyoisku Syoseki.

Nakamura, K. and Takano, T. (1996) A megacity's approach: Tokyo healthy city. In Price, C. and Tsouros, A. (eds) *Our Cities, Our Future.* Copenhagen: WHO Healthy Cities Project Office.

Price, C. and Tsouros, A. (1996) *Our Cities, Our Future: Policies and Action Plans for Health and Sustainable Development.* Copenhagen: WHO Healthy Cities Project Office.

Sondile, E. (1996) *Healthy People 2000: Meeting National and Local Health Objectives.* Public Health Reports, 111: 518–20.

Van Rockel, N. (1999) *WHO Healthy Cities. Revised Baseline Healthy Cities Indicators: Update Report.* Copenhagen: National Institute of Public Health.

Water, H. P. A. and Herten, L. M. (1996) *Bulls Eye or Achilles Heel: WHO's European Health for All Targets Evaluated in the Netherlands.* Leiden: TNO.

Wilkinson, R. and Marmot, M. (eds) (1998) *The Solid Facts.* Copenhagen: WHO Regional Office for Europe.

Wilkinson, R. and Marmot, M. (eds) (1999) *The Social Determinants of Health.* Oxford: Oxford University Press.

World Health Organisation (WHO) Healthy Cities Project Office (1996) *City Health Planning: the Framework.* Copenhagen: WHO Regional Office for Europe.

WHO Healthy Cities Project Technical Working Group on City Health Profiles and Indicators (1995) *City Health Profiles – How to Report on Health in Your City.* Copenhagen: WHO Regional Office for Europe.

WHO Regional Office for Europe (1985) *Targets for Health for All.* Copenhagen: WHO Regional office for Europe.

WHO Regional Office for Europe (1992) *Twenty Steps for Developing a Healthy Cities Project.* Copenhagen: WHO Regional Office for Europe.

WHO Regional Office for Europe (1997) *Sustainable Development and Health: Concepts, Principles and Framework for Action for European Cities and Towns.* Copenhagen: WHO Regional Office for Europe.

WHO Regional Office for Europe (1998) *City Health Profiles: A Review of Progress.* Copenhagen: WHO Regional Office for Europe.

WHO Regional office for Europe (1999) *Health 21: The Health for All Policy Framework for the WHO European Region.* Copenhagen: WHO Regional Office for Europe.

Yen, I. H. and Kaplan, G. A. (1999) Neighbourhood social environment and risk of death: multilevel evidence from the Alameda County Study. *American Journal of Epidemiology,* 149: 898–907.

Chapter 6

Indicators for Healthy Cities
Tools for evidence-based urban policy formation

Keiko Nakamura

An indicator is a tool for assessing and evaluating community interventions. Indicators are used in the assessment of baseline conditions of health in a city, the development of city health profiles to share information among the various partners, the monitoring of programme progress, and the evaluation of the impact of interventions to develop favourable conditions for the health of the population.

When defined appropriately, indicators provide evidence on various aspects of issues concerned with health. Healthy Cities address a wide range of urban issues in connection to health. Healthy Cities are usually developed through the participation of people from a variety of sectors, departments, and agencies, including ordinary citizens. It is important that these people share accurate information, discuss the issues on the basis of the shared information, and make decisions on ways to enhance the environment to promote healthy living.

It is not easy, however, to obtain solid information that covers all the various urban issues related to people's health in cities. Indicators for Healthy Cities are developed as tools to support evidence-based urban policy formation and to encourage effective application of the Healthy City approach.

This chapter describes the basis of health indicators, the use of indicators in Healthy Cities, sample analysis of health and health determinants indicators, profiling a city's health, and evidence-based urban policy formation.

HEALTH INDICATORS

Indicators that describe one or more of the diverse aspects of individual or population health are called 'health indicators'. *The World Health Organization (WHO) Health Promotion Glossary* (WHO 1998) defines health indicators as follows:

> A health indicator is a characteristic of an individual, population, or environment which is subject to measurement (directly or indirectly) and can be used to describe one or more aspects of the health of an individual or population (quality, quantity, and time).

Individual and population health comprises multifaceted aspects; therefore health measurement requires a broad approach. Health measurement covers a wide spectrum, including life and death, disease, physical functioning, mental health, subjective health, social functioning, and quality-of-life issues (McDowell and Newell 1996). Health measurement should also take into consideration the living environment, availability of healthcare services, and socioeconomic conditions that affect people's health directly or indirectly (WHO 1957).

Indicators of the health of a community are formulated based on health statistics, including vital statistics, demographic statistics from census reports, socioeconomic statistics, and results from other community-based surveys. Examples of widely used vital statistics are live-birth rates, crude death rates, infant mortality rates, age-specific death rates, neonatal death rates, under 5-year death rates, and age-adjusted death rates. Indicators of diseases and ill health include incidence rates, prevalence rates, health facility visits, and disability rates.

Indicators of functional independence, subjective well-being, and quality of life are usually developed based on various community-based surveys. Life expectancy is used as a summary statistic of a community's health status. Health expectancy, health-adjusted life expectancy, and disability-adjusted life years are overall summary statistics of mortality adjusted by disease, injury, and disability. Behaviours closely related to an individual's health status can be measured, and the aggregated results form health indicators. These include measurement of lifestyle, coping skills, health literacy, diet and eating habits, and disease-prevention activities.

The health of a community is characterised by various health determinants. The determinants of health are defined as 'the range of personal, social, economic and environmental factors which determine the health status of individuals or populations' (WHO 1998). It is also noted that 'the factors which influence health are multiple and interactive'. Health determinants are considered to include such factors as income and social status, education, employment and working conditions, access to appropriate health services, and physical environments. In a broader sense, health indicators include indicators of health determinants.

Quantitative and qualitative information regarding the following aspects is used to assess health determinants in society: demography, household, education, income and family expenses, employment and occupation, local economy and industry, infrastructure, living environment and sanitation, housing environment, environmental quality, land use, urbanisation, community activities, lifestyle and health behaviours, disease-prevention activities, prioritised health issues in local public policies, healthcare services, welfare services, environmental health services, cultural values and historical perspectives, and legislation.

USE OF INDICATORS IN HEALTHY CITIES

Indicators give us a clear, objective image of a city by reporting the needs of that city, describing the resources available in that city, and addressing the characteristics of that city. Because of the comprehensive nature of Healthy Cities, practitioners, decision-makers, and researchers need multifaceted information. Various approaches are being taken in the use of indictors in Healthy Cities (Webster and Price 1997; Doyle *et al*. 1999; WHO Western Pacific Region 2000). Box 6.1 is a list of indicators of community health and health determinants that could be used in Healthy Cities based on previous experience in various countries and regions. These indicators help people share information, particularly when people from different sectors are working together. Indicators collected by community-based assessment and evaluation are helpful to reflect a community's views.

Box 6.1.   Example list of indicators for Healthy Cities by categories

Population health
- Percentage of population who feel in good health
- Perceived overall quality of life
- Average scores of life satisfaction
- Life expectancy at birth (male, female)
- Life expectancy at 20 (male, female)
- Life expectancy at 40 (male, female)
- Life expectancy at 65 (male, female)
- Disability-free life expectancy
- Number of cases of food poisoning per population
- Number of work-related injuries per population
- Number of traffic accidents related injuries per population
- Childhood asthma hospitalisation rate
- Percentage of children with dental decay
- Percentage of population having any physical complaints
- Percentage of population perceiving stressfulness in daily life
- Students absenteeism rate
- Worker absenteeism rate
- Average annual attendance to hospitals and/or clinics
- Percentage of population consecutively regularly attending to hospitals and/or clinics for the same reason for at least 6 months
- Rate of attendance to hospitals or clinics by major illnesses (hypertensive disease, acute respiratory disease, chronic respiratory disease, diarrhoea-related disease, diabetes mellitus, dorsopathies, cerebrovascular disease, ischemic heart disease, mental disorders)
- Morbidity rates by sex and major illnesses (parasitic/infectious disease, tuberculosis, malignant neoplasms, ischemic heart disease, cerebrovascular disease, respiratory-related diseases, diarrhoea-related diseases, mental ill-health)

- Percentage of population needing personal assistance in every-day personal care
- Percentage of elderly receiving allowance for disability
- Percentage of population with disability in moving around inside of houses
- Percentage of population with disability in moving around outside of houses
- Percentage of people with disability (motor function, visual and ocular function, auditory function, speech)
- Infant mortality rate
- Perinatal mortality rate
- Stillbirth rate
- Percentage of children weighing 2.5 kg or less than 2.5 kg at birth
- Under 5 years mortality rate
- Age-adjusted mortality rates of all causes (male, female)
- Mortality rates by sex and age groups
- Age-adjusted mortality rates by sex and major causes of death (parasitic/infectious diseases, tuberculosis, all causes of malignant neoplasms, ischemic heart disease, cerebrovascular disease, malignant neoplasms of lung, malignant neoplasms of stomach, malignant neoplasms of liver, malignant neoplasms of breast, malignant neoplasms of uterus, pneumonia and bronchitis, motorvehicle accidents, suicide)
- Proportional mortality of age 50 and older (PMI50)
- Proportional mortality of age 60 and older (PMI60)
- Proportional mortality of age 80 and older (PMI80)
- Proportional mortality of age 85 and older (PMI85)
- Longevity differential index (standard deviation of the age-adjusted death rate as a function of age calculated by using a standard population)
- Traffic deaths per population
- Traffic deaths per daytime population
- Number of traffic accidents per kilometre of road
- Number of criminals per population (traffic violation excluded)
- Number of violent criminals per population
- Non-sexual assaults per population
- Sexual assaults per population
- Number of incidents of domestic violence per population
- Number of fires per building

Urban infrastructure
- Tap water service area
- Sewer diffusion rate
- Length of road per total land area
- Length of road per habitable land area
- City planning area as percentage of total land area
- Road area as percentage of total land area
- Length of guardrail per kilometre of public road
- Number of traffic signs per kilometre of public road
- Number of goods vans per kilometre of road
- Number of cars per kilometre of road
- Number of two-wheeled vehicles per kilometre of road
- Percentage of dwelling units located within 50 m of a road 6 m or more in width
- Percentage of houses which face no road or road of less than 2 m width
- Percentage of dwelling units more than 1 km away from railway station and more than 500 m away from bus stop
- Residential-zone area as percentage of total city-planning area
- Commercial-zone area as percentage of total city-planning area
- Industrial-zone area as percentage of total city-planning area
- Residential-zone area as percentage of habitable land area
- Electrification coverage rate

Environmental quality
- Number of complaints per household relating to smoke
- Number of complaints per household relating to suspended particles
- Number of complaints per household relating to external noise
- Number of complaints per household relating to vibration
- Index of higher nitrogen oxide measurement
- Annual median of atmospheric nitrogen oxides ($\mu g/m^3$)
- 98% value of the daily average of nitrogen oxides
- Annual median of atmospheric sulphur dioxide ($\mu g/m^3$)
- Annual mean concentration of atmospheric sulphur dioxide ($\mu g/m^3$)
- Annual median of suspended particulate matter (SPM) and particles below 10 micrometre (PM10) ($\mu g/m^3$)
- Annual mean of suspended particulate matter (SPM) and particles below 10 micrometre (PM10) ($\mu g/m^3$)
- Annual median of atmospheric lead concentration ($\mu g/m^3$)

- Annual mean concentration of atmospheric lead ($\mu g/m^3$)
- Noise level
- Heavy metals in air, water, soil, dust, and food
- Microbiological quality measurements of the water supply exceeding zero faecal coliforms per 100 ml as percentage of total number of measurements
- Nitrates quality measurements of the water supply exceeding 50 mg/l (NO_3) as percentage of total number of measurements
- Fluorine quality measurements of the water supply exceeding 1.5 mg/l as percentage of total number of measurements
- Benzene quality measurements of the water supply exceeding 10 $\mu g/l$ as percentage of total number of measurements
- Chlordane quality measurements of the water supply exceeding 0.2 $\mu g/l$ as percentage of total number of measurements
- Normalised difference vegetation index area-averaged by a circle of 3 km radius
- Normalised difference vegetation index area-averaged by a circle of 10 km radius
- Normalised difference vegetation index area-averaged by a circle of 19 km radius
- Distribution of plants and animals in communities

Housing, living environment and sanitation
- Percentage of sub-standard dwelling units
- Percentage of population living in sub-standard dwelling units
- Percentage of dwelling units having direct sunshine 5 hours or more per day
- Percentage of older houses
- Percentage of dwelling units with flush toilets
- Percentage of wooden houses not constructed with fire-retardant materials
- Percentage of households in detached houses
- Increase rate of detached houses
- Percentage of households in apartment flats
- Increase rate of apartment houses
- Increase rate of dwelling units in high rise apartments with six or more floors
- Percentage of dwelling units on the sixth floor and above
- Owner-occupied dwelling units as a percentage of all dwelling units
- Rented dwelling units as a percentage of all dwelling units
- Living space per household

- Living space per person
- Average number of rooms per inhabitants
- Access to regular garbage removal system
- Average daily weight of waste per population
- Recycled waste as a percentage of total weight of waste collected
- City park area as percentage of total land area
- City park area as percentage of habitable land area
- City park area per population
- Safe, open outdoor space for children as percentage of habitable land area
- Access to safe drinking water
- Estimated number of homeless people
- Risk score indicating fragileness of buildings in case of earthquake
- Fire risk score in case of earthquake
- Microbiological quality of food
- Chemical quality of food

Community action and activities
- Number of health volunteers per population
- Number of social support volunteers per population
- Number of environmental health volunteers per population
- Number of facilities available for meetings of community groups per population
- Visits at the community centres and other public facilities for community activities per population
- Number of sports facilities accessible to the public per population
- Number of indoor pools accessible to the public per population
- Recreational area per population
- Area of well-maintained gardens accessible to the public per population
- Length of bicycle paths per population
- Number of barrier-free design facilities accessible to the public
- Number of barrier-free design eating and drinking places
- Number of barrier-free design facilities for recreational use
- Number of barrier-free design facilities for educational use
- Availability of information regarding garbage recycling
- Existence of local guidelines or legislation for food safety, air quality, water quality, and hazardous substances
- Existence of environmental health information system accessible to the public

- Existence of health service information systems accessible to the public
- Existence of social support service information systems accessible to the public
- Existence of health promoting lifestyles information systems accessible to the public
- Existence of monitoring and surveillance systems for environmental quality (air, water, soil)
- Existence of monitoring and surveillance systems for housing quality
- Existence of monitoring and surveillance systems for food quality
- Existence of Geographic Information System filing health and health determinants information accessible to the public
- Existence of local health profiles accessible to the public
- Existence of inventory of community-based non-profit groups working on health, social support, and environmental health
- Number of community-based non-profit groups for health, social support, and environmental health
- Existence of support programmes for community groups
- Types of support programmes for community groups (finance, allowance for attending meetings, provision of material, assistance of professionals, use of premises, printing documents, others)
- Progress in formulating training programmes for community workers
- Existence of inventory of professionals on health promotion and environmental health available in advising community groups
- Number of recreational leaders per population
- Number of seminars on health promotion (nutrition and diet/physical fitness/relaxation/child care) per population
- Progress in formulating training programmes on skills for multisectoral work
- Number of consultations on health promotion/nutrition and diet/physical fitness/relaxation per population
- Existence of city (municipal) council and/or task group for health promotion and environmental health with the participation of residents
- Progress in formulating city (municipal) health plan
- Public awareness to city (municipal) health plan
- Progress in formulating city (municipal) health development plan
- Progress in formulating city (municipal) environmental health plan
- Representation of women in planning of the city health plan/city health development plan/city environmental health plan

- Clarification of health agenda in the city's long-term development plan
- Progress in formulating city planning scheme considering health of the residents
- Progress in formulating emergency preparedness plans
- Progress in formulating multisectoral steering committee or task group for healthy city
- Progress in establishing Healthy City project office
- Existence of a full-time Healthy City project coordinator
- Public awareness to Healthy City project
- Progress in involvement to Healthy Cities networks

Lifestyles and preventive activities
- Current smokers as percentage of total population
- Per capita cigarette tax revenue
- Per capita alcohol consumption
- Percentage of population consuming more than 14 drinks per week
- Prevalence of substance use among youth (cigarettes, alcohol, drugs)
- Existence of smoking-control policies in public places
- Percentage of population not wearing seat belts
- Percentage of population exercising 15 minutes or more per week
- Percentage of population eating everyday meals regularly
- Patterns of leisure-time activities
- Participation rate to general health check-up
- Participation rate to health check-up of stomach cancer
- Participation rate to health check-up of lung cancer
- Participation rate to health check-up of cervical cancer
- Availability of health check-up in foreign languages
- Percentage of pregnant women taking maternity health check-up regularly
- Participation rate to child health check-ups
- Participation rate of children to dental health check-ups
- Percentage of six-year-old children having received all compulsory vaccinations
- Availability of preventive health consultations in foreign languages

Healthcare, welfare and environmental health services
- Accessibility of primary health care services
- Percentage of households identifying own family doctors

- Accessibility to primary health care services during nights and holidays
- Availability of primary health care services in foreign languages
- Percentage of population covered by health insurance
- Per capita annual expenditure spent on curative medical care
- Number of medical doctors per population
- Number of public health nurses per population
- Number of midwives per population
- Number of nurses per population
- Number of hospitals per population
- Number of general hospitals per population
- Number of clinics per population
- Number of hospital beds per population
- Number of beds in general hospitals per population
- Number of beds in clinics per population
- Number of hospitals and clinics per habitable land
- Number of clinics per habitable land
- Number of dentists per population
- Number of dental clinics per habitable land
- Number of pharmacists per population
- Number of pharmacies per population
- Number of pharmacies per habitable land
- Percentage of dwelling units located 500 m or less than 500 m from medical facilities
- Emergency ambulance car callings per population
- Emergency ambulance car callings per hospital
- Emergency ambulance car callings per hospital bed
- Percentage of population having access to an emergency medical service within 30 minutes
- Welfare-assistance recipients as percentage of total population
- Number of social workers per population
- Indoor environmental inspections per year per population
- Food inspections per year per population
- Number of environmental health officers per population
- Percentage of local government's budget allocated to health care services
- Percentage of local government's budget allocated to welfare services
- Percentage of local government's budget allocated to environmental health services

Education and empowerment
- Number of students per elementary school
- Number of students per junior high school
- Number of students per high school
- Percentage of children leaving school after compulsory education
- Employment rate of junior high school graduates
- Employment rate of high school graduates
- Age-adjusted years of education
- Average years of education of people aged 25–29
- Ratio of male and female age-adjusted years of education
- Growth rate of age-adjusted years of education
- Adult literacy rate
- Number of libraries per population
- Number of volumes owned by libraries per population
- Percentage of people registered for the use of lending service of libraries
- Local budget for education per population
- School meal provision at school
- Existence of education programmes on healthy lifestyles (smoking, diet, leisure, sexuality, drug, alcohol, driving, safety, etc.)
- Availability of education programmes on healthy lifestyles in foreign language
- Existence of environmental health education programmes
- Availability of environmental health education programmes in foreign language
- Existence of maternal and child health education programmes
- Participation rate to maternal and child health education programmes by parents
- Availability of maternal and child health education programmes in foreign language
- Percentage of health education programmes using round-table discussion and/or participatory style
- Existence of basic food hygiene education programmes for food producers, handlers, and sellers
- Existence of training programmes for health promotion and environment health workers
- Existence of training programmes on health promotion and environmental health for community leaders

Employment and industry
- Unemployment rates
- Unemployment rate among people aged 20–24
- Unemployment rate among people aged 60–64
- Workforce enrolment as percentage of population aged 15–65
- People with disabilities in work force as percentage of the total number of people with disabilities in working age (15–65)
- Primary industry work force enrolment as percentage of total work force
- Secondary industry work force enrolment as percentage of total work force
- Tertiary industry work force enrolment as percentage of total work force
- Managers and officials as percentage of total work force
- Manufacturing industry workers as percentage of total work force
- Wholesale, retail trade, and eating establishment workers as percentage of total work force
- Professional and technical workers as percentage of total work force
- Average number of workers per establishment (all industries)
- Small-scale establishments (less than 4 employees) as percentage of all businesses
- Small-scale establishments (less than 10 employees) as percentage of all businesses
- Average commuting time
- Percentage of workers using public transport for commuting
- Percentage of workers using private cars for commuting
- Construction industry firms as percentage of all businesses
- Manufacturing firms as percentage of all businesses
- Percentage of workers engaged in manufacturing
- Percentage of wholesale, retail trade, and eating establishments
- Percentage of workers engaged in wholesale, retail trade, and eating establishments
- Percentage of wholesalers in sales industry
- Percentage of retail shops in sales industry
- Retail shops per area
- Retail shops per population
- Retail shops per daytime population
- Percentage of eating and drinking establishments in sales industry
- Eating and drinking establishments per area
- Eating and drinking establishments per population
- Eating and drinking establishments per daytime population

Income and family living expenses
- Annual per capita income
- Annual taxable income per taxpayer
- Annual taxable income per capita
- Annual taxable income per household
- Average annual earnings per household
- Standardised deviation of average annual earnings per household
- Family expenses for food as percentage of the total family expenses
- Family expenses for housing as percentage of the total family expenses
- Family expenses for education as percentage of the total family expenses
- Family expenses for leisure and hobby as percentage of the total family expenses
- Family expenses for fish consumption adjusted by the area-difference of food consumption
- Family expenses for meat consumption adjusted by the area-difference of food consumption
- Per capita balance of savings
- Per capita value of housing and land property
- Per capita value of consumer durables
- Percentage of families below the national poverty level

Local economy
- Local tax revenue as proportion to the total amount of revenue to the local government
- Per capita subsidy to local government from the national government
- Per capita local public debt
- Local government financial index
- Per capita local expenditure on health services
- Per capita local expenditure on welfare
- Per capita local expenditure on environmental health
- Per capita local expenditure on education
- Per capita local expenditure on civil engineering
- Growth rate of number of establishments
- Growth rate of total work force
- Increase rate of manufacturing firms
- Increase rate of workers engaged in manufacturing
- Increase rate of workers in wholesale, retail trade, and eating establishments

- Increase rate of retail shops
- Increase rate of eating and drinking establishments
- Increase rate of construction industry firms
- Housing units built per year

Demographics
- Population growth rate
- Night-time population density
- Ratio of male and female night-time population
- Daytime population density
- Age structure of the population
- Juvenile percentage of population
- Percentage of population 65 and over
- Percentage of population 75 and over
- Percentage of elderly 75 and over among the 65 and over population
- Birth rate
- Marriage rate
- Divorce rate
- Percentage of single parent families
- Number of children brought up without parents
- One-person private households as percentage of total number of households
- Aged one-person private households as percentage of total number of households
- Foreign residents as percentage of total population
- Daytime influx population as percentage of night-time population
- Daytime influx population as percentage of daytime population
- Daytime efflux population as percentage of night-time population
- Ratio of daytime population to night-time population
- Annual entries and departures of the population

The purposes of using indicators in Healthy Cities are to diagnose the community's public health needs at certain points in time, to examine trends in the health levels of the population over time by numerical data, and to set targets that should be achieved within a certain period. Indicators are used to produce city health profiles that help identify, in text and graphs, health problems and their potential solutions in a specific city (WHO Healthy Cities Project Technical Working Group on City Health Profiles 1995). Indicators are also used to examine variations in health levels among populations and communities, to examine inequality in health, to analyse the relationship between health and health determinants, and to elucidate the impact of community interventions on health.

Indicators that show changes in targets are called 'outcome indicators'. When the targets are changes in mortality, incidence, or other health-specific event, the outcomes are called 'health outcomes' or 'health impact'. When the targets are changes in lifestyle, improvement of the living environment and sanitary conditions, or changes in the quality of community activities, the outcomes are called 'health promotion outcomes' or 'intermediate health outcomes'. Indicators that reflect the processes of developing programmes are called 'process indicators'. Both outcome and process indicators are used in evaluating a healthy city.

SAMPLE ANALYSIS OF INDICATORS

Environments which have a major effect on community health may vary with social and physical conditions. In post-manufacturing urban areas, where the service industry constitutes a major part of the industrial structure, most health fundamentals are usually provided, and the health status of communities in such an area is characterised by a low birth rate, a low death rate, and a prolonged life expectancy. Urbanisation usually induces intensive land utilisation, high land prices, and high living costs; the cities often start to experience various inequity problems, including some in health.

Evidence that shows the relationship between health and health determinants in a given urban area helps to formulate concepts about particular issues needing attention. To produce such evidence, we need to identify the indicators of health and those of environments which may contribute to health, and to analyse their relationship in order to construct a model which can predict health levels on a statistical basis. The prediction model provides information which helps identify the relevant health determinants and the extent to which they contribute to health quantitatively in each community; this will be instrumental in deciding health policies which cover not only healthcare and welfare services but also various social and physical environments.

A key element in analysing health and health determinants by city-based indicators is the selection of indicators. The health of the population itself has multiple aspects, and health determinants have multiple facets. However, simply presenting the relationships among many indicators does not lead to productive policy discussions. Table 6.1 shows indicators used in the analysis of health and health determinants in the central part of Tokyo as an example of analysis in a given area (Takeuchi *et al.* 1995).

First, indicators which represent the level of health in each city-ward (health-level indicators) and various environmental indicators for each ward as potential health determinants (environmental indicators) were compiled. Data for the indicators were obtained from statistics from the national, prefectural, and municipal governments. The health-level indicators included age-adjusted death rates (standardised mortality ratios [SMRs]), the extent of inequity in health, the absenteeism rate for students and workers, per capita cigarette tax revenue, the number of traffic accidents and fires, and the number of criminals. The environmental indicators included demographic indicators, infrastructure conditions, education level, working and living environments, financial indicators, and welfare and healthcare services. The environmental indicators were then categorised into the following six categories: demography, infrastructure, amenities, education, local activities, and healthcare and welfare services. Table 6.1 also shows the results of the principal factor analysis to determine the factors which express the comprehensive characteristics of health or environment. Five factors (FH1–FH5) were obtained for health level from 27 indicators (H1–H27); three factors (FD1–FD3) were obtained for demography from six selected indicators (D1–D6); three factors (FI1–FI3) for infrastructure from seven indicators (I1–I7); three factors (FA1–FA3) for amenities from nine indicators (A1–A9); four factors (FE1–FE4) for education from eight indicators (E1–E8); five factors (FW1–FW5) for local activities from nine indicators (W1–W9); and four factors (FS1–FS4) for healthcare and welfare services from seven indicators (S1–S7). The indicators are well represented by the obtained factors: they explain from 84 to 95 per cent of the total variance of the selected indicators in each category.

Table 6.2 shows the environmental factors which have significant correlation ($P < 0.05$) to the health-level factors and health-level indicators. Each health-level factor correlates differently to the environmental factors. All the health-level factors and indicators, except for FH5, have correlating factors in the environment. FH1, FH2 and FH3 correlate to the factors of all six categories, while FH4 correlates to five categories. Correlations between environmental factors were also observed. There were 15 pairs of environmental factors which have correlation to each other with $P < 0.001$ (Pearson coefficients > 0.65).

The figures indicating the correlation between health and health determinants might vary from area to area. Also, the figures might show different features by developmental stage over several decades. However, it is universally important to select a wide range of health determinants and to recognise the existence of interrelations between health determinants and health status. These kinds of analyses are tools for evidence-based decision-making in the formation of comprehensive health programmes, such as Healthy Cities projects.

PROFILING A CITY'S HEALTH: IMAGE-DIAGNOSIS

Awareness of the importance of citizen participation in the formulation of local health policy is increasing; a multisectoral approach in developing and implementing city health plans is essential. Visualisation of the health level of the community helps people from different backgrounds to share information and to participate in decision-making regarding its city's policies.

Table 6.1. Pearson correlation coefficients between the factors and the original indicators for the health determinants

Health level (C=0.87)		FH1	FH2	FH3	FH4	FH5
H1	Death rate		−0.8**			
H2	SMR (male)	−0.98**				
H3	SMR (female)	−0.98**				
H4	SMR (malignant neoplasms)	−0.90**				
H5	SMR (malignant neoplasms of stomach)	−0.93**				
H6	SMR (ischemic heart disease)	−0.92**				
H7	SMR (cerebrovascular disease)	−0.96**				
H8	PMI	0.82**	−0.41*			
H9	PMI65	0.84**				
H10	PMI80		0.71**		0.44*	
H11	PMI85		0.76**			
H12	Birth rate	−0.50*	0.71**			
H13	Stillbirth rate					−0.72**
H14	Longevity differential index (both sides)				−0.96**	
H15	Longevity differential index (half)				−0.94**	
H16	SMR (suicide)	−0.83**				
H17	Student absenteeism rate (elementary school)		0.83**			
H18	Student absenteeism rate (junior high school)	−0.59**	0.52*			
H19	Worker absenteeism rate	0.77**				
H20	Marriage rate		0.74**			
H21	Divorce rate		0.58**	−0.56**		
H22	Per capita cigarette tax revenue			−0.59**		

H23	Traffic accidents per kilometre of road	−0.93**	
H24	Number of persons injured or killed by traffic accidents per kilometre of road	−0.93**	
H25	Number of criminals per 1000 people (traffic violation excluded)		−0.86**
H26	Number of vicious criminals per 1000 people		−0.84**
H27	Number of fires per 10,000 buildings	−0.55*	−0.47* (−0.47*)

Demography (C=0.84)

		FD1	FD2	FD3
D1	Night-time population density			0.97**
D2	Night-time population sex ratio	−0.56**	0.77**	
D3	Daytime population density	0.88**		
D4	Population growth rate	−0.83**		
D5	Elderly percentage of population (65 years of age and over)	0.86**		
D6	Rate of private one-person households		−0.79**	0.50*

Infrastructure (C=0.84)

		FI1	FI2	FI3
I1	Availability of sewerage		−0.95**	
I2	Road area as percentage of total land area			0.88*
I3	Percentage of narrow roads (under 5.5 m)	0.89**		
I4	Number of cars per kilometre of road	−0.92**		
I5	Number of post offices per 100,000 people			0.84**
I6	Percentage of wooden houses not constructed with fire-retardant materials	0.73**	0.59**	
I7	Percentage of dwelling units more than a 15-min. walk from public transportation		0.94**	

Table continued overleaf

Amenities (C=0.84)

	FA1	FA2	FA3	FA4
A1 Number of complaints per household relating to smoke	0.76**			
A2 Number of complaints per household relating to external noise		0.91**		
A3 Square kilometres of city park per square kilometre of land				0.88*
A4 Average daily weight of waste per person		0.93**		
A5 Owner-occupied dwelling units as a percentage of all dwelling units	0.65**			
A6 Average area of dwelling units per person			−0.84**	
A7 Percentage of sub-standard dwelling units			0.95**	
A8 Percentage of dwelling units located within 50 m of a road 6 m or more in width				0.86**
A9 Percentage of dwelling units with non-flush toilets	0.88*			

Education (C=0.85)

	FE1	FE2	FE3	FE4
E1 Number of students per elementary school			0.72**	
E2 Number of student per junior high school			0.89**	
E3 Number of students per high school		0.82**		
E4 Employment rate of junior high school graduates	0.88**			
E5 Employment rate of high school graduates	0.91**			
E6 Age-adjusted educational level	−0.91**			
E7 Sex ratio of age-adjusted educational level (younger than 50 years of age)				0.80**
E8 Number of libraries per 100,000 people		−0.80**		

Local activities (C=0.95)

	FW1	FW2	FW3	FW4	FW5
W1 Unemployment rate					0.97**
W2 Number of employees as percentage of population		-0.84**			
W3 Tertiary industry workers as percentage of total work force	0.91**				
W4 Managers and officials as percentage of total work force	0.89**				
W5 Number of employees as percentage of total work force		0.90**			
W6 Number of establishments per 1000 people		-0.47*	0.77**		
W7 Growth rate of total work force				0.95**	
W8 Small-scale establishments (less than four employees) as percentage of all businesses			-0.62**	-0.54**	
W9 Per capita resident tax	0.78**		0.46**		

Health care and welfare services (C=0.89)

	FS1	FS2	FS3	FS4
S1 Number of medical doctors per 100,000 people	0.92**			
S2 Number of hospital or clinic beds per 100,000 people	0.95**			
S3 Welfare-assistance recipients as percentage of total households				0.97**
S4 Percentage of medical-assistance expenditures of the total welfare-assistance expenditures	0.52**	0.74**		
S5 Percentage of people attending health examinations held by clinics			0.93**	
S6 Emergency ambulance calls per 100,000 people	0.78**			
S7 Percentage of dwelling units located more than 500 m from medical facilities		-0.75**	-0.46**	

Source: Takeuchi et al. 1995

Notes
* $P < 0.05$; ** $P < 0.01$.

Table 6.2. Correlation coefficients between the health-level factors/indicators and the health-determinant factors

	FD1	FD2	FD3	FI1	FI2	FI3	FA1	FA2	FA3	FA4	FE1	FE2	FE3	FE4	FW1	FW2	FW3	FW4	FW5	FS1	FS2	FS3	FS4
FH1				+ +					-		- -												- -
FH2	- -	- -			+		-		-				+ +		+ +						- -		
FH3	-		-	+ +			+	-										-		- -	- -		
FH4	-					-		-		-		+					-	+		- -			
FH5																							
H1	+ +					+		+				-	-		- -	- -					+ +		
H2		+ +		- -			+ +		+ +		+ +												+ +
H3		+ +		- -	+		+ +		+ +		+ +					+ +							+ +
H4		+ +		- -					+ +		+ +						+						+ +
H5		+ +		-			+		+ +		+ +				- -	- -							+ +
H6		+ +		-	+ +		+ +		+ +		+ +				- -	- -							+ +
H7	-	+ +		+			-		- -		- -				- -	- -							- -
H8		- -							- -		- -			+	+								
H9	-	- -		+					- -		- -				+								- -
H10	- -					-		- -			- -		+ +		- -	+ +					- -		
H11	- -					+ +		- -			- -		+ +		- -	+ +					- -		
H12	- -	+	-		+ +		+ +				+ +	+	+ +		-		-				- -		+
H13											+ +	+						+	+				
H14	+ +			- -		+ +		+ +											+ +	+ +			
H15	+				+ +	+ +		+			+ +									+ +			+ +
H16		+ +					+		+ +		+ +						+						+ +
H17	- -			- -			+						+ +		- -						- -		
H18	-	+ +			+ +		-		+		+ +				- -						- -		- -
H19		- -			-		-		- -		-		-	+ +	+ +	+							+ +
H20									+			+					+ +				+		
H21										+													
H22	+ +					+		+						+	+		+			+ +	+ +		
H23	+ +					+ +	+ +	+ +				- -			+		+	+		+ +	+ +		
H24	+ +					+	+ +	+ +				- -		+	+		+	+		+ +	+ +		+
H25																						+	+
H26	+					+ +									- -	+ +					+	+ +	+ +
H27	+ +		-			+ +		+ +							- -	- -	+ +			+ +		+	+ +

Notes +(−) positive (negative) correlation with P < 0.05; + +(− −), positive (negative) correlation with P < 0.01.   Source Takeuchi *et al.* 1995

Image-diagnosis is a tool for profiling data regarding community health levels and the determinants thereof (Nakamura *et al.* 1997). This tool consists of:

- mapping
- star-plotting procedures.

The mapping procedure graphically depicts regional statistics on cartograms to show geographical variations in public health.

The star-plotting procedure aims to assess the impacts of health-determining factors on people's health: depicts the relation between health level and health-determining factors; and shows the projected variations in health level resulting from specified changes in health-determining factors by animation of graphics based on models to predict health level.

Figure 6.1 maps health-level factors in central Tokyo calculated by principal-factor analysis using the 27 health-level indicators listed in Table 6.3. Figures 6.2 and 6.3 are star-plots showing the relationship between a health-level factor and health-determining factors in selected cities in central Tokyo. Table 6.4 shows indicators used to calculate health-determining factors. Star-plots first visualise the current situation of the relative health levels and the relative arrangement levels of health determinant factors of a particular city and then visualise the predicted relative health level when an intervention achieves a certain level of improvement in the condition of health determinants.

Use of the image-diagnosis tool to present urban health conditions graphically offers the advantages of:

- presenting data regarding urban community health levels in connection with geographical distribution;
- showing the relationships between health levels and health-determining factors;
- giving a graphic representation of changes in health levels following particular changes in the condition of health-determining factors.

Visual presentation of the special distribution of health-level and health-determining factors helps people understand the links between urban health conditions and health determinants. The advantage of giving information about the links between health and health-determining factors in urban development is also expected to result when we use boundaries and corresponding statistics of smaller areas such as mesh areas or areas corresponding to neighbourhoods. These smaller-area studies are understood to be necessary for obtaining a diagnosis not only for an entire municipality, but also for individual local communities, and for setting priorities for policy measures aimed at promoting health in specific areas.

Table 6.3. Health-level indicators. All the indicators were used to obtain the health-level factors

H1	Death rate
H2	SMR (male)
H3	SMR (female)
H4	SMR (malignant neoplasm)
H5	SMR (malignant neoplasm of stomach)
H6	SMR (ischemic heart disease)
H7	SMR (cerebrovascular disease)
H8	PMI50
H9	PMI65
H10	PMI80
H11	PMI85
H12	Birth rate
H13	Stillbirth rate
H14	Longevity differential index (both sides)
H15	Longevity differential index (half)
H16	SMR (suicide)
H17	Student absenteeism rate (elementary school)
H18	Student absenteeism rate (junior high school)
H19	Worker absenteeism rate
H20	Marriage rate
H21	Divorce rate
H22	Per capita cigarette tax revenue
H23	Traffic accidents per kilometre of road
H24	Number of persons injured or killed by traffic accidents per kilometre of road
H25	Number of criminals per 1000 people (traffic violation excluded)
H26	Number of vicious criminals per 1000 people
H27	Number of fires per 10,000 buildings

Source: Nakamura *et al.* 1997

Notes
SMR: Standardised Mortality Ratio.

PMIx: Proportional mortality indicator with divided age x.

Longevity differential index: standard deviation of the age-adjusted death rate as a function of age calculated by using a five-year-interval death rate with the Japanese standard population.

Fig. 6.1.   Graphic representation of health-level factors produced by the image-diagnosis mapping procedure summarising 27 health-level indicators. High health-level factor 1 (FH1) indicates lower age-standardised mortalities and higher age-adjusted proportional mortality over 50 years; high health-level factor 2 (FH2) indicates higher age-adjusted proportional mortalities over 80 years and 85 years, higher student absenteeism rate and the higher marriage rate; high health-level factor 3 (FH3) indicates smaller number of traffic accidents; high health-level factor 4 (FH4) indicates smaller differentials in years of death; and high health-level factor 5 (FH5) indicates lower rates of stillbirth and criminals. Each map displays individual city-wards by classifying into five grades according to their standardised health levels. For all five cartograms, means are set as 0 and standard deviations are set as 1 in the figures. A more densely hatched area corresponds to a city-ward of higher health levels.

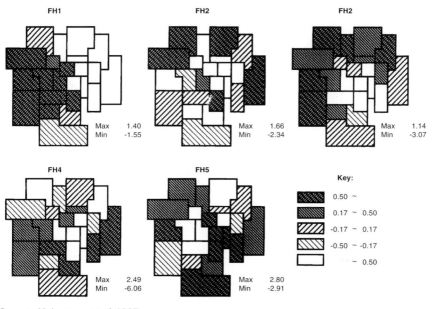

Source: Nakamura *et al.* 1997

EVIDENCE-BASED URBAN POLICY FORMATION

In order to adopt and implement effective city health policies that will improve the health status of residents, it is necessary to deal collectively with a variety of health determinants from an integrated viewpoint. To implement Healthy Cities projects in actual situations, the various sectors of society which are considered key elements in urban health management should collaborate and use common databases, and information should be shared among the various government departments and other sectors of society that are concerned with health issues.

Fig. 6.2.   Star-plots to show the relationship between the health-level factor 1 (FH1) and the health-determining factors. The size of the circle corresponds to the value of the health-level factor (FH1), mean was 0 and standard deviation was 1. The values of the health-determining factors are expressed in the length of arms, where means were set as 0 and standard deviations were set as 1. Individual factor represents the following components: −FI3 (infrastructure factor) represents a road infrastructure; −FE1 (education factor) represents a high educational-level; −FA3 (amenity factor) represents a good housing amenity; and −FA4 (amenity factor) represents a safe open space amenity. Individual diagrams show health level of FH1 and health-determining factors of a city-ward L, S and B, where health level is high, average and low.

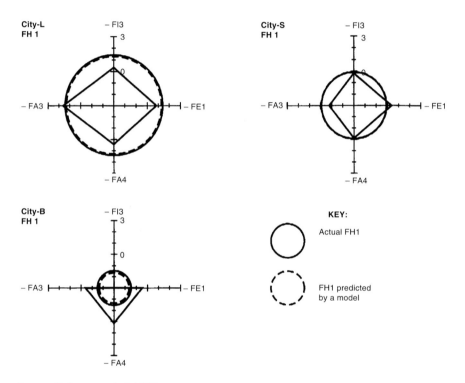

Source: Nakamura *et al.* 1997

The availability of common databases and tools for visual presentations of geographic variations of health also provides a platform for evidence-based decision-making. Tools for visual presentation of geographic variations of health help the monitoring, evaluation, and planning processes in achieving a Healthy City (Takano and Nakamura 1990; van Oers and Reelick 1992; Nakamura *et al.* 1996; Kaneko *et al.* 2003).

Fig. 6.3.   Prediction of health-level factor 1 (FH1) in City-V by the animation of
star-plots. The top-left diagram represents the relationship between an
actual health level (FH1) and health-determining factors' status (–FI3:
infrastructure, –FE1: education, –FA3: amenity and –FA4: amenity).
City-V-a is drawn as an assumption that an amenity factor (FA3)
changed from 0.58 to 0. An improvement in health level (FH1) calculated by the prediction model. City-V-b is a predicted diagram following
the change of amenity and education factors (FA3 and FE1) from 0.58
to 0 and from 1.57 to 0, respectively. Health level (FHI) improved to be
greater than 0.

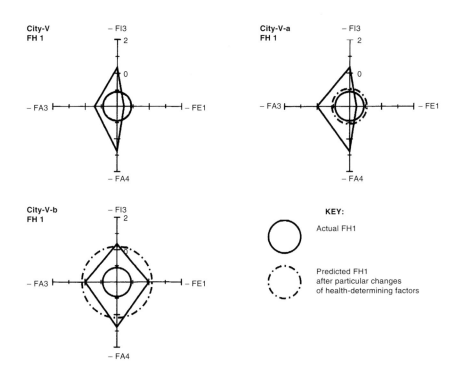

Source: Nakamura *et al.* 1997

Collection of indicators of health and health determinants that show a wider scope
of a city's health allows the production of a statistical view of the city. This data
gives evidence that is important for planning, monitoring, and evaluating a
Healthy City project. Appropriate tools for visual presentations foster evidence-
based planning.

Table 6.4. Indicators used for calculation of health determinant factors

Demography indicators
D1 Night-time population density
D2 Night-time population sex ratio
D3 Daytime population density
D4 Population growth rate
D5 Elderly percentage of population
    (65 years of age and over)
D6 Rate of private one-person
    households

Infrastructure indicators
I1 Availability of sewerage
I2 Road area as percentage of total
    land area
I3 Percentage of narrow roads
    (under 5.5 m)
I4 Number of cars per kilometre
    of road
I5 Number of post offices
    per 100,000 people
I6 Percentage of wooden houses
    not constructed with fire-retardant
    materials

Amenity indicators
A1 Number of complaints per
    household relating to smoke
A2 Number of complaints per
    household relating to external noise
A3 Square kilometres of city park
    per square kilometre of land
A4 Average daily weight of waste
    per person
A5 Owner-occupied dwelling units as
    a percentage of all dwelling units
A6 Average area of dwelling units
    per person
A7 Percentage of sub-standard
    dwelling units
A8 Percentage of dwelling units
    located within 50 m of a road
    6 m or more in width
A9 Percentage of dwelling units
    with non-flush toilets

Education indicators
E1 Number of students per
    elementary school
E2 Number of students per junior
    high school
E3 Number of students per
    high school
E4 Employment rate of junior
    high school graduates
E5 Employment rate of high
    school graduates
E6 Age-adjusted educational
    level
E7 Sex ratio of age-adjusted
    educational level (younger than
    50 years of age)
E8 Number of libraries per
    100,000 people

Working-environmental indicators

W1 Unemployment rate
W2 Number of employments as
    percentage of population
W3 Tertiary industry workers as
    percentage of total work force
W4 Managers and officials as
    percentage of total work force
W5 Number of employees as
    percentage of total work force
W6 Number of establishments
    per 1000 people
W7 Growth rate of total work force
W8 Small-scale establishments
    (less than four employees) as
    percentage of all businesses
W9 Per capita resident tax

**Health-care and welfare service
indicators**
S1 Number of medical doctors per
    100,000 people
S2 Number of hospital or clinic beds
    per 100,000 people
S3 Welfare-assistance recipients as
    percentage of total households
S4 Percentage of medical-assistance
    expenditures of the total
    welfare-assistance expenditures
S5 Percentage of people attending
    health examinations held by clinics
S6 Emergency ambulance calls
    per 100,000 people
S7 Percentage of dwelling units
    located more than 500 m from
    medical facilities

Source Nakamura *et al.* 1997

References

Doyle, Y. G., Tsouros, A. D., Cryer, C., Hedley, S. and Russell-Hodgson, C. (1999) Practical lessons in using indicators of determinants of health across 47 European cities. *Health Promotion International,* 14: 289–99.

Kaneko, Y., Takano, T. and Nakamura, K. (2003) Visual localization of community health needs to rational decision-making in public health services. *Health and Place,* 9:241–51.

McDowell, I. and Newell, C. (1996) *Measuring Health.* New York: Oxford University Press.

Nakamura, K., Takano, T., Takeuchi, S. and Tanaka, A. (1996) Assessment of health in cities by employing a Geographical Information System: Its contribution to the health policy development. In Bruce, N., Springett, J., Hotchkiss J. and Scott-Samuel A. (eds) *Research and Change in Urban Community Health.* Aldershot: Avebury, 187–94.

Nakamura, K., Takano, T. and Takeuchi, S. (1997) Image-diagnosis: visualization of community health levels and the impacts of determinants thereof. *Health and Place,* 3: 43–53.

Takano, T. and Nakamura, K. (1990) *Baseline Data for Healthy City Tokyo.* Tokyo: Gyosei.

Takeuchi, S., Takano, T. and Nakamura, K. (1995) Health and its determining factors in the Tokyo megacity. *Health Policy,* 33: 1–14.

van Oers, J. A. and Reelick, N. F. (1992) Quantitative indicators for a healthy city – the Rotterdam local health information system. *Journal of Epidemiology and Community Health,* 46: 293–6.

Webster, P. and Price, C. (1997) *Healthy Cities Indicators: Analysis of Data from Cities across Europe.* Copenhagen: World Health Organisation Regional Office for Europe.

World Health Organisation (WHO) (1957) *Measurement of Levels of Health.* Geneva: World Health Organisation.

WHO (1998) *Health Promotion Glossary.* Geneva: World Health Organisation.

WHO Healthy Cities Project Technical Working Group on City Health Profiles (1995) *City Health Profiles: How to Report on Health in Your City.* Copenhagen: World Health Organisation Regional Office for Europe.

WHO Western Pacific Region (2000) *Regional Guidelines for Developing a Healthy Cities Project.* Manila: World Health Organisation Western Pacific Region.

Chapter 7

The effectiveness of community-based health promotion in Healthy Cities programmes

Frances E. Baum

INTRODUCTION

Healthy Cities has been one of the key means by which health promotion has been implemented internationally. The movement has spread to over 1000 communities (Goldstein and Kickbusch 1996) yet the evidence base for the success of Healthy Cities projects remains small and under-developed. This is not surprising. The Healthy Cities movement is little over a decade old, it has set an ambitious task, has goals that will be achieved over decades rather than years and its activities are embedded in social, economic and political contexts that make monitoring its successes and assigning credit extremely difficult. In addition the resources devoted to research and evaluation in health promotion and in Healthy Cities specifically have not been great.

A central tenet of the Healthy Cities movement is the mandate to involve community people in health promotion initiatives. The Ottawa Charter states:

> Health promotion works through concrete and effective community action in setting priorities, making decisions, planning strategies and implementing them to achieve better health. At the heart of the process is the empowerment of communities, their ownership and control of their endeavours and destinies.
>
> Community development draws on existing human and material resources in the community to enhance self-help and social support, and to develop flexible systems for strengthening public participation and direction of health matters. This requires full and continuous access to information, learning opportunities for health, as well as funding support.
>
> (World Health Organisation [WHO] 1986)

Community-based health promotion is one of the important means by which this community action is implemented within Healthy Cities initiatives. Consequently, developing systematic means of evaluating such initiatives and so improving knowledge about factors leading to their success is important. This chapter examines the nature of community-based health promotion and presents a framework and approach for its evaluation.

This chapter commences by defining community-based health promotion. It then proceeds to consider the benefits of building an evidence base for its practice through evaluation. The challenges of evaluating Healthy Cities projects are examined and a framework for evaluation is proposed. The application of different evaluation tools is then examined and the chapter ends with a consideration of the most effective means to report and apply the evaluation findings.

WHAT IS COMMUNITY-BASED HEALTH PROMOTION?

Community-based health promotion in this chapter is taken to mean activities within Healthy Cities projects designed to promote health in a manner consistent with the principles espoused in the Ottawa Charter (WHO 1986). Health promotion, according to the Ottawa Charter, is the process of 'enabling people to increase control over, and to improve, their health'. Community-based health promotion aims to encourage empowerment amongst the community and, to this end, is based on a model of professional practice which stresses partnership rather than professional dominance. Community development is a key strategy. These approaches have been envisaged as part of Healthy Cities programmes since their early days. There is some evidence to indicate that the development of community initiatives has been more rhetorical than real and that often Healthy Cities projects are driven by the agendas of policy makers and other professionals (Baum 1993; Petersen and Lupton 1996).

So while community-based initiatives have always been envisaged as a central part of Healthy Cities projects they have not been the subject of much evaluation. This means while there are many claims for their value the evidence base to support this claim is weak. Community-based health promotion is a broad term. The characteristics of the approach have been elaborated by a number of authors (Fry 1989; Baum *et al.* 1992; Sanderson and Alexander 1995; Tesoriero 1995; Labonte 1992; Legge *et al.* 1996) and the summary of main principles and styles of practice which characterise community-based health promotion, based on a synthesis of these studies, is shown in Box 7.1.

The understanding of health underlying Healthy Cities is based on a socio-environmental approach which encompasses medical, behavioural and community development strategies (Labonte 1992). According to Labonte this approach recognises the different levels of power that groups within society hold and that power levels can influence the ability of individuals to promote their own health. Ideally, community-based health promotion initiatives are derived from issues identified from members of the community, rather than by professional health workers. Community members are also integral to the planning, implementation and evaluation of the initiatives. In practice Healthy Cities projects often start from a professional agenda and are led by the main power brokers within a city who then seek to involve the community. Immediately this means that the community-based health promotion approach is modified and we already

Box 7.1.   Main features of community-based health promotion

Principles:
- uses a socio-environmental approach to health promotion which encompasses medical, behavioural and community development strategies;
- based on a recognition of the importance of power differentials in determining health outcomes and the abilities of groups to promote their own health;
- recognises the diversity of communities and the particular needs of sub-groups within a defined area, in terms of variables such as gender, ethnicity, class and age;
- concerned with achieving equitable health outcomes;
- is informed and strengthened by the participation of local people in management, program planning, implementation and evaluation.

Style of practice:
- focuses on the health of the people in a defined geographic area or community of interest;
- community members define the issues on which the health promotion effort focuses;
- development, through a partnership between community members and professionals, of a comprehensive knowledge of local people, their environment and needs;
- uses this knowledge to identify and analyse local health issues, and to develop and implement initiatives;
- rests on models of professional practice which stress partnerships with communities and strives to overcome professional hegemony;
- involves advocacy and the provision of a public voice for the health of the local community;
- main strategies are based on community development practice.

Source: Baum 1998: 346–7.

see the complexities involved in community work that tries to live up to the ideals of participation and empowerment.

Even the definition of community is problematic (Jewkes and Murcott 1998). The 'community' may be a geographic community but can also refer to a community of interest such as people with a particular health issue or from a particular ethnic group. The term community is sometimes interpreted to include the gender, ethnicity, class and age diversities typical of contemporary societies. The interpretation of 'community' in discussions of Healthy Cities projects varies in its degree of sophistication. Some policy statements treat the term uncritically and use 'community' to evoke warm, nostalgic notions of a by-gone age and do not acknowledge the power dimensions, conflicts and diversity that typify most communities. Other commentators are far more analytical and point out that 'community' is a complex term which means different things to different groups and often masks considerable tensions, inequities and diversity (Petersen and Lupton 1996).

The Healthy Cities approach is not just concerned with promoting health per se, but also with a focus on improving the health of the least healthy (such as indigenous peoples in Australia). Healthy Cities projects focus on improving the health of the built and natural environment and argue that once this happens then the health of individuals will also improve. Health promotion, based on strategies designed to achieve behavioural change alone, may well increase health inequities because those people whose living conditions (housing, income, employment, for instance) are relatively good are the most likely to be able to incorporate lifestyle changes into their lives. It is increasingly recognised that only approaches which tackle the underlying conditions of illness will have much impact on the health of poor people. Consequently one of the ways in which to judge the success of a Healthy Cities community-based health promotion project is the extent to which it is focused on those with worst health in a city and attempts to increase equity within the city.

Typical examples of community-based health promotion are community campaigns to improve aspects of the environment, health promotion initiatives to improve health with a particular group by using community development strategies or locally based healthy settings projects such as at a workplace, school or market.

WHY AN EVIDENCE BASE FOR COMMUNITY-BASED HEALTHY CITIES INITIATIVES IS IMPORTANT

Four reasons for establishing an evidence base for community-based health promotion initiatives within Healthy Cities projects are as follows.

1. The guidelines for Healthy Cities projects produced by the various WHO regional offices all call for evaluation of project initiatives. This is recognised as particularly important because the comprehensive, city-wide projects that are part of Healthy Cities do not have a long history and so are still in the process of building an evidence base. It is important to establish the credibility of Healthy Cities approaches and of community participation aspects of Healthy Cities projects in particular. These initiatives have not been the subject

of much evaluation despite the fact that participation is seen as a crucial aspect of Healthy Cities. Evaluation is a key tool in determining the extent to which a project has been successful in integrating community people in different aspects of a Healthy Cities project.

2. Evaluation is a tool for critical reflection on practice. This can be of value to both professional and community people involved in a project or initiative. Later in this chapter I will argue for the importance of building evaluation into a project right from the beginning so that it is able to play a key role in the planning and development of a project. Reflection on practice provides participants with the opportunity to think back on their project and determine what things worked well and what things could be improved.

3. Funders of projects generally want to know that their money has been well spent and that the initiative they have funded represents value for money. This is particularly the case in community development projects because of their long-term developmental nature. The absence of monitoring and recording could lead to the impression that little progress is being made. This compares to initiatives in which direct care is offered and the impact of funding appears more obvious (even though the outcomes are as difficult to demonstrate).

4. Community-based health promotion has been growing in both popularity and credibility in public health generally, and the Healthy Cities movement specifically, in both developing and developed countries. International agencies such as the World Bank advocate the use of community-based strategies (see for example World Bank 1996). There are, however, many theoretical debates about the meaning of empowerment and the types of participation that may be implemented by international and government agencies. Community development practice in developing or developed country settings within state-funded services has always been problematic. One reason for this is that workers using community development strategies will often find themselves working on issues that bring them into conflict with the government department that funds them (Baum *et al.* 1997). Or if they do not they can be accused of being co-opted by the state or international agency. These debates need to be addressed in the assessment of the effectiveness of community-based health promotion initiatives.

Mayo and Craig (1995) pose the question of whether the use of community development is always used as a tool of democratic transformation or whether, for agencies such as the World Bank, it serves as the 'human face of structural adjustment'. It is quite likely that the World Bank uses terms such as 'empowerment' quite differently to a progressive non-governmental organisation (NGO) such as Oxfam/Community Aid Abroad. The same is true of the use of the terms within developed countries. Government departments are likely to use terms such as empowerment in a quite rhetorical way, whereas workers in a community health centre may be engaged in real attempts to work with dis-empowered people so that they can exercise a little more power in their lives. Despite these reservations and, even in the face of problematic questions such as this, Mayo and Craig (1995) recognise that community development and participation are still vital. They see these strategies being increasingly advocated in both the North and the South in 'the context of increasing poverty, polarisation and social exclusion' (Mayo and Craig 1995). These debates about the problematic aspects of community participation have not been very evident in the Healthy Cities literature. The term tends to be used uncritically and it is rare to see questions asked about the effectiveness of community participation in terms of who the participation serves, what parts of the community are involved and how equipped Healthy Cities projects are to engage in meaningful partnerships with communities. Consequently evaluations of these initiatives which seek to address such dilemmas will help to determine the value of these approaches in reducing inequities and improving health.

In recent years the importance of social capital to health has been recognised (Baum 1999; Kawachi *et al.* 1997; Campbell *et al.* 1999) and this provides a theoretical basis for assessing the impact the social development aspects of community-based health promotion may have on the broader health and life of a community. Evaluation will be helpful in addressing the ways in which health promotion can contribute to the stocks of social capital in a community.

CHALLENGES OF EVALUATING HEALTHY CITIES PROJECTS

Complexity of Healthy Cities initiatives
Healthy Cities is a long-term developmental activity, which seeks to change the ways in which organisations work and to put health and the environment at the top of their agendas. The implementation of Healthy Cities is complex and consists of multiple actions and outcomes at a number of levels. As well as empowerment, intersectoral collaboration and policy change, expected outcomes of Healthy Cities are that organisations change and that environmental and health conditions are improved (Goldstein 1998). While there is a common core of ideas in a Healthy Cities project, methods of implementation and local culture, history and circumstances differ from city to city. This is particularly true of community-based health promotion initiatives that form part of Healthy Cities projects.

The processes of community-based health promotion initiatives demonstrate levels of complexity and uncertainty that are unlikely to be precisely measurable. This complexity offers a real challenge for evaluators and needs to be incorporated into any framework. Community-based projects are based on complex social processes that have not been well theorised or researched. An example is the concept of empowerment whose complexities are little understood (Grace 1991; Yeo 1993). It is not unusual to see attempts to understand the processes of increasing community participation which do not grapple with issues of power. Often it is as important to study the dynamics of the organisation that is trying to increase participation as it is to study the community itself. Policy change, which is also central to Healthy Cities and may be the aim of some community-based health promotion, often involves long and complicated processes which reflect a mix of pragmatism, planning and politics. It is very rare that policy-making processes can easily be studied or attributed to specific interventions in isolation (Walt 1994).

Appropriate research approaches

There has been considerable methodological debate in public health and health promotion in the past two decades. From this a consensus has emerged that the most valuable public health research is based on approaches which select the most appropriate methods to answer a particular research question (Baum 1995). Invariably this implies using a mix of qualitative and quantitative methods. Juggling these different approaches is not easy. Generally a Healthy Cities evalua-tor will find themselves straddling very different methodological worlds when they discuss their evaluation approach. On the one hand some players will have a firm belief in a logical positive view of the world and believe that unless an intervention can be precisely measured and subject to some form of at least a quasi scientific design, then the evaluation will not produce useful knowledge. This view is much less prevalent than when I first dipped my methodological foot in to the Healthy Cities evaluation waters in the 1980s but it is nonetheless still sufficiently preva-lent to require addressing. The other extreme is a constructivist view of the world in which knowledge is understood as 'speculative, informing, rich in depth and contextualised' (Scott and Weston 1998). In this view, perhaps best exemplified in the work of Lincoln and Guba (1985) and their advocacy of fourth generation eval-uation, the job of the evaluator is less to come up with an objective view of what changes have been achieved than to describe the context and its politics and cul-tures and represent different interpretations of the world that is the focus of the evaluation. In addition within public health there has been growing recognition of the value of community-based research (see Israel *et al.* (1998) for a review of these approaches and their benefits and see de Koning and Martin (1996) for examples of its application). Its key principles have been defined as follows.

1. Recognises the community as a unit of identity.
2. Builds on the strengths and resources within the community.
3. Facilitates collaborative partnerships in all phases of the research.
4. Integrates knowledge and action for mutual benefits of all partners.
5. Promotes a co-learning and empowering process that attends to social inequalities.
6. Involves a cyclical and iterative process.
7. Addresses health from both positive and ecological perspectives.
8. Disseminates findings and knowledge gained to all partners (Israel *et al.* 1998).

The compatibility between these principles and the philosophy of the Ottawa Charter and the Healthy Cities movement is obvious. This tradition of research is very readily adaptable to evaluation.

Participatory and constructivist paradigms of evaluation have gained much more credibility recently and Healthy Cities evaluators will often find themselves trying to combine aspects of quite contradictory paradigms. Thus they may represent the views of key players about how successfully community people have been involved in the project and rely on a standard laboratory measure to demonstrate how effectively pollution in a river has been reduced. Using this mix of measures inevitably means there are some methodological tensions (Baum 1995) but these are manageable and likely to produce an evaluation accepted by a broader constituency than one which uses only qualitative or quantitative data. The resulting evaluation is also likely to be more convincing.

The value of qualitative and interpretive methods to social and health evaluations is now well recognised (Patton 1990; Wadsworth 1991). Equally it is accepted that healthy settings projects are unlikely to be amenable to evaluation using conventional epidemiological techniques such as randomised controlled trials. The strength of RCTs is based on the assumption that the process of randomisation will produce two comparable populations. In community trials this is rarely achievable. As soon as the experimental and control populations are different there is the possibility that any differences observed between the two groups is due to the differences between the populations rather than to the intervention. In the case of community-based health promotion, which is based on the premise that the initiative will develop in light of community input and each stage will build on the previous in a manner unlikely to be foreseen in advance, a control group would make little sense. Consequently, while RCTs have conventionally been seen as the gold standard for epidemiological research, this is not necessarily the case for the evaluation of health promotion in a community setting. Nutbeam *et al.* (1993) report that in the evaluation of the Heartbeat Wales health promotion project the community selected as a control community decided to institute its own heart health programme, thus undermining its value as a control. Additionally it is likely in most health promotion interventions that the randomisation process will not be able to compare the health promotion intervention with a situation in which there is no health promotion intervention at all, but rather to compare the value of one form of intervention over the other.

Community-based interventions have to deal with the complexities of the social world. Projects involve many components, and much of the focus is on changing organisational process and methods of operation or on encouraging more meaningful community participation. These process changes are important stages on the road to health and environmental outcomes. They are best studied using a range of methodologies including interpretative, qualitative and quantitative methods.

Assigning causality

Determining the impact of a healthy settings project on health status and the quality of the social and physical environment is extremely complex. It is relatively straightforward to produce a set of indicators but making inferences about the causes of any changes in the indicators monitored is far more hazardous. In order to attribute any change to a particular intervention it is necessary to be able to show that these factors were directly causally related. Rarely will there be a clear and undisputed pattern of causality. Consequently, this appreciation has to form the basis of evaluation of Healthy Cities. This means that evaluation has to be to based on an acceptance that understanding and assessing complex change processes cannot be based on a linear model of causality. Duhl (1992) notes:

> Linear change is a rare phenomenon. It occurs only when time is short, goals clear and scale small. Urban issues are instead complex, unclear, confused and ever changing. Change is full of ambiguous goals on multiple time lines. In fact, control of the intervention process is close to impossible.

Changes in population health and environmental health may only become evident some time after the initiatives that brought them about. Evaluations are rarely funded over the long term. Also the precision of measurement of most community indicators will often not be great enough to compare two similar communities and monitor change over a few years. Rather any framework for evaluating Healthy Cities initiatives has to consider complicated feedback loops and systems that cannot be explained by simple one-direction causal links. The next section presents a framework which is designed to cope with these complex patterns of causality.

FRAMEWORK FOR EVALUATION

One of the weaknesses of the global Healthy Cities movement to date has been that there has been little cumulative and comparative evaluation data available. Pawson and Tilley (1997) note that most evaluations are one-off affairs and that the lack of cumulative evaluation data impedes the development of projects in the future. Healthy Cities evaluators have stressed the need for process evaluation in the shorter-term as well as longer-term impact and, eventually outcome, evaluation (Baum and Brown 1989; Draper and Curtis 1993; Kelly and Davies 1993). Werna and Harpham (1996) note that short-term process evaluation is important because it allows the assessment of projects, early identification of problems and helps keep the morale of participants high by demonstrating and monitoring progress. The longer-term evaluation is equally as important to add to knowledge about those factors that make a project sustainable and effective over the long term. So any framework has to incorporate both process and intermediate and longer-term outcomes.

A process for evaluating Healthy Cities was proposed by Baum and Brown (1989) and indicates the need for a dynamic evaluation approach that sees evaluation as a continual process designed to refine and improve the project over time. The approach draws on components of action research (in that it stresses the use of research as a learning tool) and organisational development models which also emphasise a continual learning and adjustment cycle. The framework proposed here (Healthy Cities Evaluation Outcome Framework) builds on the work of Baum and Brown (1989) and on that of Nutbeam (1999) and Goldstein (1999). Goldstein suggests that the evidence base for Healthy Cities projects will be strengthened if a predictive model is used to predict the likely outcomes of Healthy Cities initiatives. The process involved in applying this approach is shown in Box 7.2. One of the objections to adopting a predictive model in relation to community-based health promotion has been the development nature of the projects which appears to be at odds with predetermining outcomes. The framework discussed here attempts to combine some of the rigour offered within a predictive model with the flexibility required within community-based health promotion.

The Healthy Cities Evaluation Outcome Framework adopts three types of evidence (similar to those suggested by Nutbeam 1999): process evaluation and short-term impacts, intermediate term health and well-being outcomes and health and development outcome measures. The latter two categories of outcomes would be determined by the project staff and community people involved based on their prediction of the likely outcomes of their initiatives.

The Healthy Cities Evaluation Outcome Framework is also based on the premise that there are some links between intervention and outcomes that can be supported and given credibility by reference to previous research. For example there is a considerable body of research relating to the benefits to health of improving social contact between people who are relatively isolated. So if a community-based project could show that those involved had more social contacts and that these led to ongoing relationships it would be a fair assumption to say that this improved social contact was likely to translate to improved health outcomes. The proposed framework encourages the project implementers and the evaluators to make such assumptions explicit. This process of making explicit the rationale for particular parts of a community-based health promotion project being linked to health or environmental health outcomes will strengthen the validity and credibility of the eventual evaluation findings. In turn this will lead to the development of stronger evidence of effectiveness and enhancement of community-based health promotion initiatives. In addition the use of this framework will provide the basis for comparative evaluations of Healthy Cities projects.

Examples of the use of the framework are shown in Figure 7.1 and 7.2. Figure 7.1 applies the model to a community-based campaign for the clean up of a polluted river and Figure 7.2 to the development of a community-based strategy developed by a district health service to promote the health of mothers and children under the age of eight.

Box 7.2. Stages of predictive model for Healthy Cities evaluation framework

1. In the initial phase of the project, 5–7 health issues are selected for priority action by the multisectoral task force.
2. For each priority issue selected, one or more activities that will be carried out are identified. These are expected to focus on health promotion activities such as education and training, social mobilisation (including group facilitation and community development), and advocacy.
3. A selection of short-term indicators to measure the impact of each type of activity will be made, based on the predicted (or hoped for) effect.
4. For each activity, a predictive model specifies: (a) what impacts are expected (based on review of existing studies) on each indicator, and (b) what is the expected effect of changes in the short-term indicators on longer-term social and health outcomes.
5. With careful attention to research methods (sampling, instrument design, etc.), a baseline measurement of each indicator is made.
6. The project activities are implemented.
7. A follow-up measurement of the short-term indicators is made after 3–6 months, and a comparison of expected to actual values is made.
8. Across all the activities, an assessment of the measured changes in short-term impacts, and the predicted effects on long-term health and social outcomes is made.

Source: Goldstein 1999

Assessment of implementation (short-term impacts)

The examples in Figures 7.1 and 7.2 show the short-term impacts that were expected from each of the stated objectives. In the case of the example in Figure 7.1 (river clean-up campaign) the short-term impacts would include:

- an audit of the numbers and types of community people involved;
- an assessment of the structures that have been established to support the community;
- an assessment of the applicability of the strategies established to secure resources and funding;
- the existence of a list of justified and prioritised mechanisms to achieve the river clean-up.

Fig. 7.1. Healthy Cities evaluation outcome framework – community-based campaign for clean-up of river

Project objectives	Short-term impacts (implementation)	Intermediate term health and well-being outcomes (predicted)	Health and development outcomes
Involvement of community in campaign	No./type of community people involved	Community people report increased confidence/ new skills/new networks	Improved individual health
Structures to support community	Committee/support from officials	Bureaucracies more supportive/ encouraging of community	Community better able to organise on future issues
Secure funding/ resources	Strategies for securing funding/resources in place	Some funding/resources available	Cleaner river • Less hard rubbish • Water pollution improved
Determine priorities Mechanisms of clean-up	List of priorities and predicted outcomes Mechanisms determined e.g. community day to clean up hard rubbish Wetlands New policies on pollution output from industry	Some mechanisms implemented	

= Link based on prediction or support by previous research

Source: Based on previous work by Nutbeam 1999, Goldstein 1999, and Baum and Brown 1989.

Fig. 7.2. Healthy Cities evaluation outcome framework – development of a community-based strategy by a district health service to promote the health of mothers, and children under eight years old

Project objectives	Short-term impacts (implementation)	Intermediate term health and well-being outcomes (predicted)	Health and development outcomes
Involve community in determining strategies and implementation	Plan of strategies developed including time-line and evidence of community involvement	Community management mechanisms	Increased confidence levels/ skills in community
Make the mother/child clinic more user friendly	Staff development programme	Change in staff behaviour, clinic, environment Increased use	Evidence of improved health of mothers and children and of their living environments
Increased awareness of benefits of clinic in community	Information available in appropriate and accessible form	Increased use of clinic	
Develop health promotion strategies in a variety of sites in district	Document sites and activities and predict outcomes	Evidence of predicted outcomes Will be developed as project progresses	

⟹ = Link based on prediction or support by previous research

Source: Based on previous work by Nutbeam 1999, Goldstein 1999, and Baum and Brown 1989.

Each of these is a process indicator and important in terms of programme development. It is also important to determine whether or not short-term impacts have occurred because in any evaluation it is necessary to determine that the initiative has been implemented as initially envisaged. Those working within a logical positive paradigm would refer to this circumstance as a Type III error. Tones (1998) defines such an error as the 'tendency to deny the effectiveness of a health promotion programme when that programme was inadequately designed and therefore doomed to fail'. An example would be if a Healthy Cities initiative used the rhetoric of participation and the involvement and empowerment of community people but in practice little effort was made to involve people and the professional people involved did not actually believe that participation was possible. Typical comments they might make would be 'the people are too apathetic', 'they do not have any skills that would be useful', 'participation is too time-consuming'.

Feedback to programme implements on Type III errors is a crucial aspect of an evaluator's role. There is little point looking for outcomes if the project has not been implemented in accordance with the original plan or underlying Healthy Cities philosophy. If at this point any of the objectives have not been achieved then it is necessary for the initiative's implementers to re-think their approach or revise their objectives if they are, for whatever reason, not applicable. The evaluation report should document changes in strategies or revision of objectives.

Intermediate term health and well-being outcomes and health and development outcomes

The next step in the evaluation is to determine the likely intermediate term health and well-being outcomes and the longer-term health and development outcomes. The evaluator works with project participants (including community members) to produce a series of predictions about what the project will achieve in terms of intermediate impacts and final health and development outcomes. In some cases the link between the intermediate impacts and outcomes will be made on the basis of previous research. These will be determined through a process of prediction (that intervention A will led to outcome B) and will usually (but not always) be supported by previous research or theory. In the case of the example of the community-based river clean-up campaign the kind of likely intermediate outcomes are that community people involved will report increased confidence, new skills and effective networks. The project could then argue that for these individuals these changes are likely to lead to improved health over the longer term and contribute to the overall health of the community. The structures and support from organisations over the longer term is predicted to lead to a community that will be more capable of organising itself on issues which affect its health and well-being. If the intermediate goal of securing funding and resources and so implementing some of the clean-up mechanism then this should lead to a cleaner river with less hard rubbish and water pollution.

In the example of the health promotion programme for mothers and children under eight (Figure 7.2) intermediate health and well-being outcomes are evidence of effective community management mechanisms, changes in the staff behaviour towards the mothers and children and clinic environment so that the clinic is more welcoming and friendly, and increased use of the clinic. The health and development outcomes would be increased confidence levels and skills in the community, and evidence of improved health in the mothers and children and of their living environments.

The advantage of the framework is that it encourages a systematic approach to evaluation and acknowledges the value of both process and outcome information. The engagement of the project participants in predicting the desired outcomes encourages participation in the evaluation. These predictions could also be modified as the project develops. Consequently there is a need for regular project review and assessment and review of the emerging picture from the available evaluation data.

EVALUATION TOOLS

A variety of evaluation tools should be used within the Healthy Cities Evaluation Outcomes Framework. These tools should draw on qualitative and quantitative techniques as appropriate. Causality can be established through quasi-experimental methods (where this is feasible) and also through the use of observation and description and subsequent deductive argument.

The tools developed should be acceptable to project participants, be feasible and not too time-consuming to use and produce the type of information required by funders, project managers, intersectoral partners and community members. The tools used within the framework should also enable the evaluation to lead to knowledge development amongst the project participants and the broader Healthy Cities community (Poland 1996).

The range and type of evaluation methods that might be used is illustrated by the example provided in Figure 7.2. This example is of the development of a community-based strategy by a district health system to promote the health of mothers and children under eight. The project has identified a series of short-term, intermediate and longer-term health and development outcomes. They are concerned with the processes of involvement, the involvement of multiple sites within the community, the improvement of confidence levels and skills and improvement in the health of the mothers and children and of their living environments. To do justice to this initiative a bevy of evaluation tools and methods will be required. Evaluation tools may provide evidence on a specific impact or outcome or may provide evidence for a number of them. Box 7.3 provides an indication of the methods and their application in relation to the example.

The use of multiple methods will build up a picture of the community-based health promotion initiative. The process is akin to doing a jigsaw puzzle in which each evaluation tool adds a few pieces to the overall picture. In building this jigsaw it is important to be aware of both the benefits of different evaluation tools as well as their limitations and difficulties. Each tool is reviewed in more detail below.

Box 7.3.   Tools for use in the evaluation of a health promotion
            campaign for mothers and children under eight years old

Method/tool	Impact/outcome measured
Audit of sites involved and activities at each site	Assessment of short-term impact to determine how the initiative has been implemented
Audit of clinic (before and after)	User friendliness Client statistics to determine if more people using it
Journal kept by project co-ordinator	Would provide data on the process of implementation and aspects of project such as the success of strategies to involve the community
Face-to-face interviews with project management committee	Determining the participants assessment of the initiative's success or otherwise. Information on skill and confidence development from community members
Focus group discussion with staff and community members (before and after) in clinic and health promotion sites	Assessing their orientation towards community members and style of professional practice in terms of their acceptance of community knowledge and expertise
Story/dialogue analysis with community people involved and staff in each site and any management committees	Assessing effectiveness of community management mechanisms, the extent to which people believe their skills and confidence levels have been increased and assessing perceptions of improved health of mothers and children and living environments and why these came about

Health status survey (before and after)	Monitor changes in health status (but note problem of attribution)
Survey of selected living environments (schools, clinics, homes) (before and after)	Monitor the extent to which the living environment is health enhancing

Audits

These are relatively straightforward mechanisms because the focus is on description and producing information for the short-term impact analysis. These may focus on specific topics such as the audit of community participation suggested above or the attendance record of meetings.

A useful tool for a project to use in assessing whether the participation objectives of a community-based health promotion project have been implemented is one of the many participation continuum that have been developed to illustrate the degree of participation in a particular project. An adaptation of one of these continuums to a Healthy Cities project is shown in Box 7.4. An audit tool to support deciding where a project is located on the continuum would be useful. Such a tool has been developed in Australia for using in relation to hospitals and could be adapted to the needs of a Healthy Cities project.[1] The audit tool determines the extent to which an organisation is equipped to support community participation, particularly the participation of groups who are usually marginalised.

Bjaras *et al.* (1991) have also proposed a methodology to assess the extent to which community people are involved in different aspects of a project (needs assessment, leadership, organisation, resource mobilisation, and management). This could be used as part of a Healthy Cities evaluation to determine the degree of community participation. These tools can be used at various points in the project to determine if there has been a shift in the level of participation.

Journals

Journals kept by key people such as project personnel can be very helpful in opening up the black box of the evaluation and highlighting aspects of the process of implementation. They provide a form of participant observation. An example of the way a journal was used in an evaluation of a healthy hospital project was that the evaluator noted that when a health information centre was opened some of the medical staff were vehemently opposed to it and one wrote to the 'Board of Directors asking them to withdraw support because the hospital should not be offering this type of service to the community when funding was so scarce for all the patient care areas' (Johnson 1998). She was also able to document that such

Box 7.4.   The Healthy Cities ladder of participation

Degree	Participants' action	Examples
High	Has control: ⟶	Healthy Cities initiative asks community to identify the problem and to make all the key decisions on goals and strategies. Offers help to community at each step to accomplish goals.
	Has delegated: ⟶	Healthy Cities initiative identifies and presents an issue to the community, defines the limits and asks community to make a series of decisions, which can be embodied in a plan it can accept.
	Plans jointly: ⟶	Healthy Cities initiative presents tentative plan subject to change and open to change from those affected. Expect to change plan at least slightly and perhaps more subsequently.
	Advises: ⟶	Healthy Cities initiative presents a plan and invites questions. Prepared to modify plan only if absolutely necessary.
	Is consulted: ⟶	Healthy Cities initiative tries to promote a plan. Seeks to develop support to facilitate acceptance or give sufficient sanction to plan so that administrative compliance can be expected.
Low	Receives information: ⟶	Healthy Cities initiative makes a plan and announces it. Community is convened for informational purposes. Compliance is expected.
	None: ⟶	Community not involved.

Source: Adapted from Arnstein, 1971: 216–25; Brager and Specht 1973

opposition was rare and the majority of staff were very supportive of health promotion initiatives.

Face-to-face interviews

Face-to-face interviews are an extremely good method of collecting qualitative data which provide a very detailed view of an initiative (Minichiello *et al.* 1990). Generally they can only be used sparingly in an evaluation because their collection and analysis is very time and resource consuming.

Focus group

Focus groups are increasingly used as part of health evaluations. They are essentially a group interview of up to ten people. The discussion in them is usually guided by a facilitator and would be based on approximately five questions. They are an efficient means to collect qualitative data and the interaction between the people in the group generally enhances the data (Morgan 1988).

In the case of the health promotion initiative for mothers and young children focus groups would be a very suitable means to gain data from paid staff working in the various agencies that might become involved in the initiative. This is likely to be staff and community people in the health clinic, schools and perhaps any work sites that employ mothers of young children. A focus group held earlier on in the initiative would ask them to speculate about what they predict the outcomes might be for their site and how they felt about the initiative. For example staff might be asked how they felt about the involvement of community members, what their fears were about this and what they believed the community involvement would bring to the project. The community members would be asked about their feelings about their future involvement, why they had decided to become involved in the first place and what they thought the project would achieve.

This qualitative information will provide a very rich and textured portrayal of how different actors feel about the initiative. These data will allow the evaluator to provide a full picture of the initiative's implementation and a detailed view of what worked and what needed improvement. All projects contain a mix of both. The focus groups held earlier on will be an important mechanism of project development and a report based on them would form a useful basis for a review of the initiative's process and an early trouble-shooting exercise. Those held at the end of the initiative (or its evaluation) would contribute to cross-validating any intermediate or health and development outcomes and provide a form of triangulation for data from other sources.

Story/dialogue analysis

This method was developed by Ron Labonte and colleagues (Labonte *et al.* 1999) for the specific purpose of evaluating community-based health promotion initiatives. The method is based on a structured group discussion based on case stories of community-based health promotion practice. The structure enables those involved in the discussion to analyse the case study and to derive both specific evaluation information and general, theoretical points from the case. The method is based on a circle of description, explanation, synthesis and planning for future action. The method can be used for knowledge development and evaluation. Its application to Healthy Cities projects holds much promise especially as it allows for debate and discussion about the perceptions of different stakeholders.

Before and after surveys

A standard method of evaluation is to measure a phenomenon before and after an intervention and then compare the results. We have already seen that the use of randomised control trials in community settings is rarely possible. This means that the strength of before and after surveys is diminished. However, their value can be increased if project participants have *predicted* the changes that are noted in before and after surveys. This enables the problem of attribution to be overcome. In the example, if the project management committee had predicted that, as a result of a campaign to increase knowledge and acceptance of immunisation in the community, immunisation rates had been increased following the implementation of the campaign then attributing the increase to the campaign would be valid. Another example would be if the project management committee had predicted that the introduction of an informal discussion and friendship group for mothers at the local health clinic would lead to increased use of the clinic and that this would lead to improved growth and weight monitoring and so to a decrease in underweight babies. In this instance a before and after survey of the weights of children under two which showed a decrease in underweight babies could be attributed to the discussion and friendship group. But the attribution is still not straightforward. The evaluator should document any developments that might affect the predicted outcomes of an initiative. For example if there had been a poor harvest in a community in a rural area or a sudden increase in unemployment in an urban area then this factor, quite outside the initiative, could affect the weight of children under two regardless of any health promotion interventions.

Measuring disease, health and well-being is far from easy. Bowling (1991, 1995) provides guides to the complexities of doing so and also provides a review of tools that can be used to make these measurements.

Unintended outcomes

The evaluation should also monitor any unintended or unpredicted outcomes of the initiative. For example it could be that from a mother's discussion and friendship group (established as one strategy in the example in Figure 7.2) some women decide to start a community garden to increase the available food supply. This would, of course, be an indicator of the predicted outcomes of increased confidence and skills but would have come about in a manner not predicted at the outset of the project.

Realistic evaluation
With any evaluation it is important to be realistic about what can be achieved given the available budget. Most often the evaluation cloth will have to be cut to suit the budget. So that in the example above, while believing that all the methods would produce useful information, the evaluator may have had to decide not to use them all because of the cost and then have to make judgements about which would be the most important.

Reporting and using the evaluation findings
Producing the final evaluation report is generally the most challenging part of an evaluation. It is the point where the different parts of the jigsaw are assembled to produce a complete picture. It requires skills in critical analysis, political sensitivity and the ability to make sense of divergent perspectives from different forms of data. Oakley (1991) suggested that evaluations of community-based initiatives should address questions of:

- *efficiency:* has the initiative been 'value for money'?;
- *effectiveness:* refers to the extent to which the predicted outcomes have been achieved or, in terms of longer-term outcomes, are likely to be achieved in the future;
- *self-reliance:* has the initiative helped to break dependency (which has characterised much health and welfare work in the past) and so promoted self-awareness and confidence and sense of control which will help people to examine their problems and be positive about solutions?;
- *coverage:* given that in the past health promotion has tended to be more successful in reaching those who are already relatively healthy, how successful has the initiative been in involving people who are often excluded? Are there any key players who haven't been involved and the evaluator considers should be?;
- *sustainability:* Healthy Cities is a long-term development project so the sustainability of initiatives and their outcomes is of crucial importance in judging the success of a Healthy Cities project. An evaluation should examine whether the mechanisms have been put into place to ensure that sustainability happens. If the initiative is not sustainable the evaluation should suggest why this is the case and what may have ensured sustainability.

Each of these is relevant to the Healthy Cities initiative. In addition the ideology of Healthy Cities, derived from the Ottawa Charter for Health Promotion, provides other criteria which an evaluation report may wish to address (Tones 1998). These are the extent to which an initiative:

- contributes to the reduction of inequalities and promotes equity;
- builds on a positive and holistic definition of health and a healthy society and focuses on social and environmental determinants of health;

- has an emphasis on active participating communities and self-empowerment (overlaps with Oakley's concept of self-reliance).

A report that addresses each of these issues should be of value to the various project participants, to funders and to those interested in the broader development of the Healthy Cities movement and in knowledge about it.

Evaluation reports are often criticised because their findings are not used to inform practice. The extent to which they do depends on the manner in which the evaluation is conducted. If project participants feel they have been part of the process of producing the evaluation then they are likely to have some commitment to its findings. To this end some authors (Wadsworth 1991) have advocated action evaluation frameworks which involve the project participants directly in the evaluation. However, while this approach may be desirable philosophically it is also very challenging. Boutilier *et al.* (1997) describe a number of these challenges and argue that the perspectives of academic researchers, practitioners (managerial and frontline) and community members differ and argue that to be effective action research requires considerable negotiation and reflection on practice. Community participation and control of research processes may lead to some conflicts with the demands of scientific rigour (Allison and Rootman 1996) as community people are generally not experts in research and evaluation or primarily interested in their validity. Evaluators should address such tensions so that evaluations are both scientifically acceptable and achieve some degree of participation. Of course this is only possible when there is sufficient time and the project community participants are keen to be involved. Participatory evaluation is well suited to community-based initiatives (for an example in the context of a Healthy Cities project see Kennedy 1994). It requires the evaluators to be skilled at working alongside others and at being a facilitator of the evaluation process. But it should also be acknowledged that both paid staff and community members might not be overly interested in the process of evaluation or have the time to devote to being an active participant. In such cases the evaluator will have to develop techniques of reporting back to the project participants and ensuring that they are aware of the progress of the evaluation and are not surprised at its findings. The issue of power between evaluators and communities in the context of a Healthier Communities initiative in New Mexico has been very honestly examined by Wallerstein (1999). She examined an evaluation process she had been involved in (as an academic evaluator) and showed how the communities whose projects were being evaluated felt they were being judged on criteria unacceptable to them. She notes that community-based research and evaluation 'is full of potential pitfalls, conflicts and pain'. She offers in explanation:

> Community-based research and evaluation doesn't take place in a vacuum: relationships are based on institutional history and links between the academic setting and the community; on the history of previous research in the community; on the particular origins of the research and on the negotiations among community and academic

> stakeholders. Community-based evaluation adds the important question of who judges and interprets the data, with an eye on how the evaluation will be used.
>
> (Wallerstein 1999: 49)

Her solutions lie in professional evaluators becoming more skilled at developing 'power with' rather than 'power-over' relationships with communities and in being more reflective about the cultural, political class and institutional meanings which shape the relationships between communities and academics. She concludes that if researchers are using the language of empowerment then they have to learn 'how to walk the talk'.

A good evaluation report is likely to be the result of a creative and lateral thinking and able to assess the initiative within its local social and political context. Healthy Cities projects are invariably tied up with the local politics of bureaucracies and formal political processes. These aspects of Healthy Cities initiatives should not be ignored and the evaluation should be set in the local context. Unlike other forms of research, evaluation is very context dependent and it is hard for outsiders particularly to make sense of an evaluation without having at least some understanding of the context. The data will not speak for itself and needs to be interpreted through the perspective of the evaluator who can be greatly assisted in this process by discussing the findings with participants. The evaluator:

> assumes the position of being an orchestrator of opinion, an arranger of data, a summariser of what is commonly held, a collector of suggestions for change, a sharpener of policy alternatives.
>
> (Parlett 1981: 234)

If the evaluator is able to achieve this and do so in partnership with the key players, then evaluation can become part of the knowledge development process which will lead to improved health promotion practice in the future.

The dissemination of evaluation findings is also an important issue. My experience suggests that many people will not have the time to read a full report. Consequently reports need to be supplemented by other means of distributing the information. One method colleagues and I have used is to present the results on colourful posters. The posters reported on a collaborative evaluation effort between project staff and researchers. The pictures, diagrams and text presented the evaluation results in a friendly, easy to understand and attractive format. Our role was to provide technical support through the process (Baum *et al.* 1998). Community members and senior executives in the local health department alike applauded the poster mechanism as an effective method of reporting the results. They have been displayed in health centres and the central office of the health department and received far more attention than a standard report would. Whatever method is used to report and disseminate the evaluation results the crucial thing is that people are engaged and inspired to act on the basis of the findings. Seminars and workshops to allow discussion of the results can also be effective and allow a time for critical reflection on the project.

Dissemination of evaluation findings should also happen beyond the immediate Healthy Cities project to the broader Healthy Cities community. Knowledge exchange and consequent project development has been a feature of the Healthy Cities movement (see for example Doyle *et al.* 1999 for description of the application of indicators across 47 European Healthy Cities). Future evaluation findings should be widely disseminated to increase the evidence-base for Healthy Cities. It should be noted that most evaluations find a mixture of successes and failures in projects. Both should be reported so that others can learn from the experiences of the projects. This requires considerable honesty and self-reflection from project participants and they should feel comfortable about the way in which their project is reported. Any evaluation that only reports the good aspects of the project is unlikely to be taken seriously and may be seen as a whitewash. Consequently honest appraisals are likely to have most credibility.

CONCLUSION

This chapter has presented a framework for the evaluation of community-based health promotion within Healthy Cities initiatives. The framework combines aspects of traditional positivist research approaches with those more closely aligned to a constructivist position. The tensions of this approach have been acknowledged but the chapter has provided the argument in favour of methodological pluralism. The chapter has also stressed the importance of examining the extent to which the key principles (equity, a socio-environmental perspective on health and participation) underlying the Healthy Cities movement have been advanced through the initiative being evaluated.

It is important that frameworks of the type advocated are used to evaluate community-based health promotion because, in an age when accountability is so strongly stressed, it is vital that a credible evidence-base to support the effectiveness and efficiency of these initiatives is developed. Evaluation based on the Healthy Cities Evaluation Outcome Framework should lead to improved community-based practice within Healthy Cities projects and increase the credibility and legitimacy of these approaches.

Note

1 This tool was developed by the Australian National Resource Centre for Consumer Participation in Health, Room 517, Health Sciences Building 2, La Trobe University, Bundoora, Victoria 3083, Tel 03 9479 3614, Fax 03 9479 5977, Email m.wohlers@latrobe.edu.au. http://www.participateinhealth.org.au/how/practical_tools.htm

References

Allison, K. R. and Rootman, I. (1996) Scientific research and community participation in health promotion research: are they compatible? *Health Promotion International,* 11: 333–40.

Arnstein, S. Q. (1971) Eight rungs on the ladder of citizen participation. In Cahn, S. E. and Passett, B. A. (eds) *Citizens Participation. Effecting Community Change.* London: Paeger.

Baum, F. (1993) Healthy Cities and change: social movement or bureaucratic tool? *Health Promotion International,* 8: 31–40.

Baum, F. (1995) Researching public health: behind the qualitative-quantitative methodological debate. *Social Science and Medicine,* 40: 459–68.

Baum, F. (1998) *The New Public Health: an Australian Perspective.* Melbourne, Australia: Oxford University Press.

Baum, F. (1999) Social capital: is it good for your health? Issues for a public health agenda. *Journal of Epidemiology and Community Health,* 53: 195–6.

Baum, F. and Brown, V. (1989) Healthy Cities (Australia) Project: Issues of evaluation for the new public health. *Community Health Studies,* 13: 140–9.

Baum, F., Cooke, R. and Murray, C. (1998) *Community-based Health Promotion: Evaluation and Development.* Adelaide: South Australian Community Health Research Unit.

Baum, F., Fry, D. and Lennie, I. (1992) *Community Health Policy and Practice in Australia.* Sydney: Pluto Press in conjunction with Australian Community Health Association.

Baum, F., Sanderson, C. and Jolley, G. (1997) Community participation in action: an analysis of the South Australian Health and Social Welfare Councils. *Health Promotion International,* 12: 125–34.

Bjaras, G., Haglund, B. J. A. and Rifkin, S. B. (1991) A new approach to community participation assessment. *Health Promotion International,* 6: 199–206.

Boutilier, M., Mason, R. and Rootman, I. (1997) Community action and reflective practice in health promotion research. *Health Promotion International,* 12: 69–78.

Bowling, A. (1991) *Measuring Health: A Review of Quality of Life Measurement Scales.* Milton Keynes: Open University Press.

Bowling, A. (1995) *Measuring Disease.* Milton Keynes: Open University Press.

Brager, G. and Specht, H. (1973) *Community Organising.* New York: Columbia University Press.

Campbell, C., Wood, R. and Kelly, M. (1999) *Social Capital and Health.* London: Health Education Authority.

de Koning, K. and Martin, M. (eds) (1996) *Participatory Research in Health: Issues and Experiences.* London: Zed Books.

Doyle, Y. G., Tsouros, A. D., Cryer, P.C., Headley, S. and Russell-Hodgson, C. (1999) Practical lessons in using indicators of determinants of health across 47 European cities. *Health Promotion International,* 14: 289–99.

Draper, R. and Curtis, L. (1993) *WHO Healthy Cities Project: Review of the First Five Years (1987–1992) – A Working Tool and a Reference Framework for Evaluating the Project.* Copenhagen: World Health Organisation, Regional Office in Europe.

Duhl, L. (1992) Healthy Cities: myth or reality? In Ashton, J. (ed.) *Healthy Cities.* Milton Keynes: Open University Press, 17.

Fry, D. (1989) *Is There a Distinctive Community Health Approach to Health Promotion? Health Promotion – the Community Health Approach.* Melbourne: Australian Community Health Association.

Goldstein, G. (1998) *Report on DGIS/UNDP/LIFE/WHO Healthy Cities Project Meeting.* Nijmegen, 7–10 December, 1998.

Goldstein, G. (1999) WHO Healthy Cities – a global program. Paper presented to a Consultation on the Healthy Cities Program in Nairobi, Kenya, 15–19 November 1999: 3.

Goldstein, G. and Kickbusch, I. (1996) A healthy city is a better city. *World Health,* 49: 35–7.

Grace, V. (1991) The marketing of empowerment and the construction of the health consumer: a critique of health promotion. *International Journal of Health Service,* 21: 329–42.

Israel, B., Schulz, A. J., Parker, E. A. and Becker, A. B. (1998) Review of community-based research: assessing partnership approaches to improve public health. *Annual Review of Public Health,* 19: 173–202.

Jewkes, R. and Murcott, A. (1998) Community representatives: representing the 'community'? *Social Science and Medicine,* 46: 843–58.

Johnson, A. (1998) Reorienting a hospital to be more health promoting: a case study of the Women's and Children's Hospital, Adelaide [unpublished PhD thesis]. Adelaide, South Australia: Department of Public Health, Flinders University of South Australia.

Kawachi, I., Kennedy, B. P., Lochner, K. and Prothrow-Stith, D. (1997) Social capital, income inequality, and mortality. *American Journal of Public Health,* 87: 1491–8.

Kelly, M. T. and Davies, M. P. (1993) Healthy Cities: a modern problem or a post modern solution? In Davies, M. P. and Kelly, M. T. (eds) *Healthy Cities: Research and Practice.* London: Routledge, 159–67.

Kennedy, A. (1994) *Practising 'Health For All' in a Glasgow housing scheme: The Drumchapel Community Health project 1990–1992.* Glasgow: The Drum Chapel Community Health Project.

Labonte, R. (1992) Heart health inequalities in Canada: models, theory and planning. *Health Promotion International,* 7: 119–27.

Labonte, R., Feather, J. and Hills, M. (1999) A story/dialogue method for health promotion knowledge development and evaluation. *Health Education Research,* 14: 39–50.

Legge, D., Wilson, G., Butler, P., Wright, M., McBride, T. and Attewell, R. (1996) *Best Practice in Primary Health Care.* Melbourne: Centre for Development and Innovation in Health and Commonwealth Department of Health and Family Services.

Lincoln, Y. S. and Guba, E. G. (1985) *Naturalistic Inquiry.* Beverly Hills, California: Sage.

Mayo, M. and Craig, G. (1995) Community participation and empowerment: the human face of structural adjustment or tools for democratic transformation? In Mayo, M. and Craig, G. *Community Empowerment: A Reader in Participation and Development.* London: Zed Books, 1–11.

Minichiello, V., Aroni, R., Timewell, E. and Alexander, L. (1990) *In-Depth Interviewing.* Melbourne: Longman Cheshire.

Morgan, D. L. (1988) *Focus Groups As Qualitative Research.* Portland: Sage.

Nutbeam, D. (1999) Health promotion effectiveness – the questions to be answered. In Boddy, D. (ed.) *The Evidence of Health Promotion Effectiveness. Shaping Public Health in a New Europe, Part Two Evidence Book.* Brussels: European Commission.

Nutbeam, D., Smith, C., Murphy, S. and Catford, J. (1993) Maintaining evaluation designs in long term community based health promotion programmes: Heartbeat Wales case study. *Journal of Epidemiology and Community Health,* 47: 127–33.

Oakley, P. (1991) *Projects with People.* Geneva: ILO, 17–18.

Parlett, M. (1981) Illuminative evaluation. In Reason, P. and Rowan, J. (eds) *Human Inquiry*. Chichester: John Wiley & Sons, 234.

Patton, M. Q. (1990) *Qualitative Evaluation and Research Methods*. Newbury Park: Sage.

Pawson, R. and Tilley, N. (1997) *Realistic Evaluation*. London: Sage.

Petersen, A. and Lupton, D. (1996) *The New Public Health: Health and Self in the Age of Risk*. St. Leonards, NSW: Allen and Unwin.

Poland, B. (1996) Knowledge development and evaluation in, of and for Healthy Communities initiatives. Part 1: guiding principles. *Health Promotion International*, 11: 237–47.

Sanderson, C. and Alexander, K. (1995) Community health services planning. In Baum, F. (ed.) *Health for All: the South Australian Experience*. Adelaide: Wakefield Press, 161–71.

Scott, D. and Weston, R. (1998) *Evaluating Health Promotion*. Cheltenham: Stanley Thornes, 148.

Tesoriero, F. (1995) Community development and health promotion. In Baum, F. (ed.) *Health for All: the South Australian Experience*. Adelaide: Wakefield Press, 268–80.

Tones, K. (1998) Effectiveness in health promotion. In Scott, D. and Weston, R. (eds) *Evaluating Health Promotion*. Cheltenham: Stanley Thornes.

Wadsworth, Y. (1991) *Everyday Evaluation on the Run*. Melbourne: Action Research Issues Association Inc.

Wallerstein, N. (1999) Power between evaluator and community: research relationships within New Mexico's healthier communities. *Social Science and Medicine*, 49: 39–53.

Walt, G. (1994) *Health Policy: an Introduction to Process and Power*. London and New Jersey: Zed Books.

Werna, E. and Harpham, T. (1996) The implementation of the Healthy Cities project in developing countries: lessons from Chittagong. *Habitat International*, 19: 223.

World Bank (1996) *The World Bank Participation Sourcebook*. Washington DC: the World Bank.

World Health Organisation (WHO) (1986) Ottawa Charter for Health Promotion. *Health Promotion*, 1(4): i–v.

Yeo, M. (1993) Toward an ethic of empowerment for health promotion. *Health Promotion International*, 8: 225–35.

Chapter 8

Applicability of information technologies for health

Keiko Nakamura

INTRODUCTION

The use of advanced technology in urban society benefits residents by increasing their quality of life. Examples of the use of technology in Healthy Cities programmes are:

- health-promoting equipment and information services;
- improved care support systems for senior citizens and people with disabilities;
- high-quality and accessible medical services;
- enhanced management of living environments;
- improved systems for monitoring the city's health and environmental conditions;
- a city health and environment information system accessible by the public;
- an information system, such as a geographic information system (GIS), for monitoring and evaluation of health;
- user-friendly devices to support citizens' health-promotion practices at home;
- a health-information network system, such as e-health;
- an information exchange system among people involved in Healthy Cities programmes at various levels (city, country and worldwide).

The recent development of information and telecommunications technology is now causing rapid changes to people's everyday lives. Our daily lifestyle will be very different in several years; the changes over the next few years could be greater than those in the past several decades. Health is closely related to people's everyday activities, such as working, eating, commuting, shopping, leisure-time activities, and sleeping. The conditions for these everyday activities will be radically changed by advanced technology.

To create cities that provide supportive environments for the health of its citizenry, it would be effective to make use of information technology. This chapter illustrates the effectiveness of using information technology in home healthcare and discusses IT's potential values in promoting health.

TELECARE AND TELEHEALTH

The term 'telecare' refers to the provision of home medical treatment, home nursing, nursing care guidance, and nutritional and other types of care and guidance as directly accessed by patients who live at home and their families. The provision of health-promotion information, patient education, consumer education, and related items is sometimes also referred to as 'telehealth', but there are frequently no clear divisions between telecare and telehealth. Moreover, within telehealth, access to easily understandable medical information and to information regarding medical institutions by general consumers and patients using the Internet and other information technology is also referred to as 'e-health', and this field is exploding into a large market.

HOME HEALTHCARE AND TELECARE NEEDS

In home healthcare, communication and coordination between clients and care providers and among care providers themselves facilitate clients' independence and the provision of appropriate care. Therefore, a large percentage of the healthcare needs of senior citizens involves consultations and management of chronic illness and disability. The measurement of mobility, sleep patterns, and domiciliary behaviour, such as cooking, washing, and toileting, can properly identify changes in the functional health status of the client at home. These everyday activities reflect clients' independence in living and are essential for them to regain their social life skills. Obtaining emotional and social support is identified as a major home-care problem. Consultations, assessments pertaining to the performance of daily living tasks, practical advice to facilitate independent living, and emotional support are all needed in home healthcare.

Home healthcare often requires frequent visits by healthcare professionals, which necessitate the participation of a wider range of professionals. There are great time demands made on the professionals involved. Coordination of services provided to a client by different professionals has helped eliminate duplication and mismatch of services. However, the senior citizen population is growing rapidly, and existing services do not meet growing client demands for more frequent communications with professionals and detailed supervision of their health and their acquisition of everyday life skills. It is becoming crucial to improve the quality of home healthcare by using resources wisely.

Thanks to recent advances in telecommunications, interactive audiovisual transmission – videophone technology – between households and healthcare providers has become available. The application of this technology to healthcare services or telecare, particularly in the home-healthcare field, seems likely to widen the choices of better care for those senior citizens who need long-term consultation with healthcare professionals.

The use of videophone technology helps match information with an individual's needs in a timely manner. This technology has been applied in different clinical settings and is changing access issues in medical care. In the field of home health-care for senior citizens, home telecare employing videophone technology has the potential better to match the knowledge and skills of health professionals with the growing needs of senior citizens seeking care at home.

ASSESSMENT OF EFFECTIVENESS OF HOME TELECARE

An intervention study was conducted to evaluate add-on benefits to home health-care from a videophone system (Nakamura *et al.* 1999). We compared improvement in the functional independence of clients and the time spent by professionals in providing home-healthcare services with and without videophones.

The intervention group cases were provided home-healthcare services with videophone in addition to conventional services, and they were compared with the reference group cases which were provided regular home-healthcare services only. The former cases were defined as telecare cases and the latter as usual-homecare cases. Telecare cases and usual-homecare cases were selected from communities where home healthcare usually includes physician home visits, visiting nurse services, meals on wheels, and household services.

Clients of home telecare were requested to participate in a three-month study of videophone use for their services and an evaluation study of home healthcare. Individual services were provided by a physician, a public health nurse, a visiting nurse, a physical therapist, an occupational therapist, a speech therapist, a social worker, and one to three home helpers according to individual needs.

The usual-homecare cases were selected as reference cases from ordinary home-healthcare cases provided with ordinary home-healthcare services. Among newly enrolled clients in home healthcare in any month except February, June, and October, those matching the telecare cases on the criteria of sex, age (three-year range), and level of independence as assessed by the Katz index of ADL (Katz 1963) were requested to participate in an evaluation study of home healthcare. Individual home-healthcare services were provided by a physician, a public health nurse, a visiting nurse, a physical therapist, an occupational therapist, a speech therapist, a social worker, and one to three home helpers according to individual needs.

The following services are usually planned and provided based on the regulations of a municipality: physician home visits, public health nurse visits, visiting nurse services, visits by physical therapists, visits by occupational therapists, home-visiting services by home helpers, daycare service for frail senior citizens, meals on wheels, mobile shower and bathing service, in-house bathing service for bed-ridden senior citizens, a group rehabilitation programme for senior citizens with disabilities, and others.

We used videophone sets transmitting colour images using 128 Kbps ISDN (Fujitsu VS-700) – video camera, codec, and monitor – for the services for the telecare cases. Videophone sets were installed in the homes of the individual telecare clients and the offices of home-healthcare professionals, namely, the physicians, public health nurses, physical therapists, occupational therapists, and social workers.

The following were offered as services using videophone: medical consultation about clients' health problems; instructions regarding physical exercise; communication exercises; assessment and instructions regarding ADL; assessment and instructions regarding communication; assessment and instructions regarding daily activities; assessment and instructions regarding clients' social activities; assessment and instructions regarding nutrition; assessment and instructions regarding caregiving techniques; advice and instructions for visiting healthcare staff; advice and instructions for volunteers; advice on the effective use of health and welfare resources; and emotional support for clients and their families. Those clients having difficulties in handling the videophone by themselves were supported by their family members in the use of the videophone.

The following assessments were performed both at the first and second assessment visits and in both the intervention telecare cases and the reference usual-homecare cases: ADL independence measured by the 13 motor items in the Functional Independence Measure (FIM), including self-care, sphincter control, transfer and locomotion; communication independence measured by the two communication items in the FIM; and social cognition independence measured by the three social-cognition items in the FIM (Keith *et al.* 1987). We compared differences in the before-and-after improvements between matched pairs of intervention telecare cases and reference usual-homecare cases using paired t-test, controlling for sex, age, and the baseline Katz index of ADL.

Records of home visits, outpatient care, and consultation via videophone were filed and used for this analysis. According to the dates and hours that clients received services by physicians, public health nurses, physical therapists, occupational therapists, social workers, visiting nurses, and home helpers at home, and services via videophone, person-minutes spent by physicians, public health nurses, physical therapists, occupational therapists, social workers, visiting nurses, and home helpers were calculated for each case, including time spent at clients' homes; time spent for examinations, treatment, and instructions for a single client at outpatient settings, such as physician's clinics, hospitals, or day-rehabilitation centres (in the case of a group session of t_1 minutes cared for by n_1 professionals and attended by n_2 clients, time spent for a single client (t) was calculated as follows: $t = (t_1 \times n_1)/n_2$); and time spent for communication via videophone. Weekly average person-minutes per case were calculated for the telecare and usual-homecare groups.

RESULTS OF THE ASSESSMENT

A total of 39 clients used videophones. The selection of telecare cases from the 39 telecare cases according to the baseline ADL and case matching defined 16 matched pairs for the analysis. They were five pairs of male clients and 11 pairs of female clients. The average age of the telecare clients was 72.1 years and that of the usual-homecare clients was 73.0. Although two cases of home-telecare cases were categorised as G level in the Katz index of ADL, case matching was not successful with ordinary home-healthcare cases.

The ADL independence scores of the telecare group improved from 61.4 to 62.9 (91 points as maximum score) on average, while those of the usual-homecare group declined from 60.8 to 60.4; the improvement in the telecare group was statistically significant ($p<0.05$). The communication and social cognition independence of the telecare group during the three-month trial period measured by the FIM improved from 10.4 to 11.4 points (14 points as maximum score) and from 14.2 to 16.1 points (21 points as maximum score) on average, respectively; these were significantly greater than those of the usual-homecare group ($p<0.05$).

Communication via videophone facilitated the following assessments and responses: assessment of weight loss and prompt provision of advice; evaluation of nutritional balance and everyday meals at home; assessment of everyday life schedule and change of physical condition during the day; supervision of physical exercise suited to clients' everyday physical condition; advice on health of family caregivers; provision of everyday face-to-face speech exercise; advice on everyday homemaking activities; encouragement of regular physical exercise at home; and others.

Average weekly total person-minutes required for face-to-face intervention and intervention via videophone by professionals working with the telecare group was 229 minutes per case, while that by professionals working with the usual-homecare group was 219 minutes per case ($p>0.05$). Time spent for communicating via videophone was 66 minutes per week. Time spent providing visiting services and travelling in the telecare cases was 186 min/week/case and that in the usual-homecare cases was 255 min/week/case ($p>0.05$). When time for travelling to and from clients' homes and for pick-up service to provide transportation from clients' homes to care centres was included in the calculation, the average weekly total person-minutes required was 303 minutes per case with the telecare group and 316 minutes per case with the usual-homecare group. Average weekly person-minutes required by professionals were as follows.

- Physicians: 15 minutes (3 minutes via videophone) in the telecare group and 18 minutes in the usual-homecare group.
- Public health nurses, visiting nurses, physical therapists, occupational therapists: 151 minutes (63 minutes via videophone) in the telecare group and 109 minutes in the usual-homecare group.
- Home helper: 120 minutes in the telecare group and 170 minutes in the usual-homecare group.

As regards the number of consultations, the telecare group received 7.0 consultations per week (3.8 consultations via videophone and 3.2 consultations as home visiting and ambulatory services) while the usual-homecare group received 3.6

consultations as home visiting and ambulatory services. The frequency of received consultations was significantly greater in telecare cases than in usual-homecare cases (p<0.01).

EFFECTIVENESS OF HOME TELECARE

Home healthcare using videophone, in addition to home visiting and ambulatory services, was more successful in improving the independence of clients than care under conventional support programmes provided through home visiting and ambulatory services. Improvements in clients' functional independence were realised without requiring extra time by the professionals involved. This evidence shows the potential for telecommunications technologies to improve the quality of home healthcare.

Our experience in this study suggests that services via videophone cannot replace all in-person visits. The net time professionals contributed in services via videophone was 29 per cent of the total time spent with clients (face-to-face in-person services and services via videophone). The frequency of consultations, regardless of the time spent for the consultation, was significantly increased with the application of telecare. This might have increased opportunities to respond to clients' needs in a timely fashion.

Results of the time study showed that the total person-time required per case for the telecare cases was not greater than that for the usual-homecare cases. Although the total cost of home healthcare requires inclusion of other direct and indirect costs, it is significant that telecare cases did not require additional person-time compared with usual-homecare cases. This is because videophone communication replaced some of the visiting services. If telecare were widely provided as one of the regular styles of home healthcare, more efficient use of time and personnel could be realised.

POTENTIAL ADDED VALUE IN HEALTH PROMOTION

The development of personal skills through the provision of information, education for health, and other enhancement of life skills helps people exercise more control over their own health and over their environment and make choices conducive to health. In rehabilitation at home, task-specific activities based on the client's personal interests are important. Home-based therapy values purposeful activities that promote adaptation and competence in older adults with chronic disabilities. Communication independence, particularly independence in expression, was improved. Videophones enable communication via body language, physical expression, and appearance. Therefore, repeated opportunities to speak with others via a medium that includes a visual component contributed to the improvement of clients' personal skills in communication. The use of such an audiovisual medium was thought to increase compliance, encourage clients, and facilitate health professionals' decision making.

A senior citizen's ability to communicate is closely related to his or her physical and interpersonal environment. Support from friends and neighbours is associated with mental and physical health outcomes. Communication via videophone focuses one's concentration on one's interlocutor. Videophone communication widens clients' social network, and so they can regain their independence in society. Videophone communication requires greater independence than direct personal communication by visiting or ambulatory services because the client must organise the call. In addition, it is easier to develop better human relationships and greater self-esteem by use of videophone.

In terms of controlling the quality of home healthcare, telecare would facilitate timely assessment by supervisors and/or outside reviewers. As most home-healthcare services are provided at individual households without constant monitoring by outside reviewers, review of services via videophone is a possible option to protect clients' rights and guarantee quality services.

Differences in level of home healthcare by geographical area are thought to lead to unequal access to care. Telecare can alleviate regional differences by making high-quality assessment and supervision of home healthcare available regardless of the distance a client lives from a well-staffed home-healthcare centre and by providing on-the-job training and case supervision and advice to visiting staff by well-trained supervisors.

The add-on effectiveness of videophones in home-healthcare services was found to be significant. Evidence showed that the use of information technology in home healthcare increased the ability of the senior citizen and their families to control and improve their health. The further potential of information technology fundamentally to increase the control of the general public on their health was inferred (Brennan 1999). Appropriate use of information technology is likely to increase opportunities for multiple sectors to participate in decision making in individual as well as population health. Innovative thinking regarding the best use of emerging technology will create new opportunities for health promotion.

References

Brennan, P. F. (1999) Telehealth: bringing healthcare to the point of living. *Medical Care,* 37: 115–16.

Katz, S. (1963) Studies of illness in the aged: the index of ADL, a standardized measure of biological and psychosocial function. *JAMA,* 185: 914.

Keith, R. A., Granger, C. V., Hamilton, B. B. and Shervin, F. S. (1987) The functional independence measure: a new tool for rehabilitation. In Eisenberg, M. G. and Grzesiak, R. C. (eds) *Advances in Clinical Rehabilitation.* Vol 1. New York: Springer-Verlag.

Nakamura, K., Takano, T., Akao, C. (1999) The effectiveness of videophones in home healthcare for the elderly. *Medical Care,* 37: 117–25.

Chapter 9

Nurturing Healthy Cities

Research responsibility and accountability

Evelyne de Leeuw

Dear Dr de Leeuw,

[...] Unfortunately, we are unable to fund your research proposal on Healthy Cities. As you should be aware, our organisation only funds public health intervention research. To our mind, Healthy Cities is not an intervention, but rather a vision or philosophy, and we are therefore not in a position to make out a grant.

Dear Evelyne,

[...] After long deliberations we have decided not to honour your proposal to fund your inquiry in which you would compare Healthy Cities effects in four matched municipalities in the south of our province. We will instead fund a proposal which will apply validated social psychological theories in the field of community intervention in those towns.

A friend of mine had worked for many years in the field of environmental health promotion in Latin America and the Middle East. She decided that the Healthy City idea would possibly be very applicable to her work, and enrolled in a British school of public health with enormous global repute in order to pursue a PhD in that field. Her advisors told her: 'forget Healthy Cities. They're active for over a decade, and no-one so far has ever attempted to evaluate it. For a reason, we suspect. You would fail any PhD in that direction.'

Anyone active in the field of Healthy Cities research must have been confronted with tales like the above. It seems that social scientific research in public health is already having a hard time, let alone undertaking such research in a realm which is still considered by numerous funding agencies 'ideological', 'erratic', 'unfocused' or even 'unresearchable'.

Perhaps we are doing something wrong. For research in, with, for and on Healthy Cities is as old as the movement itself, and by now a considerable body of evidence is amassed. Certainly, this evidence is not the kind of irrefutable 'proof' advocated by fans of 'evidence-based medicine'. Nor are measures that are all too common in epidemiology or the more hardline health services research field easily found in the Healthy Cities body of evidence.

WHAT ARE WE AFTER?

The sheer number of cities, globally, that has embraced the Healthy Cities per-spective since 1986 is evidence in itself that we must have something in our hands that *works*. Compare it with any other product: if Sony had launched, somewhere in the 1980s, a palm-size sound reproduction system called 'walkman' which did not live up to its promise the Japanese multinational would never have continued to market such systems in the twenty-first century.

So – if we are to solve the riddle 'do Healthy Cities work?' we must consider a number of issues before we can proceed to answer the question.

1. We will have to review the core values of Healthy City projects, whether they are European towns designated by the World Health Organisation (WHO), members of networks of Healthy Cities in Europe or elsewhere, or lone pio-neers of the movement in countries that have not yet fully adopted modern health policy approaches.
2. We will have to connect those essential merits with the notion of evidence. What should we consider appropriate or sufficient evidence to judge Healthy Cities as something that works?
3. Once we know which evidence is acceptable in judging the efficacy of Healthy Cities, could we develop a meaningful research framework, or even research agenda? What types of questions would we ask, what data would we need, which theories might be appropriate, what methodologies would be advisable? And most important, for whom are we producing such evidence?
4. We will explore which areas in the proposed framework or agenda are rea-sonably well filled in, and which fields are still white spots in our knowledge.
5. Ultimately, one possible framework will be presented: it is the MARI frame-work currently in use in the European network of WHO designated cities. MARI stands for Monitoring, Accountability, Reporting, and Impact assess-ment; though developed specifically for Europe, the general vision and mission of MARI might be applicable to other Healthy Cities as well.

WHAT UNITES THOUSANDS OF HEALTHY CITIES?

In her seminal research piece *Innovations in a Fuzzy Domain* (1998) Marleen Goumans asked politicians and civil servants in ten British and Dutch cities what their perception of their town being a Healthy City was (cf. also Goumans and Springett 1997). No two perceptions were alike. Had she included community leaders and non-government organisation (NGO) representatives, as did de Leeuw *et al.* (1998), the picture would have been even fuzzier. Responses range from 'good local governance' to 'ecological urban planning', and from 'commu-nity consultation' to 'healthy public transport'.

Looking at writings that are used to underpin Healthy City projects globally, there appears to be somewhat more consistency, but even here the sets of core values range from a number of merely four (WHO/EURO 1998) to seven (Ashton 1991), three (Werna *et al.* 1998: 18), six (WHO 1995, similar to the core principles of the Health for All strategy) or eleven (Tsouros 1992), see Figure 9.1.

In a way, it is peculiar that that which has become known as 'The Healthy Cities Movement' (e.g. Tsouros 1992) seems to have such a limited sense of history – or maybe this is exactly what constitutes a movement: a perceived lack of (theoretical) foundation which is compensated by enormous enthusiasm. A quick guesstimate among colleagues involved in Healthy City implementation both in academia and in practice would indicate that there is very little sense of the sheer innumerable quantity of booklets, brochures, books published by quite reputable companies, by WHO, and by passionate believers, newsletters and articles, which over the years have produced a reasonably solid foundation for the movement. Yet, there is a continuous process of re-invention of the Healthy City which seems utterly useless. Why am I saying this?

Most if not all about the foundation of the Healthy City concept has been laid down in a series of WHO publications, most notably the 'yellow booklets' that

Fig. 9.1.   Eleven qualities a Healthy City should strive to provide

THE QUALITIES OF A HEALTHY CITY **a city should strive to provide:**
1   a clean, safe physical environment of high quality (including housing quality)
2   an ecosystem that is stable now and sustainable in the long term
3   a strong, mutually supportive and non-exploitive community
4   a high degree of participation and control by the public over decisions affecting their lives
5   the meeting of basic needs (food, water, shelter, income, safety and work) for all people
6   access to a wide variety of experiences and resources, for a wide variety of interaction
7   a diverse, vital and innovative city economy
8   the encouragement of connectedness with the past, and heritage of citydwellers and others
9   a form that is compatible with, and enhances, the preceding characteristics
10 an optimum level of appropriate public health and sick care services accessible to all
11 high health status (high levels of positive health and low levels of disease)

Source: Tsouros 1992

were published in the late 1980s (Hancock and Duhl 1988; Kaasjager *et al.* 1989; Kickbusch 1989; WHO 1988a; WHO 1988b). Reviewing the material over a decade later, it is striking how much of these writings should still be considered inspirational and validated observations on the creation and maintenance of health promotion in the urban context. Hancock and Duhl (1988: 23) point out that a healthy city can only be identified by encountering it:

> It must be experienced, and we must develop and incorporate into our assessment of the health of a city a variety of unconventional, intuitive and holistic measures to supplement the hard data. Indeed, unless data are turned into stories that can be understood by all, they are not effective in any process of change, either political or administrative.

Since the beginning of the Healthy Cities Project in Europe there have been less or more successful efforts at evaluation of the achievements of the network cities and the Project as a whole (for review, see Curtice 1995 and Tsouros 1994). Research in, with, for and on Healthy Cities over time has become an important issue in the movement. There is no conference, seminar or meeting where the research issue has not been debated (de Leeuw *et al.* 1992). Currently, there still is very little empirical work on Healthy City evaluation, work by Werna and Harpham (1995, 1996) being the exception rather than the rule. However, equivocal notions of what Healthy Cities are all about have obscured the development of a reasonable and validated research paradigm.

Judging all this contextualism and diversity, it might be tempting even to the rational investigator to adopt the words by Italian author Italo Calvino in his *The Invisible Cities*:

> [...] è inutile stabilire se Zenobia sia da classificare tra le città felici o tra quelle infelici. Non è in queste due specie che ha senso dividere le città, ma in altre due: quelle che continuano attraverso gli anni e le mutazioni a dare la loro forma ai desideri e quelle in cui i desideri o riescono a cancellare la città o ne sono cancellati.
>
> (Italo Calvino, *Le città invisibili, Le città sottili* 1972: 2)

or in my own limited English translation:

> [...] it is useless to establish whether Zenobia should be classified as one of the happy cities, or one that is unhappy. It does not make sense to divide cities into these two types, but it does into two others: cities that through the years and changing times still shape longing, and cities in which longing manages to wipe away the city, or is being wiped away itself.

Yet, the quote itself is useful in determining the values that unite Healthy Cities globally: they are the values that cities shape themselves for their healthful futures, and developmental perspectives they are trying to avoid in order to secure a healthy existence in the future. Such values find their foundation in community action, empowerment, sustainable development, equity, and generally in a locality-based strategic and systemic approach of all determinants of health and disease. Hancock and Duhl (1988) have proposed the following working definition:

> A healthy city is one that is continually creating and improving those physical and social environments and expanding those community resources which enable people to mutually support each other in performing all the functions of life and in developing to their maximum potential.

This so-called 'working definition' might – even though all-encompassing and inspirational – be regarded as a trifle normative rather than scientifically operative (i.e. a definition which would enable us to formulate theoretical presuppositions and their subsequent research questions). In order to develop a more operational definition, we would want to develop a more generic Healthy City logic. Breaking down the logic of Healthy Cities world-wide, then, would lead us to the following.

- The geographical set-up in which most people live is the town or city.
- Towns and cities have certain degrees of authority and governance to create, recreate and maintain their social and physical infrastructures.
- Towns and cities are more often than not the lowest level of formal (democratically elected, and therefore accountable to communities) authority in a country.
- Thus, actions and policies of city authorities impact on the options people have for living.
- The above options are also known as 'determinants' (cf. Marmot and Wilkinson 1998) of health.
- Local authorities are thus in an ideal position to formulate and implement policies impacting on determinants of health, thereby potentially improving health; however, 'top-down' approaches in policy-making and intervention development are doomed to fail (Boutilier, Cleverly and Labonté; de Leeuw 2000).
- Full involvement of local communities in formulation, implementation and evaluation of health programmes is therefore imperative in order to achieve equity in local health.

In spite of the enormous number of (normative) definitions and recipes for Healthy Cities (or whatever they are called, such as for instance *'Comunidades Saludables'* in the Americas) we propose here as a unifying 'constituent' definition:

> a locality-based strategic and systemic approach of social, physical and individual determinants of health and disease incorporating the full involvement of communities in the formulation, implementation and evaluation of policies and interventions aiming at equity in health and sustainable development.

Apart from defining the concept of Healthy Cities, however, it is also important to identify its primary objective(s). As we have stated in an earlier major Healthy City evaluation (de Leeuw *et al.* 1998) one can only evaluate what one has set out to do in the first place. Thus: if a health education intervention sets out to reduce the number of eighth-grade pupils from taking up smoking, this is what should be evaluated, and not whether these pupils happen to eat more potato chips in the course of not smoking.

As we have observed above, there are thousands of municipalities and urban governance levels that are now sharing the Healthy City vision. Whether they have committed themselves to achieving specific objectives is an issue that cannot be answered; we are unaware of any exploratory global surveys mapping the existence of specifically formulated individual Healthy City objectives.

A global publication (WHO 1995: 11) states that the core objective of Healthy Cities is 'to improve the health of urban dwellers, and especially low income urban dwellers, through improved living conditions and better health services'. However commendable this objective might be, we do not find that it conveys a vision or innovative networking perspective, which is so direly needed in urban health.

The only group of Healthy Cities that has agreed upon a clearly stated objective is the network of European WHO designated Healthy Cities. In their commitment to a rigorously applied set of designation requirements (WHO 1997: see Box 9.1 for overview) they share these overarching objectives:

> The WHO Healthy Cities project is a long-term international development project that seeks to put health on the agenda of decision-makers in the cities of Europe and to build a strong lobby for public health at the local level. Ultimately, the project seeks to enhance the physical, social and environmental well-being of the people who live and work in the cities of Europe. The project is one of WHO's main vehicles for giving effect to the strategy for Health for All (HFA).
>
> (Tsouros 1994: 1)

> The strategic objectives for the second phase include the speeding up of the adoption and implementation of policy at city level based on the European HFA policy and its targets; strengthening national and subnational support systems; and building strategic links with other sectors and organizations that have an important influence on urban development.
>
> (Tsouros 1994:11–12)

While investigating European Healthy Cities at a comparative level, therefore, only these policy oriented (i.e. 'health on the agenda') issues can be the research objective. Many of these issues have been addressed in an investigation funded by the European Union (e.g. de Leeuw 1999). An important finding of that study was produced by a research team from Milan, demonstrating that the mere involvement of a city in Healthy City networks impacted positively on its capacity to address health and its determinants. One might wonder why this finding in itself would not be convincing enough evidence for anyone to start participation in the Healthy City movement.

Box 9.1.   Designation requirements: Healthy Cities WHO European Regional Office

A: Endorsement of principles and strategies

A.1   Cities must have sustained local government support and support from key decision-makers in other sectors to the principles and goals of the project.

A.2   Cities must have in place mechanisms which ensure an integrative approach to health planning, with links being made between their health policies and other key city-wide strategies, and their health strategies and city-based work on Agenda 21.

A.3   Cities should develop policies and strategies based on health for all for the twenty-first century. Particular emphasis should be placed on the three issues of 1) reducing inequalities in health, 2) working to achieve social development, and 3) commitment to sustainable development.

A.4   Cities should select **at least one** additional target of health for all for the twenty-first century, which has particular local importance. Progress towards this target should be carefully monitored.

B: Establishment of project infrastructures

B.1   Cities must have an intersectoral steering group involving political/executive-level decision-makers.

B.2   Cities must have a full-time identified project coordinator or equivalent and administrative/technical support for the project. The project coordinator must have proven fluency in English.

B.3   Cities must identify and give commitment to the package of resources required to implement the strategies and action plans for Phase III.

B.4   Cities should review project management processes and implement a programme of action to address identified weaknesses.

B.5   Cities should demonstrate increased public participation in the decision-making processes that affect health in the city, thereby contributing to the empowerment of local people.

B.6   Cities should establish mechanisms for the engagement of the business sector in local action for health, at both policy and operational levels.

B.7a Cities should implement a communications strategy, involving a range of communications mechanisms, to stimulate visibility for health issues and public health debate within the city; this strategy should be evaluated to assess its impact; **and/or**

B.7b Cities should implement an ongoing programme of training/capacity-building activities for health and healthy public policy making; this programme should have two strands: involving key decision-makers across the different sectors in the city, and involving local communities and opinion leaders; the impact of this programme should be evaluated.

C: Commitment to specific goals, products, changes and outcomes

C.1 Cities must produce and implement a city health development plan during the third phase, which builds on previous integrative city health planning and reflects the values, principles and objectives of health for all for the twenty-first century and Local Agenda 21; relevant national health strategies; and local city-specific priorities. This plan must have clear long term and short term aims and objectives and a system on how the city will monitor whether these objectives have been met (indicators and evaluation framework).

C.2 Cities should implement a programme of systematic health monitoring and evaluation, integrated with the city health development plan, to assess the health, environmental and social impact of policies within the city. In addition, cities should strengthen health accountability mechanisms and measures.

C.3 Cities should implement a programme of action targeted at reducing health inequalities within the city.

C.4 Cities should carry out a programme of action to promote healthy and sustainable urban planning policies and practice within the city.

C.5 Cities should develop and implement a tobacco control strategy, in line with WHO's identification of tobacco as a strategic priority.

C.6 Cities should implement and evaluate a comprehensive programme of activity to address **at least one** of the following priority topics: social exclusion, healthy settings, healthy transport, children, older people, addictions, civil and domestic violence, accidents.

D: Investment in formal and informal networking and cooperation

D.1   Cities must give executive and political commitment for the attendance of the project coordinator and nominated politician at WHO business meetings and symposia. At each, the city should be represented, as a minimum, by the coordinator and politician responsible.

D.2   Cities should ensure that their Mayor (or lead politician) attends the Mayors' meetings at start of the phase (1998) and midway through it (in the year 2000).

D.3   Cities should be connected to the Internet and electronic mail, and ideally should have access to video-conferencing facilities.

D.4   Cities should participate actively in different networking activities (thematic, sub-regional, strategic, twinning, etc.) during the phase, including the development of close links with national networks. Cities should demonstrate practical contributions to these networks throughout the phase.

Source: de Leeuw 2001

Creating evidence for Healthy Cities

Formulation of the above definition, and identification of European Healthy City objectives, has not made things easier. In its operational version, the definition could imply almost anything. Possibly this aspect of Healthy Cities has scared away more traditional academics and research funding; what these actors would call 'anecdotal' evidence (i.e. proof that comes about by pure luck) indicates that thousands of cities have enthusiastically embraced the idea, and that probably hundreds of thousands of people in those cities are involved in this miracle programme. Then, when trying to comprehend the recipe, they find out that each city or town may be doing radically different things under the same banner. This, of course, is not what most scientists like. Scientists like controlled conditions, and randomised assignment of interventions to extremely homogeneous experimental and control groups ('matching'). Nothing of the kind would probably ever be found in Healthy Cities.

Or wouldn't there? Some authors have argued that the diversity of perspectives of the Healthy Cities movement is its strength, and that precisely this strength should be mapped and understood. Such mapping has been going on since the very beginning of the programme, in 1986. Enormous collections of 'best practices' have been amassed, which lead a rather successful life in themselves as sources of inspiration of Healthy City officers and community leaders (e.g. Price and Tsouros 1996).

Still, inspiration by a good story is only one piece of evidence. Epidemiologists would be tempted to refute a story as proof of the efficacy of an intervention; they would go for the randomised control trials, hard numbers, small α's and even smaller p-values. This seems to be a conflict never to be resolved.

Tones (1997) has endeavoured to bridge this apparent gap between a good story and the validated numbers. He calls for a 'judicial perspective' on evidence. Just as much as any reasonable scientist in the footsteps of Karl Popper would acknowledge that truth is transient (i.e. only true until the theory upon which it is based is falsified), Tones asserts that particularly in the health sciences and health promotion the belief of a notion of truth is only created on the bases of a number of different sources of information. Rather than taking a pure scientific view, Tones asserts that evidence is needed to guide the actions of intervention developers and decision-makers, not just those of scientists. This view is shared by Nutbeam and Vincent (1998) and McQueen and Anderson (1999). Intervention developers and decision-makers by their very nature draw upon a variety of sources of information, and Tones' perspective therefore mimics that of a court of law. He calls it the 'judicial perspective'. The outlook calls for 'proof beyond reasonable doubt' derived from witness accounts, expert testimony, scientific work, and circumstantial evidence. However, it is of course not obvious what relative weight different actors would attribute to different sources of evidence; a politician might sooner decide to take action on the basis of the expressed satisfaction by his constituency, whereas an intervention developer would want to have proper information on cost-effect ratios.

One perspective worth mentioning here is how differently scientists and policy-makers present scientific data required for policy change. Jasanoff (1990) and Shackley and Wynne (1990) have investigated differences in such presentation: scientists present research materials not committing themselves to many certainties. Scientists, external observers to the game of transforming scientific findings into policy realities, are addicted to probabilities and unable to make unequivocal statements. Policy-makers using the very same research materials tend to use totally unambiguous statements as to the certainty of the outcomes of investigations. One lesson to be learnt for the debate on whether Healthy Cities 'work' or not is therefore to identify and interpret the messenger. Apart from framing the message itself we have demonstrated elsewhere (de Leeuw 1993) that networking and power distribution among participants in the policy game determine the output of the policy formulation process. This is consistent with observations by Kingdon (1995) and Stone (1997) who assert that policies are the result of seemingly irrational processes which can only be understood as functions of symbolic exchanges between institutions (people, agreements, bodies) in the policy arena.

Applying this notion of a variety of sources of evidence to the Healthy City concept developed above, we can now induce the following: adequate evidence to answer the question whether Healthy Cities 'work' can only be provided once all components of the Healthy City vision are judged positively from the various sources of evidence required.

One possible way, then, to solve the problem that we have created is to build a matrix in which these components are each assessed. A rather preliminary attempt to do this is presented in Table 9.1. We have reviewed in a rather superficial way the just over 1000 annotated entries in the bibliographies produced by the WHO Collaborating Centre for Research on Healthy Cities (Polman *et al.* 1992; Sanders *et al.* 1994; Salgado and de Leeuw 1998), and all twelve issues of the *Research for Healthy Cities Newsletter* published by same. Yet, a validated meta-analysis of the available data is still to be produced.

In line with Tones' (1997) argument, we have juxtaposed sources of evidence to components of the Healthy City definition presented above. Typically, a witness account would be a story from a community group, expert testimony might come from committed welfare workers or family practitioners, scientific work normally would be published in serious academic journals (with SSCI impact factors!), and circumstantial evidence could be provided, for instance, by structural changes documented by maps, papers, and local perceptions.

The realm of research in, with, for and on Healthy Cities seems to have much to gain from a rigorous use of the matrix presented here.

One thing becomes strikingly clear when reviewing Table 9.1. In spite of what some academics seem to believe, there is a considerable body of evidence arguing in favour of Healthy City components; the field which is most diverse in providing conclusive evidence is that of community action (e.g. Minkler 1997; Bracht 1999; Boutilier *et al.* 2000).

On the other hand, we would argue that answering the question of whether Healthy Cities 'work' is not the simple sum total of various positive and negative expressions of evidence. As stated above, we believe that such information only becomes convincing evidence through the interpretation by the end users. Clearly, as the call for further production of evidence does not weaken there is also a need for what we might call 'synergistic evidence': particularly the meaningful re-combination of sources of evidence in a larger framework would produce a more profound insight into the adequacy, efficacy and efficiency of Healthy City projects.

It is further worth pointing out that the uniqueness of Healthy Cities does not lie in their application of models of community action, or of determinants-based health education campaigns, or of a policy-driven urban perspective. Goumans (1998) has demonstrated that in their operational functions, Healthy Cities can be divided as falling into three models: the *health* model, the *city* model, and the *vision* model. In the health model, Healthy Cities use the WHO vision in order to develop and implement innovative health promotion interventions. In the city model, Healthy Cities feel enabled to use the concept to develop and improve intersectoral urban policies for health. And finally, in the vision model, the Healthy City becomes a vehicle to enhance the health of the city (economically, ecologically, psychologically, etc.) rather than only that of its population. This means that the question whether the Healthy City (as a generic concept) 'works' could never be answered: evidence in its synergy would have to demonstrate how each city reaches the specificity of its own objectives.

Table 9.1. General estimate of availability of sources of evidence for Healthy City components

Healthy City component	Source of evidence							
	Witness accounts		Expert testimony		Scientific work		Circumstantial evidence	
Strategic and systemic	–	x	o	xx	o	x	–	xxx
Determinants of health	–	xx	–	xx	o	xxx	o	xx
Community action	–	xxx	ooo	x	o	xx	o	xx
Equity in health	–	–	o	x	o	–	–	x
Sustainable development	o	xx	–	xx	o	xx	o	xx

Notes   – no adequate rule

o few negative data
oo considerable negative data
ooo conclusive negative data

x few positive data
xx considerable positive data
xxx conclusive positive data

A REVITALISED AGENDA FOR RESEARCH IN, WITH, FOR AND ON HEALTHY CITIES

In 1992, a group of research experts gathered in Maastricht to develop a Healthy Cities Research Agenda (de Leeuw *et al.* 1992). It should be noted that the group of 'research experts' was made up of individuals with strong academic backgrounds, but not always in academic positions. Housing executives, senior community centre managers and independent business consultants were invited to be members of the expert group in order to facilitate outcomes of the meeting that were to be scientifically profound, but also socially relevant (cf. for instance, the debate in the public health training literature in the 1990s where it was purported that schools of public health were to be centres of relevance rather than only centres of excellence: Barnard and Köhler 1994; de Leeuw 1994). Figure 9.2 was one of the most important outcomes of that meeting. The figure acknowledges that the type of research into Healthy Cities is dependent on community needs, willingness and possibilities to fund specific projects, and on the composition of the research team: epidemiologists may want to study different issues than those of interest to political scientists, for instance. That very context creates a domain in the central rectangle of the figure in which level of analysis is connected to the phenomenon under study (or rather, the preferred type of research product). The expert meeting also established the observation that researchers at the time were not doing enough to market their work and its outcomes. There was a call for further 'vulgarisation' of the research process, its mission, and its outcomes in order to connect better with political, community and funders' needs for proper research action; consistent with earlier findings (Tarenskeen 1991) it was agreed that 'practical' people such as politicians have problems understanding and interpreting information provided to them by scientists. They seek refuge instead in information gathering from sources such as tabloids and incidental talks with

Fig. 9.2.   A model to structure Healthy City research needs

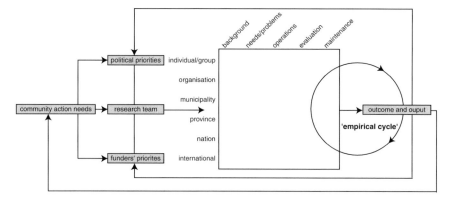

Source: de Leeuw *et al.* 1992

their constituencies. There is frustration on both sides: epidemiologists, for instance, complain that politicians do not take their analyses seriously whereas politicians deplore the inability of epidemiologists to explain clearly what the problem really is. 'Vulgarisation' of research should bridge that gap (cf. also de Leeuw 1993). Other authors have in addition argued that it is not just the outcomes of research that should be vulgarised, but also that the formulation of the primary research question should be developed in closer contact with practice (Kok and Green 1990). This observation takes us to the expert meeting establishing that there is a marked difference between research in, with, for and on Healthy Cities.

This differentiation between research in, with, for and on is not merely a semantic one. It denotes the delineation of roles in the research endeavour, and follows roughly the same parameters I have set out elsewhere for the respective roles of bureaucrats, scientists and community representatives in the initiation and implementation of community action for health (de Leeuw 2000).

Research *on* Healthy Cities would be the typical, almost clinical, perspective on the research enterprise. It would regard issues and situations in the urban environment as separable from reality, as if a true experiment in a petri dish were possible. No involvement of local politics, consultation with inhabitants, nor any form of exploratory research are deemed necessary in Research on Healthy Cities. Pure epidemiological research, involving measures of morbidity, mortality and odds ratio calculations would be an example of such research.

Research *for* Healthy Cities does not necessarily have to take place in the Healthy City itself. This research type could be regarded as foundation-building inquiry that would contribute to the adequate and responsive operations of Healthy City activities. Fundamental research into cognitions, attitudes and beliefs which could contribute to intervention development could be regarded Research for Healthy Cities. Experimental social psychological investigations into, for instance, risk perception and ways in which to modify such ideas, could be exemplary for this type of Healthy City research.

Research *with* Healthy Cities would be the type of inquiry hinted at above, in which the formulation of the research problem is established in close collaboration between academics and research principals. It should be observed, though, that in our view Research with Healthy Cities still distinguishes between an academic world and something 'out there' which should be structured and reconstituted in order to suit a more traditional scientific paradigm in which the randomised control trial is still considered the penultimate in appropriate scientific technology. The *American Journal of Health Promotion*, for instance, uses an evidence rating with which its reviewers would be enabled to judge whether research materials provide proper evidence:

- *conclusive evidence* (*****) is: the cause–effect relationship between intervention and outcome is supported by a substantial number of well-designed studies with randomised control groups;

- whereas *weak evidence* (*) is that research in which evidence supporting relationships is fragmentary, non-experimental and/or poorly operationalised.

Such a position would consequently mean that policy research by definition yields weak evidence: in policy studies experimental and control groups are virtually impossible.

Research *in* Healthy Cities, finally, would best meet the needs of communities and politicians; however, such interactive and exploratory research is not easily brought under such standards as routinely (or arrogantly, *sic*) applied by mainstream quantitative experimentation-driven research institutions and their funders. Research in Healthy Cities, by definition, is respectful of community concerns, even if this would mean that a randomised control trial would be totally besides the point. Fortunately, however, there is an emerging scientific tradition that takes account of such issues.

EVIDENCE AND RESEARCH

These observations led to the conclusion that there was a strong need for further application of so-called Fourth Generation Evaluation to Healthy Cities research (Guba and Lincoln 1981, 1989). Such evaluation is developed in close discourse with research clients. Fourth Generation Evaluation assumes the following steps in the research development process:

1. contracting
2. organising
3. identifying stakeholders
4. developing within-group joint constructions
5. enlarging joint stakeholder constructions through new information/increased sophistication
6. sorting out resolved claims, concerns and issues
7. prioritising unresolved items
8. collecting information/adding sophistication
9. preparing agenda for negotiation
10. carrying out the negotiation
11. reporting, and
12. recycling.

Guba and Lincoln not only postulate a new generation of evaluation approaches. They have also ascertained what the moral and ethical position of the research endeavour should be: the academic community should work with its clients through the entire inquisitive process, from problem identification and phrasing until the implementation of processes of change, their evaluation, and beyond.

Though these observations hold true in the twenty-first century, the judicial evidence perspective introduced above adds a new dimension, and would necessarily lead to a revitalisation of the research agenda.

We can now acknowledge that such a meaningful framework must serve a number of clients and purposes. Researchers, politicians, and probably most prominently communities are the clients, whereas the purpose of a reference framework is primarily to produce evidence, which (when used with the canons of good reasoning and principles of valuation) answers the question *why*, when asked of a judgement, decision, or action.

This has implications for a new Healthy Cities Research Agenda: it is not sufficient merely to take into account the agendas, wishes and constraints of communities, politicians, and research principals, but we would have to add to our agenda a more profound recognition of the fact that evidence may come from a variety of (sometimes unexpected) sources. The central cube in what we could call the '2000β version' of the Healthy City Research agenda (i.e. a version that is still subject to change and debate) connects the various scientific perspectives and levels of analysis from the original model with the range of sources of evidence identified above (see Figure 9.3).

For different stakeholders in the Healthy City research process, then, the '2000β version' would provide an opportunity to connect perceptions and perspectives among Healthy City participants into a validated strategic manoeuvre in social entrepreneurship (cf. de Leeuw 1999).

MONITORING, ACCOUNTABILITY, REPORTING AND IMPACT ASSESSMENT (MARI)

Healthy Cities need to show their communities, their politicians and their partners that their work yields real results. Showing results, that is being accountable, can be done in different ways. It is a true, and shared, responsibility for Healthy City

Fig. 9.3.   Healthy City research agenda: the 2000β version

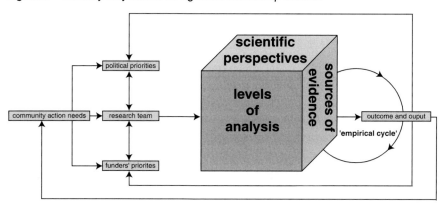

operators and researchers. We feel that the research community should nurture the Healthy City movement more than it has done so far. Until now, academia has looked upon Healthy Cities with justifiable criticism. Good research, however, would intend to support Healthy City endeavours, and identify their weak points with constructive critique.

In Phases I and II of the Project cities were required to produce Health Profiles and City Health Plans. For the first (1986–92), second (1993–8) and third phase (1998–2002) of the Healthy City programme cities had to demonstrate political commitment to Health for All and the Healthy City vision, appropriate resource allocations to secure a full-time project coordinator and support staff in a Healthy City Office, and commitment to specific objectives leading to the establishment of local health policies. In the first phase, among the most important of such objectives was the establishment of an urban health profile (Doyle *et al.* 1996; Garcia and McCarthy 1994; WHO/EURO 1998). In the second phase, designated cities were supposed to be working on the creation of City Health Plans (e.g. de Leeuw 1999), and the third phase committed Healthy Cities to the production of a City Health Development Plan and a process of more rigorous internal and external monitoring and evaluation. The mere production of such reports was a major step towards accountability in itself. Profiles and Health Plans showed the need for action in health, social and sustainable development. However, a city would need to go beyond such needs assessments in order to show that its activities have an impact.

Impact can be determined in different ways. Traditionally, the impact of health interventions was measured in terms of morbidity and mortality outcomes: the presence or absence of death and disease are considered relatively simple proxies for health status in a specified area. However, description of morbidity and mortality measures is in no way an indicator for the degree to which health, well-being and quality of life are currently enjoyed or pursued by communities and cities. Health determinants analyses, and sound and responsible approaches towards influencing determinants of health, would provide relevant and important information on the impact of Healthy City interventions.

Such sound and responsible approaches have now been identified as core principles of the Healthy Cities Project. Cities designated for participation in the Third Phase of the Project have subscribed and committed themselves to such principles.

However, mere commitment and good will are no longer sufficient. The Healthy Cities movement has expanded enormously. At last count, more than 5000 cities globally and over a thousand in the European Region alone have declared themselves Healthy Cities. This puts a responsibility on the group of forerunners: officially WHO designated cities will have to show the way forward. Studies into Healthy Cities dynamics will play an important role in this process.

Research in, with, for and on Healthy Cities has always been a crucial component of the European Project. In the First Phase, cities were invited to contribute to our overall knowledge by filling out a 'Healthy Cities Questionnaire'. The responses to that questionnaire have led to the production of a number of publications, most notably the *Twenty Steps* and *A Project Becomes a Movement* (Tsouros 1992) books; these publications continue to play a very inspirational role in setting up and maintaining Healthy City projects.

In the Second Phase, research and evaluation have been even more prominent. Over this five-year period, various studies were undertaken to assess Healthy City processes. Analyses of health profiles and health plans were supplemented by studies of, among others, policies and networks in Healthy Cities, research needs and research capacities of cities themselves, inventories of project management and national networks, and reviews of tobacco initiatives and city progress reports. The collection of case studies and models of good practice is growing every day. Currently, a project is under way to pull together the findings of these thousands of pages of research.

The Third Phase of the Project has committed itself to a systematic and continuous approach to monitoring and evaluation. Such an approach would serve the following purposes:

- it would assist cities in determining factors of success, and help them in being accountable towards their communities, political decision-makers, and local partners;
- it would enable the WHO Healthy Cities Project Office to keep track of local developments, tune its policies to local realities, and stand accountable to its counterparts and governing bodies;
- it would facilitate the establishment of a common body of knowledge in Healthy City development, maintenance, and evaluation in order to assist interested communities and local bodies to establish successful new Healthy City projects.

Research, thus, is not about methodology and theory (although, when applied properly, they might come in handy). Research is about being accountable, showing benefits and pitfalls, and areas of improvement. It is an integral part of the developmental process in Healthy Cities. Research is therefore not the exclusive territory of a band of academics. Anyone can, and should, be involved in research. The MARI document suggests the kinds of questions cities could ask themselves in order to be accountable and conscientiously contribute to that developmental process.

In establishing a framework for the monitoring and evaluation of Healthy Cities MARI builds on previous experiences, and is conscious of the context in which Healthy Cities are currently developing. These prerequisites are the following.

- Throughout the existence of the Healthy Cities movement, there have been four essential elements of Healthy City work:
  - endorsement of principles and strategies
  - establishment of project infrastructure

- – commitment to specific goals, products, changes and outcomes
  - – investment in formal and informal networking and cooperation.
- In the eligibility and designation assessment process, cities have demonstrated their commitment to specific and operational aspects of each of these elements linked to Phase III
- Past Healthy City studies have shown the validity of distinguishing between different types of research:
  - – relatively simple 'what is there?' studies
  - – studies looking at processes of change (who is doing what, where, why, and under which conditions?)
  - – studies aiming at the identification of results, outcomes, impact (change itself)
  - – studies connecting the other three (what is there ◄——► process of change ◄——► change itself) comprehensively.

In Europe, 'designated' cities have shown their commitment and activities to be valued partners in the international movement. Being designated, however, is not just 'having passed the test'. Adherence to the criteria applies throughout the Third Phase, and commitment and activities should remain to be carefully monitored. This is a process of mapping and plotting, answering continuously the 'what is there?' question. For instance, will political commitment still be as strong in 2001 as it was in 1998? Are commitments to undertake specific actions really followed through? Are necessary resources still there in 2002?

A second layer of research questions addresses the change processes noted above. Are activities really implemented? By whom and how? Are stakeholders satisfied with such activities?

Ultimately, we are of course all interested in the results of our actions and commitments. This is the top layer of the model.

Clearly, even an army of researchers designated to each Healthy City would have a lifetime of work. Thousands of questions can be asked, and they would still probably yield more questions than answers. In a way, this is a highly favourable situation. It means that the Healthy Cities movement provides very fertile ground for a thriving research domain.

However, some structure should be applied to this enormousness of potential research. We have chosen, as outlined above, to take two starting points for such a structure.

1. The four elements of Healthy Cities action, and their subsequent Phase III designation criteria.
2. The three types of interest identified above.

The result of these structural prerequisites is found in the MARI grid (see Figure 9.4): 'General questions derived from designation criteria: MARI issues cities may want to address'. Each page of the list follows components of the designation

Fig. 9.4.   Page 1 of the MARI grid for European WHO designated Healthy Cities

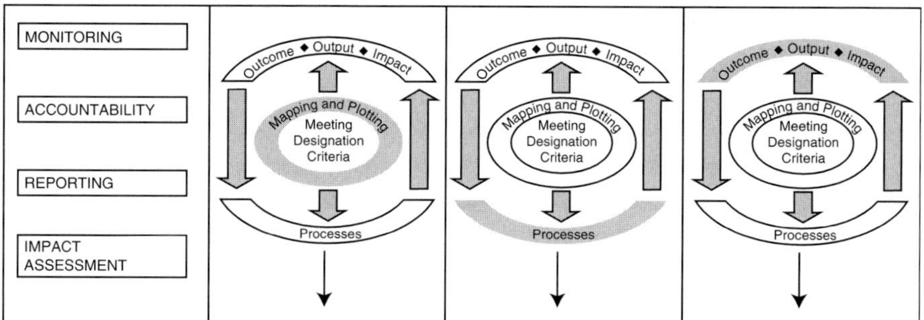

MONITORING

ACCOUNTABILITY

REPORTING

IMPACT ASSESSMENT

(Diagram: each column headed by a cycle showing "Outcome ◆ Output ◆ Impact", "Mapping and Plotting", "Meeting Designation Criteria", and "Processes")

Type of questions / Phase III designation criteria	Questions on presence of policies, adherence to principles, and involvement of actors	Questions involving processes of change	Questions aimed at the identification of results, impact, outcomes and outputs
A.1 Cities must have sustained local government support and support from key decision-makers in other sectors to the principles and goals of the project.	A1A. Have Mayor, lead politicians and heads of sectors recently (re-)endorsed Healthy Cities?	A1B. Are actions undertaken to involve politicians and other sectors in Healthy City activities and policy decisions?	A1C. Have there been any changes in tangible resource allocations for Healthy Cities?
A.2 Cities must have in place mechanisms which ensure an integrative approach to health planning, with links being made between their health policies and other key city-wide strategies, and their health strategies and city-based work on Agenda 21.	A2A. Is there a formal mechanism to structure the integration of different stakeholders in the municipality into Health City policies and activities (including Agenda 21)?	A2B. How do stakeholders contribute to an integrative approach to health planning? Is their contribution required on ad-hoc bases, or is there a continuous and sustained consultative mechanism to involve such stakeholders?	A2C. Can the involvement of stakeholders from various sectors be assessed in terms of their continued involvement in Healthy City activities? And in terms of their resources allocations to Healthy City activities?
A.3 Cities should develop policies and strategies based on health for all for the twenty-first century. Particular emphasis should be placed on the three issues of 1) reducing inequalities in health, 2) working to achieve social development, and 3) commitment to sustainable development.	A3A. Is there a formal policy addressing inequalities in health? Does the municipality have a formal policy on social development? Is there a formal decision to work on sustainable development?	A3B. What is the process that safeguards a continued commitment to the reduction of inequalities in health, social development and sustainable development?	A3C. Are there policies based on sound (scientific) data acquisition and analysis? Is progress in these fields monitored and fed back into the policy process?
A.4 Cities should select at least one additional target of health for all for the twenty-first century, which has particular local importance. Progress towards this target should be carefully monitored.	A4A. What is this additional HFA-target and why was it chosen?	A4B. What is the process that safeguards a continued commitment to achieving this target?	A4C. Is the pursuit at this target based on sound (scientific) data acquisition and analysis? Is progress monitored and fed back into the policy process?

criteria documentation. Of course, cities often do much more than is required by designation criteria. A final category of questions is therefore found on a fifth page: research questions that cities can phrase in order to meet their individual unique needs.

It is in no way suggested that cities answer all these hundreds of questions each year. The MARI grid must be considered as a self-assessment instrument and a tool for research stimulation. Cities are at complete liberty to determine their own research priorities within the framework, and re-phrase questions in the boxes to meet their own needs.

However, determining what is important within this framework must be a conscious, conscientious and strategic endeavour. Answering one question one year, and a question from another row and column in another year would not contribute to increased understanding of Healthy Cities processes and (expected) outputs. Therefore, it is suggested that cities convene a research planning meeting (and possibly establish their own evaluation advisory committees) in order to set priorities and areas of potentially successful research.

At a more aggregate level, WHO will naturally be interested in local research endeavours and progress in Healthy Cities. This interest is reflected in the Annual Reporting Template (ART) which is dealt with in the next section. The Template is directly linked with the original MARI grid, but deals with issues at a much more comparative and requisite level. A continuous interest by cities in their own research actions would facilitate the monitoring and evaluation enterprise that WHO is intending to carry out on the basis of the ART.

CONCLUSION: THE FUTURE OF HEALTHY CITY RESEARCH

More research in, and into, Healthy Cities is needed, particularly at a comparative and cross-cultural level. Each city is unique, that much is true. Establishing a causal logic between the adoption of the Healthy City vision by a town, and changing status of health and quality of life is not simple, and probably not even possible. Researchers have therefore embarked with enthusiasm on the path of collecting 'best practices', advocating especially case study designs in Healthy City research methodology.

There is, however, no reason for complacency. Empirically, we haven't progressed dramatically since the very first attempts at Healthy City evaluations. Case studies are, in that respect, only to be regarded as one source of evidence in a range of 'proofs'. Multiple case studies would generate more validity in research findings, and possibly more possibilities to formulate generic presuppositions for Healthy City practice, development and intervention implementation. Only for this reason it is important that increasing numbers of towns join the international Healthy City movement: the generation of more 'cases' will enable researchers to identify increasing numbers of indicators and proxies for the success of Healthy Cities.

One important condition in this field, however, is the recognition by Healthy Cities themselves (i.e. their communities, political leadership, and project operators) that research will in fact nurture their project, and will be no threat to Healthy City activities. So far, it seems that many cities are apprehensive of embarking on an evaluation or investigation of their project. In a way, this is understandable. Some of the most outspoken critics of the Healthy City movement have come from academic domains with little 'connectedness' to the social dynamics of urban community health action: clinical epidemiologists, (quasi-) experimental researchers, and the like. One thing we hope to have demonstrated with this paper is the fact that there are many more perspectives on the scientific endeavour, and that we find, with many others, that research in, with, for and on Healthy Cities should primarily take up the responsibility to show that *it works*, and secondly, *how*.

Maybe there is some truth in the lyrics from a song by cult band *Klaatu*:

> Mama don't need no PhD
> To know a revolution is happening in the street

or phrased in another way: academics interested in Healthy Cities should also be healthy citizens interested in academia.

References

Ashton, J. (1991) *Healthy Cities*. Milton Keynes: Open University Press.

Barnard, K. and Köhler, L. (1994) Creating a good learning environment – a review of issues facing schools of public health. In *Training in Public Health. Strategies to Achieve Competences. Training and Research in Public Health Dialogue*. Series no. 2, April 1994. Edited by WHO/EURO. WHO Regional Office for Europe, Copenhagen/Centre for Public Health Research, Karlstad.

Boutilier, M., Cleverly, S. and Labonté, R. (2000) Community as a setting for health promotion. In Poland, B., Rootman, I. and Green, L. (eds) *Settings for Health Promotion*. Beverly Hills: Sage.

Bracht, N. (1999) *Health Promotion at the Community Level*, 2nd edition. Beverly Hills: Sage.

Curtice, L. (1995) *Towards the Evaluation of the Second Phase of the WHO Healthy Cities Project*. WHO Internal document, January 1995.

de Leeuw, E. (1993) Health policy, epidemiology and power: the interest web. *Health Promotion International*, 8: 49–52.

de Leeuw, E. (1994). A framework for competence requirement based on the European strategy for health for all, pp. 43–68. In Garcia-Barbero, M., Bury, J. and Leeuw, E. de (eds) *Training in Public Health. Strategies to Achieve Competences*. Training and Research in Public Health Dialogue Series No. 2, WHO Regional Office for Europe/Centre for Public Health Research, Copenhagen/Karlstad.

de Leeuw, E. (1999) Healthy Cities: urban social entrepreneurship for health. *Health Promotion International*, 14: 261–9.

de Leeuw, E. (2000) Beyond community action: communication arrangements and policy networks. In Poland, B., Rootman, I. and Green, L. (eds) *Settings for Health Promotion*. Beverly Hills: Sage.

de Leeuw, E. (2001) Global and local (glocal) health: the WHO Healthy Cities Programme. *Global Change and Human Health*, 2 (1): 34–53.

de Leeuw, E. Abbema, E. and Commers, M. (1998) *Healthy Cities Policy Evaluation. Final Report*. World Health Organisation Collaborating Centre for Research on Healthy Cities, Maastricht.

de Leeuw, E., O'Neill, M., Goumans, M. and de Bruijn, F. (1992) *Healthy Cities Research Agenda*. Proceedings of an Expert Panel. RHC Monograph Series No. 2, Maastricht.

Doyle, Y., Brunning, D., Cryer, C., Hedley, S. and Russell Hodgson, C. (1996) *Healthy Cities Indicators: Analysis of Data from Cities across Europe*. Edited by Webster, P. and Price, C. Copenhagen: World Health Organisation European Regional Office.

Garcia, P. and McCarthy, M. (1994) *Measuring Health. A Step in the Development of City Health Profiles*. Copenhagen: World Health Organisation European Regional Office.

Goumans, M. (1998) *Innovations in a Fuzzy Domain. Healthy Cities and (Health) Policy Development in the Netherlands and the United Kingdom*. PhD Thesis, Universiteit Maastricht, Maastricht.

Goumans, M. and Springett, J. (1997) From projects to policy: 'Healthy Cities' as a mechanism for policy change for health? *Health Promotion International,* 12: 311–22.

Guba, E. and Lincoln, Y. (1981) *Naturalistic Evaluation, Improving the Usefulness of Evaluation Results through Responsive and Naturalistic Approaches*. San Francisco: Jossey-Bass Publishers.

Guba, E. G. and Lincoln, Y. S. (1989) *Fourth Generation Evaluation*. Newbury Park: Sage.

Hancock, T. and Duhl, L. (1988) *Promoting Health in the Urban Context*. WHO Healthy Cities Papers No. 1. Copenhagen: FADL Publishers.

Jasanoff, S. (1990) *The Fifth Branch: Science Advisers as Policymakers*. Cambridge: Harvard University Press.

Kaasjager, D. C., van der Maesen, L. J. G. and Nijhuis, H. G. J. (eds) (1989) *The New Public Health in an Urban Context. Paradoxes and Solutions*. WHO Healthy Cities Papers, No. 4. Copenhagen: FADL Publishers.

Kickbusch, I. (1989) *Good Planets are Hard to Find*. WHO Healthy Cities Papers, No. 5. Copenhagen: FADL Publishers.

Kingdon, J. (1995) *Agendas, Alternatives and Public Policies*, 2nd edition. New York: Harper Collins College Publishers.

Kok, G. and Green, L. W. (1990) Research to support health promotion in practice: a plea for increased co-operation. *Health Promotion International,* 5: 303–6.

McQueen, D. V. and Anderson, L. M. (1999) What counts as evidence? Issues and debates on evidence relevant to the evaluation of community health programs. In Rootman, I., Goodstadt, M., Hyndman, B., McQueen, D., Potvin, L., Springett, J. and Ziglio, E. (eds) *Evaluation in Health Promotion: Principles and Perspectives*. Copenhagen: WHO/EURO.

Milewa, T. and Leeuw, E. de (1995) Reason and protest in the new urban public health movement: an observation on the sociological analysis of political discourse in the 'healthy city'. *British Journal of Sociology*, 47: 657–70.

Minkler, M. (ed.) (1997) *Community Organizing and Community Building for Health*. New Brunswick, New Jersey, London: Rutgers University Press.

Nutbeam, D. and Vincent, N. (1998) Evidence-based health promotion: methods, measures and application. Paper, 16th World Conference on Health Promotion and Health Education. IUHPE, San Juan, Puerto Rico.

Polman, L., Goumans, M. and Leeuw, E. de (1992) *Healthy Cities Research Bibliography*. RHC Monograph Series No. 1, World Health Organisation Collaborating Centre for Research on Healthy Cities, Maastricht (ISBN 90-74590-01-2).

Price, C. and Tsouros, A. (1996) *Our Cities, Our Future: Policies and Action Plans for Health and Sustainable Development*. World Health Organisation European Regional Office, Healthy City Project Office, Copenhagen.

Salgado, J. and Leeuw, E. de (1998) *Healthy Cities Research Bibliography. Supplement 1998*. RHC Monograph Series No. 16, World Health Organisation Collaborating Centre for Research on Healthy Cities, Maastricht (ISBN 90-74590-17-9).

Sanders, M., Leeuw, E. de and Polman, L. (1994) *Healthy Cities Research Bibliography. Supplement 1994.* RHC Monograph Series No. 8, World Health Organisation Collaborating Centre for Research on Healthy Cities, Maastricht (ISBN 90-74590-10-1).

Shackley, S. and Wynne, B. (1990) Representing uncertainty in global climate change science and policy: boundary-ordering devices and authority. *Science, Technology and Human Values*, 21: 275–302.

Stone, D. (1997) *Policy Paradox. The Art of Political Decision Making.* New York/London: W.W. Norton.

Tarenskeen, H. (1991) De visie van lokale politici op gezondheidsbevordering. In Leeuw, E. de (ed.) *Gezonde Steden. Lokale Gezondheidsbevordering In Theorie, Politiek en Praktijk.* Assen/Maastricht: Van Gorcum.

Tones, K. (1997) Beyond the randomized controlled trial: a case for 'judicial review'. *Health Education Research,* 12: 1–4.

Tsouros, A. (1992). *World Health Organization Healthy Cities Project: a project becomes a movement.* SOGRESS, Milan

Tsouros, A. (1994). *The WHO Healthy Cities Project: State of the Art and Future Plans.* Copenhagen: WHO/EURO/HCPO.

Werna, E. and Harpham, T. (1995) The evaluation of Healthy City projects in developing countries. *Habitat International,* 19: 629–41.

Werna, E. and Harpham, T. (1996) The implementation of the Healthy Cities project in developing countries: lessons from Chittagong. *Habitat International*, 20: 221–8.

Werna, E., Harpham, T., Blue, I. and Goldstein, G. (1998) *Healthy City Projects in Developing Countries. An International Approach to Local Problems.* London: Earthscan.

World Health Organisation (WHO) (1995) *Building a Healthy City: a Practioners Guide. A Step-by-Step Approach to Implementing Healthy City Projects in Low-income Countries.* A manual prepared by the Unit of Urban Environmental Health, Division of Operational Support in Environmental Health, WHO, Geneva (WHO/EOS/95.10).

WHO Healthy Cities Project (1988a) *Five-Year Planning Framework.* WHO Healthy Cities Papers No. 2. Copenhagen: FADL Publishers.

WHO Healthy Cities Project (1988b) *A Guide to Assessing Healthy Cities.* WHO Healthy Cities Papers No. 3. Copenhagen: FADL Publishers.

WHO/EURO (1998) *City Health Profiles. A Review of Progress.* World Health Organisation European Regional Office, Copenhagen.

Chapter 10

Examples of research activities for Healthy Cities

Takehito Takano

A basis of evidence is necessary to develop Healthy Cities for policy-making, rational decision-making, plan formation, effective implementation, efficient allocation of resources, visible evaluation of outcomes, and fruitful exchange of experiences among many cities. Sharing an established database of evidence facilitates intersectoral collaboration, involvement of various actors, obtaining political support, and community participation. The results of Healthy Cities research comprise major parts of the evidentiary database for the development of Healthy Cities. Research conducted on priority issues for a Healthy Cities programme will proffer results that are useful in developing such programmes.

As described in the other chapters of this book, in recent years Healthy Cities research has addressed diverse issues including health and sustainability gains from urban regeneration and development, analysis of health determinants, indicators for Healthy Cities, effective community-based health promotion, application of information technology, and accountability issues.

Participatory research is recommended in Healthy Cities since it will foster essential understanding among key players in various sectors. Participatory research is sharing activities, collaborating on every step of that research to some extent: identifying research needs, bringing together research members, developing research plans, formulating research design, establishing research purposes, defining setting of the study, settling methodologies and procedures, conducting data collection and/or fieldwork, analysing data, discussing policy implications, and disseminating results.

This chapter introduces several examples of participatory research of Healthy Cities.

EXAMPLE 1
WIDE RANGE OF HEALTH DETERMINANTS IN REAL SITUATIONS TO FACILITATE INTERSECTORAL COLLABORATION

Research needs
Cities provide living conditions for their residents in complex ways. Health levels, which are largely dependent upon residents' living conditions and lifestyles, must be dealt with as a complicated interaction of a variety of health determinants – physical, economic, and social – in residential environments.

To implement Healthy Cities projects in real situations, collaboration among various government agencies and sectors of society concerned with health issues – considered a key element of urban health management – is helpful in that common databases can be utilised and information shared. An interdisciplinary and collective approach to a variety of health determinants is vital to adopt and implement effective municipal health policies that will improve the health status of residents.

Explaining and understanding the current diversity of health statuses within a given population requires a common database showing the relations between various health determinants and the health status of cities.

Purposes
The objectives of this study were to:

1. identify and categorise, in accordance with the concept of health determinants, the various city indicators that are related to health levels;
2. demonstrate the extent of influence these categorised health determinants have on health;
3. demonstrate both the interactive associations among the health determinants and the magnitude of influence of each health determinant on people's health.

Design of research
All administrative units in Japan with populations exceeding 100,000 were selected as study areas to analyse the relation of health and health determinants. Thirty-five health indicators were used to formulate the health index, and 71 indicators were used to formulate health determinant indices by factor analyses. Regression analysis was used to examine the extent of influence of health determinants on the health index; correlation analysis was used to examine the interrelations between the health determinants and the health index.

Primary findings

Primary findings are shown in Tables 10.1 to 10.3 and Figure 10.1. Obtained health index explained 31.2 per cent of the variance among 35 health indicators. These nine health determinant indices explained 51.6 per cent of the variances of the health index as a whole in the cities studies. The health determinant indices showed interrelations, in addition to the high correlation of individual health determinant indices with the health level index of the population.

Key messages from the research

The nine, broad range of health determinants that we studied – healthcare resources, preventive health activities, environmental quality, housing, urban clutter, local economy, employment, income, and education – as a whole explained more than 50 per cent of the variances in the index of the health of the population. Both individually and collectively the health determinants are closely related to the health status of a population, and the individual determinants interact. Simultaneous analysis of the interrelations among health determinants would help evidence-based decision-making in formulating urban health policies. An integrated perspective based on an understanding of the relations between health and health determinants would widen policy interventions founded on collaboration between different sectors of society. To substantially improve health status, intersectoral collaboration is inevitable.

Feedback and dissemination

It is universally important to select wider range determinants of health and to recognise the existence of causal web-like interrelations between health determinants and health status. This kind of analysis is necessary as a tool for evidence-based decision-making in the formation of comprehensive health programmes such as Healthy Cities projects. Various entities should participate in selecting appropriate indicators to be analysed for the individual sets of cities under consideration. A model application of indicator-based Healthy City plan formation was implemented in Suginami City, in Tokyo. Details of the research results were shared among members of Suginami Healthy City project, in which all agencies of the city government are participating. The research results contributed to form a conceptual basis of Healthy City projects that would broadly tackle health issues and also determine an evaluation framework.

Fig. 10.1.   Interrelationship between the health determinants and health status is shown. 'Health status' is represented by the health index. The nine health determinant indices each represented the following aspects. (1) healthcare resources: existence of adequate healthcare resources; (2) preventive health activities: preventive health activities are conducted; (3) environmental quality: good physical environmental factors, such as air and water quality; (4) housing: existence of new, good quality housing ; (5) urban clutter: urban area that is densely crowded and congested; (6) education: the level and quality of education in the population is high; (7) employment: good employment opportunities are available; (8) income: the population has a high income; (9) local economy: local business is growing and local financial conditions are good. Fine arrows indicate pairs of health-determinant indices with statistically significant correlation with Pearson correlation coefficients. Thick arrows show relationship between health-determinant indices and the index of health with Pearson correlation coefficients.

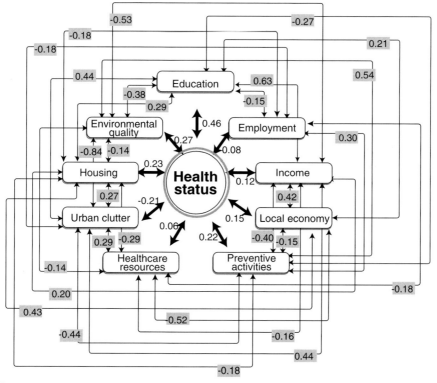

Source: Takano and Nakamura 2001a

Table 10.1. Pearson correlation coefficients of health indicators and health index

Health indicators	Health index
Male life expectancy at birth	0.748
Female life expectancy at birth	0.866
Male life expectancy at 65	0.881
Female life expectancy at 65	0.877
Male age-adjusted mortality rate of all causes	−0.760
Female age-adjusted mortality rate of all causes	−0.905
Male age-adjusted mortality rate of malignant neoplasms	−0.595
Female age-adjusted mortality rate of malignant neoplasms	−0.575
Male age-adjusted mortality rate of malignant neoplasms of stomach	−0.556
Female age-adjusted mortality rate of malignant neoplasms of stomach	−0.463
Female age-adjusted mortality rate of malignant neoplasms of uterus	−0.395
Male age-adjusted mortality rate of ischemic heart disease	−0.277
Female age-adjusted mortality rate of ischemic heart disease	−0.290
Male age-adjusted mortality rate of cerebrovascular disease	−0.246
Female age-adjusted mortality rate of cerebrovascular disease	−0.234
Male age-adjusted mortality rate of pneumonia and bronchitis	−0.761
Female age-adjusted mortality rate of pneumonia and bronchitis	−0.822
Male age-adjusted mortality rate of motorvehicle accidents	−0.177
Male age-adjusted mortality rate of suicide	−0.246
Female age-adjusted mortality rate of suicide	−0.307
Male proportional mortality of age 50 and older	0.192
Male proportional mortality of age 65 and older	0.323
Male proportional mortality of age 80 and older	0.178
Male longevity differential index	0.373
Female longevity differential index	0.459
Stillbirth rate	−0.203

Source: Takano and Nakamura 2001a

Notes
Health indicators having statistically significant correlation ($p<0.01$) with the index of health are listed.

Other health indicators used to formulate the index of health were:

- Female age-adjusted mortality rate of malignant neoplasms of breast
- Female age-adjusted mortality rate of motorvehicle accidents
- Female proportional mortality of age 50 and older
- Female proportional mortality of age 65 and older
- Female proportional mortality of age 80 and older
- Male proportional mortality of age 85 and older
- Female proportional mortality of age 85 and older
- Infant mortality rate
- Perinatal mortality rate.

Table 10.2. Pearson correlation coefficients of healthcare, urban residential, and socioeconomic indicators and health determinants indices

Indicators	Health determinants indices
	Healthcare resources
Number of hospitals and clinics per population	0.899
Number of hospitals per population	0.505
Number of general hospitals per population	0.377
Number of clinics per population	0.867
Number of dental clinics per population	0.818
Number of hospital and clinic beds per population	0.474
Number of beds in general hospitals and clinics per population	0.546
Number of hospitals and clinics per habitable land	0.546
Number of clinics per habitable land	0.534
Number of dental clinics per habitable land	0.439
Number of medical doctors per population	0.775
Number of dentists per population	0.764
Number of pharmacists per population	0.783
Percentage of households less than 500 m from the nearest medical facilities	0.476
	Preventive activity
Participation rate to general health check-up	0.348
Participation rate to health check-up of stomach cancer	0.799
Participation rate to health check-up of lung cancer	0.569
Participation rate to health check-up of cervical cancer	0.497
Number of public health nurses per population	0.410
Number of community welfare volunteers per population	0.472
School meal provision at junior high school	0.487
	Environmental quality
Percentage of houses which have sunshine at least five hours a day	0.740
Normalised difference vegetation index area-averaged by a circle of 3 km radius	0.854
Normalised difference vegetation index area-averaged by a circle of 10 km radius	0.958
Normalised difference vegetation index area-averaged by a circle of 19 km radius	0.933
Index of higher nitrogen oxide measurement	−0.922
98% value of the daily average of nitrogen oxide	−0.914

Indicators	Health determinants indices
	Housing
Percentage of houses constructed after 1975	0.953
Index of newer houses	0.973
Percentage of houses not facing at least 2 m width	0.480
Percentage of houses with flush toilet	0.426
Sewer diffusion rate	0.266
	Urban clutter
Length of road per total land area	0.719
Length of road per habitable land area	0.635
Number of goods vans per kilometre of road	0.817
Number of cars per kilometre of road	0.819
Percentage of houses less than 1 km away from railway station and less than 500 m away from bus stop	0.636
Percentage of houses less than 50 m away from road of more than 6 m width	0.536
Percentage of non-wooden houses	0.462
Percentage of city planning area	0.451
Households in apartment flats with six or more floors	0.816
	Education
Age-adjusted years of education (male)	0.946
Age-adjusted years of education (female)	0.942
Average years of education of male aged 25–29	0.918
Local budget for education per population	0.376
Local budget for education per population aged 5–19	0.403
	Employment
Male work force enrolment as percentage of male aged 15–65	0.857
Female work force enrolment as percentage of female aged 15–65	0.780
Work force enrolment as percentage of population aged 15–65	0.908
Unemployment rate	−0.638
Unemployment rate among population aged 20–24	−0.654
Unemployment rate among population aged 60–64	−0.644
Manufacturing industry workers as percentage of total work force	0.502
Wholesale, retail trade, and eating establishment workers as percentage of total work force	−0.323

Indicators	Health determinants indices
Employment (cont.)	
Professional and technical workers as percentage of total work force	−0.333
Managers and officials as percentage of total work force	−0.239
Family expenses for meat consumption adjusted by the area-difference of food consumption	−0.383
Income	
Per capita income	0.896
Average annual earnings per household	0.812
Standardised deviation of average annual earnings per household	0.876
Per capita balance of savings	0.736
Per capita value of housing and land property	0.845
Per capita value of consumer durable	0.684
Local economy	
Growth rate of number of establishments	0.805
Growth rate of total work force	0.791
Medium- to large-scale establishments (five and more employees) as percentage of all businesses	0.733
Local government financial index	0.697
Local tax revenue as proportion to the total amount of revenue to the local government	0.730

Source: Takano and Nakamura 2001a

Notes
Indicators having statistically significant correlation ($p<0.01$) with individual health-determining factors are listed.

Other indicators used to formulate individual health-determining factors were:
- Family expenses for fish consumption adjusted by the area-difference of food consumption for employment
- Indoor swimming pool with courses of 25m and more per population for healthcare resources
- School meal provision at elementary school for preventive activities
- Number of public health nurses per clinical nurse for preventive activities.

Table 10.3. Explained variances of the health index by sets of health determinants

Set of health determinants and the order of input into a regression model equation	Adjusted R Square
HC	0.055
ENV	0.134
SES	0.241
HC + ENV	0.276
HC + SES	0.321
ENV + SES	0.479
HC + ENV + SES	0.516

Source: Takano and Nakamura 2001a

Notes
HC: healthcare related indices

ENV: urban residential indices

SES: socioeconomic indices

Adjusted R square represents explained variances of individual dependent variables by the defined set of health determinants indices.

EXAMPLE 2
THE IMPORTANCE OF WALKABLE GREEN-FILLED SURROUNDINGS IN URBAN PLANNING

Research needs
It is well accepted that public green spaces provide comfortable and pleasant living environments for urban residents. However, there is a controversy as to whether substantial positive health outcomes result from living in locales with public green spaces.

Health promotion of the elderly in a megacity has become a prime concern of Healthy Cities in an aging society. That a sedentary lifestyle is a key risk of premature morbidity and mortality is well known. To maintain a healthy population in general before individuals become sedentary patients, we considered whether certain physical environmental conditions were conducive to physical activity and healthy living.

There is a growing concern for physical environmental factors in facilitating or modifying different behaviours conducive to health. We were particularly interested in studying whether walkable green spaces provide a supportive environment that promotes the health of senior citizens in densely populated urban areas. We conducted a longitudinal cohort study in cooperation with the community to obtain evidence showing the health consequences of living in a residence with walkable green-filled surroundings.

Purposes

The objective of this study was to investigate, by a cohort study of elderly people, the association between walkable green spaces and the longevity of senior citizens in a densely populated, developed megacity. This study aimed to provide facts for evidence-based policy-making and to advance intersectoral collaboration in urban planning so as to promote the health of senior citizens.

Design of the research

Five-year survival of 3144 people born in 1903, 1908, 1913 or 1918 who consented to a follow-up survey from the records of registered Tokyo citizens was analysed in relation to baseline residential environment characteristics in 1992. At the baseline survey, questions were asked relating to residential environment: nearby areas for taking a stroll, nearby parks and tree-lined streets, noise from automobiles and factories closeby, the level of crime in the community, hours of sunlight at the residence, existence of a garden at the residence, whether the residence was on a road with regular bus service, interaction among neighbours, and preference for continuing to live in the current community. Survival of the respondents was followed up by official residence records furnished by local governments (each individual had provided prior informed consent).

Primary findings

Primary findings are shown in Tables 10.4 to 10.6. We confirmed 2211 survivors and 897 deaths (98.9 per cent follow up). The probability of five-year survival of the senior citizens studied increased with the availability of nearby strolling areas (p<0.01), parks and tree-lined streets near the residence (p <0.05), and preference to continue to live in their current community (p <0.01). The principal-component analysis from the baseline residential environment characteristics identified two environment-related factors: walkable green streets and natural, green-filled surroundings, and a positive attitude toward one's own community. After controlling for the residents' age, sex, marital status and socioeconomic status, the presence of walkable green streets and green spaces near the residence indicated significant predictive value for the survival of urban senior citizens over the following five years (p <0.01).

Key messages from the research

This study revealed that the longevity of senior citizens is positively influenced by living in areas with walkable green-filled surroundings, independent of an individual's age, sex, marital status, baseline functional status, and socioeconomic status. This evidence was considered useful in supporting a decisive shift in the ongoing urban planning policy debate in favour of the proponents for public policies that put priority on health.

Table 10.4. Five-year survival percentages of the older people by selected characteristics of residential environment

Age at baseline	(n)	Female/Male Five-year survival % 3001	X² test	K-W test	Female Five-year survival % 1689	X² test	K-W test	Male Five-year survival % 1312	X² test	K-W test
All	(3001)	71.1			75.2			65.9		
Space for taking a stroll near the residence										
Enough space available	(1425)	73.8			76.5			70.5		
Some space available, not enough	(1314)	70.1	**	**	75.7	*	ns	62.5	**	**
Very little space available	(249)	67.9			72.3			61.4		
None	(79)	55.7			59.6			48.1		
Parks and tree-lined streets near the residence										
Plenty	(915)	74.2			77.3			70.4		
Some	(1328)	70.0			74.9			63.7		
Little	(583)	70.8	*	*	74.0	ns	ns	66.4	ns	ns
Very little	(231)	66.2			69.8			60.9		
Noise from automobiles and factories near the residence										
Have no trouble	(882)	73.7			74.2			73.1		
Seldom have troubles	(1127)	70.4			75.2			64.2		
Sometimes have troubles	(780)	69.6	ns	ns	75.6	ns	ns	61.9	**	**
Usually have troubles	(247)	71.3			76.4			63.6		
Safety against crimes in the community										
Perceived as very safe	(701)	71.8			75.5			67.2		
Perceived as relatively safe	(2159)	71.3			75.4			66.0		
Perceived as relatively unsafe	(183)	68.3	ns	ns	69.4	ns	ns	66.1	ns	ns
Perceived as unsafe	(11)	72.7			87.5			33.3		
Hours of sunlight at the residence (April–June)										
5 hours and longer/day	(1703)	72.5			76.5			67.8		
3–5 hours/day	(760)	70.8			75.5			64.4		
1–3 hours/day	(432)	70.4	**	*	73.3	ns	ns	65.4	*	*
less than 1 hour/day	(153)	59.5			65.3			48.1		
Types of area use around the residence										
Detached houses with gardens	(1542)	73.1			76.2			69.1		
Detached houses, densely built	(798)	70.6			74.6			65.1		
Condominium	(180)	65.0			71.4			57.3		
Apartment complex	(176)	68.8			72.2			64.6		
Shopping street area	(188)	71.3			76.1			63.4		
Small-scale factory area	(60)	61.7			65.6			57.1		
Garden at the residence										
Have garden 2 units and larger	(1785)	71.3			74.4			67.6		
Have garden less than 2 units	(349)	71.1	ns	ns	77.8	ns	ns	62.3	ns	ns
None	(867)	70.9			75.6			63.6		

Age at baseline	(n)	Female/Male Five-year survival % 3001	X² test	K-W test	Female Five-year survival % 1689	X² test	K-W test	Male Five-year survival % 1312	X² test	K-W test
Residence facing a road with a regular bus service										
No	(2251)	71.3	ns	ns	74.5	ns	ns	67.0	ns	ns
Yes	(782)	71.5			77.0			64.3		
Active communication among neighbouring residents										
Very good	(857)	71.5			75.6			66.3		
Relatively good	(1366)	73.1	ns	ns	78.6	**	*	66.3	ns	ns
Not so good	(836)	60.0			70.2			64.3		
Almost none	(122)	70.5			69.3			72.1		
Preference to continue to live in the current community										
Would like to continue to live	(2599)	72.2			76.6			66.7		
Would not like to continue to live	(104)	69.2	**	[–]	69.1	**	[–]	69.4	ns	[–]
Not know	(330)	65.5			67.4			61.7		

Source: Takano *et al*. 2002

Notes
  * : p<0.05; ** : p<0.01   ns: not significant;   [–]: not applicable
  K-W test: Kruskal-Wallis test

Table 10.5. Factor loading for selected living environmental factors

	Factor 1	Factor 2
Space for easy street walk around the residence	0.822	0.040
Parks and green lining streets around residence	0.822	0.034
Less noise from automobiles and factories near the residence	0.553	0.117
Longer hours of sunlight at the residence	0.360	0.261
Active communication among neighbouring residents	0.006	0.798
Preference to continue to live in the current community	0.158	0.686
R²	0.326	0.174

Source: Takano *et al.* 2002

Notes
Results of the factor analysis with Varimax rotation by the selected living environmental factors.
Factor 1 was considered to represent 'walkable green streets and spaces near the residence'.
Factor 2 was considered to represent 'positive attitude to one's own community'.

Table 10.6. Influence of residential environment factor of walkable, neighbour-hood green spaces on five-year survival of older people

Subjects entered in the logistic model	Walkable green spaces		
Independent variables in each model	Odds ratio	95% confidence interval	
All participated in the follow-up			
Residential environmental factors	1.15	1.06–1.25	***
Residential environmental factors, age and sex	1.16	1.07–1.27	***
Residential environmental factors, age, sex and living arrangement	1.16	1.07–1.27	***
Residential environmental factors, age, sex, living arrangement and living expenses	1.13	1.03–1.24	**
Subjects who did not need help to get out of bed at baseline			
Residential environmental factors	1.16	1.07–1.26	***
Residential environmental factors, age and sex	1.17	1.07–1.28	***
Residential environmental factors, age, sex and living arrangement	1.17	1.07–1.28	***
Residential environmental factors, age, sex, living arrangement and living expenses	1.14	1.03–1.25	*

Source: Takano *et al.* 2002

Notes
* p<0.05; ** p<0.01; *** p<0.001
Dependent variable (survival = 1; deceased = 0)
Independent variables were coded as follows:
  Residential environment factors were [walkable green spaces] and [positive attitude to one's own community] (factor scores obtained by the factor analysis)
  Age (5 years interval as one unit)
  Sex (female = 1; male = 0)
  Marital status (living with spouse = 1; others = 0)
  Living expenses (7 gradient score according to the amount of monthly living expenses).

From a Healthy Cities viewpoint and through intersectoral collaboration, neigh-bourhood, pedestrian-friendly, public green spaces should be further stressed in the development and redevelopment of densely populated areas in a megacity. The present evidence warrants closer and more effective collaboration among health, construction, civil engineering, planning, and other relevant sectors including government agencies, which has been minimal until now.

Feedback and dissemination
Collaboration of the health and urban planning sectors has been more firmly grounded when evidence that urban planning can actualise health-promoting

outcomes of particular environments was shared. This research furnished strong, logical factors for consideration in urban planning decision-making and facilitated intersectoral collaboration in urban planning of Tokyo.

Tokyo Metropolitan Government's 'New City Planning Vision for Tokyo', adopted in 2001, established 'Creation of Safe and Healthy Living Environment' as one of five major pillars of proactive implementation of policy-driven urban development. The concept of Healthy Cities was introduced in this pillar; moreover, planning for conservation and further creation of green space and redevelopment of highly concentrated areas of wooden housing were established. Creating an urban environment supportive of the health of city dwellers had become firmly set into place as a consideration in the urban planning of Tokyo.

EXAMPLE 3
DEMONSTRATING TO HEALTH PERSONNEL THAT HEALTH LEVELS RELATE TO THE NATIONAL FINANCIAL ADJUSTMENT POLICY

Background and research needs
Since 1965, health levels, represented by life expectancies, in the rural prefectures have increased sharply, while the health level of the nation's capital city, Tokyo, has marked only moderate change. The ranking of the health level of Tokyo, which once was one of the highest in the country, has declined since 1980. An interesting query is why Tokyo's health-level ranking has declined in spite of the city's economic productivity.

It is widely recognised that the determinants of health are diverse, including healthcare; welfare; education; housing; the infrastructure, such as roads, water supply and sewage; and the level of development of the local economy. Local governments and the central government provide a greater proportion of public services for these health determinants. Availability of revenue affects the ability of a local government to implement programmes to develop and maintain relevant infrastructure and services.

The national system for adjusting finances among the local prefectural governments is necessary to redress imbalances in the revenues of local governments. This will ensure balanced development nationwide and maintain public services above the minimum level all across the country.

Financial adjustment is achieved mainly through the local allocation tax (local grant tax) and treasury disbursements (grants to local governments). The local allocation tax system allocates to the local governments a certain percentage of the taxes collected by the national government. Financial resources are thereby equalised and available to individual local governments to implement necessary public services. Treasury disbursements consist of a variety of grants from the national government to local governments for specific purposes, including public investment to develop social overhead capital, social security, and education.

Health personnel tend to view these financial matters as outside their area of competence and therefore outside their concern; they are simply interested in direct countermeasures against threats to public health.

Purposes

The study examined the effects of the national adjustment system during the 1965–95 periods, both on redressing imbalances in local revenues and on health-level trends (the latter as measured by mortality rates and life expectancy by prefecture). The objective of this study was to examine:

1. trends arising from the flow of financial assistance from the national government to local governments;
2. mortality rates and life expectancy trends among prefectures;
3. the effect on mortality rates and life expectancy of the national financial adjustment policy in equalising both the revenues of local governments and variations in the health levels among the prefectures.

Design of the research

We calculated prefectural income, gross domestic expenditure, the amount of national taxes collected, financial assistance from the national government to local governments, and age-adjusted mortality rates and life expectancies of all of the prefectures in Japan from 1965 through 1995. Financial assistance from the national government to local governments consists of two components: local allocation tax and treasury disbursements.

We defined a prefectural contribution as the net amount of money transferred from a prefecture to the national coffers. A prefectural contribution was calculated as follows:

> Prefectural contribution = (total amount of national taxes collected in a prefecture) – [(local allocation taxes to that prefecture and to municipalities in that prefecture) + (treasury disbursements to the prefecture and its municipalities)].

We analysed the relationship between economic indicators – prefectural income and prefectural contribution – and health level indicators. Pearson correlation coefficients between per capita prefectural income and the age-adjusted mortality rates, and that between per capita prefectural contribution and the age-adjusted mortality rates were calculated for each year at five-year intervals from 1965 through 1995.

Primary findings

Primary findings are shown in Tables 10.7 to 10.9. Under the financial adjustment policy, financial assistance from the national government to the local governments, which consists of the sum of the local allocation tax and treasury disbursements, increased from ¥1831 billion in 1965 to ¥31,116 billion in 1995. During that same period, the age-adjusted mortality rate per 100,000 people decreased from 1168.9 (1965) to 545.3 (1995).

There was a significant statistical correlation between higher prefectural incomes and lower mortality rates from 1965 until 1975 ($p<0.05$), whereas this correlation was unclear in the 1980s and has not been observed since 1990.

The relative health level of Tokyo has declined among all the prefectures, from the highest in 1965 to below average in 1995.

Key messages from the research

The national financial adjustment policy to balance the revenues of local governments has increased the health levels of rural prefectures, and it is likely that the policy has worked to equalise the health levels of prefectures throughout the country. However, the policy has precluded the nation's capital city from applying its economic resources as local government expenditures to deal with the health-impacting urban issues faced by such a megacity. We are concerned that if appropriate policies are not adopted and implemented, the relative health level of Tokyo will experience further decline.

Feedback and dissemination

Health personnel tend to focus their attention on health services. They generally do not pay attention to local economic issues. Yet this plays a role as a health determinant. Results of this study helped direct attention to financial policy in discussions about resources for promoting the health of residents.

The results of this research have been shared among health personnel, who wished to apply a wide-angle lens to health determinants and have supported our research. Aware health personnel in Tokyo are sharing the following views:

- the central government should consider modifying the overly effective mechanism that siphons economic gains from Tokyo and impedes health promotion for Tokyo residents;
- economic benefits could be more effectively used to contribute to the health of Tokyo's residents through the introduction by the Tokyo government of a local tax earmarked for investment in health infrastructure and activities;
- the earmarked tax collected in Tokyo should be reallocated to municipalities within Tokyo with scarce resources to develop infrastructure for health promotion and to reduce disparities of health levels among its municipalities.

Table 10.7. Prefecture-wide trends in the total amount of prefectural financial indicators

Year	1965	1970	1975	1980	1985	1990	1995
Total amount of prefectural income[a] of all the prefectures (billion ¥)	26,290	59,502	124,412	199,225	263,859	363,296	391,524
Per-capita amount of prefectural income (thousand ¥)	268	574	1,111	1,702	2,180	2,939	3,118
Gross domestic expenditure[b] (billion ¥)	32,800	73,345	148,327	240,176	320,419	430,040	483,220
Total amount of national taxes collected[c] (billion ¥)	2,787	6,906	13,479	25,740	36,887	60,471	52,575
Total amount of financial assistance from the national government to local governments[d] (billion ¥)	1,831	3,879	10,292	18,619	19,868	24,957	31,116
Total amount of local allocation taxes given to local governments[e] (billion ¥)	743	1,798	4,471	8,114	9,450	14,328	16,153
Total amount of annual treasury disbursements[f] (billion ¥)	1,088	2,081	5,821	10,505	10,418	10,629	14,963

Source: Takano and Nakamura 2001b.

Notes

a Income generated by residents, businesses, and other entities that reside or exist in a prefecture
b Equivalent of gross domestic products based on the System of National Account (1968 SNA)
c Income tax, cooperation tax, and other national taxes collected
d Total amount of money transferred from the national coffers to prefectures (sum of e and f).
e Local allocation tax money given to each local government from the national government
f Subsidies to the local governments from the national government

Table 10.8. Relative decline of the health level of Tokyo

Year			1965	1970	1975	1980	1985	1990	1995
Ranking of the life expectancy at birth, male, Tokyo	rank		1	1	1	4	5	14	20
Ranking of the life expectancy at birth, female, Tokyo	rank		1	3	2	7	11	27	33
Deviation of the age-adjusted death rate[a] of Tokyo residents from the average for all prefectures	per 100,000 population		-144.3	-96.0	-76.0	-53.2	-31.2	-4.3	2.1
Standardised age-adjusted death rate[b] of Tokyo residents			-1.97*	-1.76*	-2.03*	-1.69*	-1.11	-0.19	0.09
Reduction percentage of the age-adjusted death rate by 10 years[c] for the Japanese population	per 10 years per 100,000 population				25.2484	27.1546	25.3737	22.9407	16.0923
Reduction percentage of the age-adjusted death rate by 10 years[c] for the Tokyo residents	per 10 years per 100,000 population				22.2819	25.4697	22.2152	17.7878	11.6242
Standardised reduction percentage of the age-adjusted death rate by 10 years[d] for the Tokyo residents					-1.08	-0.72	-1.22	-2.22*	-1.86*

Source: Takano and Nakamura 2001b.

Notes

a Age-adjusted death rate calculated based on a 1985 model population
b Standardised value of a
c Reduction of age-adjusted death rate during the previous 10 years divided by the value at the beginning of this 10-year period
d Standardised value of c

* The indicated value is out of mean ± 1.67 × SD.
Okinawa Prefecture was not included in the analysis because the area was not a part of Japan in 1965 and 1970.
Hyogo Prefecture was not included in the analysis of year 1995 because of the earthquake which occurred in that year.

Table 10.9. Correlation between the age-adjusted mortality rate and prefectural financial indicators

Year	1965	1970	1975	1980	1985	1990	1995
Correlation coefficient between death rate[a] and per-capita prefectural income[b]	−0.398*	−0.555*	−0.482*	−0.353	−0.240	−0.120	−0.158
Correlation coefficient between death rate[a] and per-capita prefectural contributions[c]	−0.467*	−0.560*	−0.471*	−0.352	−0.151	−0.012	−0.042

Source: Takano and Nakamura 2001b.

Notes
a Age-adjusted death rate calculated based on a 1985 model population
b Per capita amount of income generated by residents, businesses, and other entities that reside or exist in a prefecture
c Per capita net amount of money transferred from a prefecture to the national coffers
* $p < 0.05$

Okinawa in 1965 and 1970 and Hyogo in 1995 were excluded for calculation.

EXAMPLE 4
APPLYING GEOGRAPHIC INFORMATION SYSTEM FOR RATIONAL DECISION-MAKING IN HEALTH PLANNING

Research needs
Community health needs are not uniformly distributed geographically because such needs depend on a wide range of demographic, life, and environmental factors that differ among areas. Thus it is not efficient to provide uniform public health services to an entire area.

The geographic information system (GIS) has been applied to obtain spatial analyses of supply and demand in market research for retail businesses, real estate evaluation, employment, the development of a transport system, the allocation of public service facilities, and urban planning. Using a smaller-scale, more detailed GIS to evaluate community health needs would be efficient in matching needs with services. To enhance rational decision-making in public health policies, we considered that a new assessment procedure to visualise the geographical distribution of community health needs and to evaluate means of matching needs with services in smaller geographical units would be of great social benefit.

No single indicator can explain community health needs since these needs are known to be associated with multiple factors, including demography, health, socioeconomic conditions, living conditions, and environment. Therefore combining multiple parameters that relate to a particular issue should be undertaken in the geographical assessment of community health needs be done by.

Purposes
The objectives of this study were to:

1. build a geographical database that would cover demographic, life, and environmental factors for the assessment of community health needs;
2. visualise the locations of these community health needs;
3. develop a community health needs assessment GIS for rational decision-making in public health services.

Design of the research
The study area was the Northeast Tokyo Secondary Medical Area, which is divided into 476 'cho-chome' units. We compiled census data, digital data of basic planning maps, digital data of topographic maps, contents of registers of medical and welfare facilities, and statistics of establishments into a geographical database in cooperation with various sectors of local governments. To examine specific community needs at the local level, we identified sets of indicators for assessment. We employed a method to make use of order statistics, analysed geographic patterns and location of specific community needs, and quantified geographic concentration of need by the nearest neighbour method.

Primary findings

The database identified 3400 items of demographic, life and environmental factors. Examples of specific community health needs that have been analysed by community health needs GIS were health check-ups and industrial safety programmes for small-scale manufacturing firms (O1), fire prevention (E1), services for working mothers in nuclear families (C1), and sexually transmitted diseases prevention activities in entertainment areas (S1). Thematic maps display cho-chome units according to specific community needs variables by using the following indicators and the estimation model for community needs locality. Individual maps are illustrated according to calculation with the following specially defined sets of indicators.

- Map O1: density of small-scale industrial firms, percentage of multipurpose houses per total number of houses, average floor space per person in owner-occupied houses, and percentage of manufacturing firms per total number of establishments.
- Map E1: population density of elderly inhabitants, ratio of elderly/juvenile population, level of congestion of low-rise buildings, and percentage of wooden houses per total number of buildings.
- Map C1: population density of children under six years of age living in nuclear families, percentage of nuclear families per total number of households, percentage of households living in apartment houses or flats per total number of households, and expected percentage of female married workers.
- Map S1: population density of individuals 15–24 years of age, percentage of households living in non-public rented houses (less than 30 m²), percentage of non-exclusive residential-use buildings per total number of buildings, and number of amusement facilities.

Thematic maps and clustering values showed different patterns of geographical distribution of the need of individual communities.

Key messages from the research

Using these processes, we developed a community health needs assessment GIS that consisted of a geographical database and a needs-assessment procedure of community health. The results suggested that visual localisation facilitates the illustration and analysis of the geographical distributions of community health needs at the local level.

Geographical distributions of health needs should be taken into account when planning and implementing specific health measures. For this purpose, the community health needs assessment GIS provides geographical evidence of where public health services are needed. The community health needs assessment GIS will support appropriate resource allocation, intersectoral collaboration, and greater transparency in decision-making in public health policy and services. The principles of the community health needs assessment GIS are applicable to different communities.

Feedback and dissemination
The community health needs assessment GIS provided evidence on the distribution of needs, which revealed diverse patterns to both practitioners and members of the community. Visualisation was persuasive to people from different backgrounds and to both professionals and non-professionals alike. Some city governments are now trying to adopt this technique for rational decision-making in planning and implementing public health services. Available data may differ from city to city given that institutional mechanisms, administrative structures, and administrative boundaries are not always the same.

EXAMPLE 5
EVALUATING THE INTANGIBLE ACHIEVEMENTS OF A COMMUNITY EDUCATION PROGRAMME

Research needs
Various health education programmes that involve ordinary, non-professional community members have been tried. The advantages of adopting a health education programme through community participation have been widely reported. However, one weakness is the lack of numerical evidence for the results of the programme since quantifying the outcome of an education programme is difficult in the usual scheme of administration education. Therefore annual budgets for health education programmes tend to be reduced or cut by city governments experiencing financial strain. However, a health education programme is one of most important activities in developing community health promotion. Thus we conducted a survey to examine lifestyles and health literacy of participants in a community leaders' programme and in the general population in cooperation with community health centres and members, and analysed the effectiveness of this health education programme.

Purposes
The purpose of this study was to evaluate the effectiveness of the community leaders' health education programme among middle-aged women in terms of changing their:

1. attitudes toward a healthy lifestyle;
2. behaviour regarding access to health-related information;
3. attitudes and health literacy irrespective of socioeconomic status.

Design of the research

In this research, we focused on an education programme involving ordinary people of the community as members of a 'community leaders' committee'. As a group they have opportunities to gain knowledge about, and skills in, healthy lifestyles and undertake volunteer activities to serve the community. The programme includes training committee members to become health promotion leaders, following an initial period of leadership by local governments. A programme intervention sample (INT group) was selected from programme participants from 13 municipalities in an urban area. A questionnaire survey was carried out with the INT group and a general population group (REF group). The data obtained for female respondents, aged 30–59 years, in the two sample populations (n = 662 and 1361, respectively) were analysed using the chi-square test, the Kruskal–Wallis test, and multivariate log-linear methods.

Primary findings

Primary findings are shown in Tables 10.10 to 10.14. The population in the INT group were pursuing healthier lifestyles than those in the REF group; current non-smokers who engaged in physical exercise and who ate regular meals appeared more conscious of a healthy lifestyle and were more interested in the relationship between food and health. From the INT group and REF groups, 22 and 4 per cent of people, respectively, frequently obtained information from health professionals, and 29.8 and 10.8 per cent, respectively, were satisfied with their access to health-related information. Results of multivariate log-linear analysis showed that significantly more people in the INT group were exercising, eating regular meals, paying attention to nutritional balance and food additives, were interested in health and were satisfied with access to health information after excluding the effects of age and socioeconomic factors ($p < 0.05$).

Key messages from the research

It was evaluated numerically that the people who participated in the health education programme were significantly more likely to pursue a healthier lifestyle and to have greater health literacy than those who did not participate, regardless of socioeconomic status. This community participation approach, employing a committee style, was effective in improving health-related behaviour and in promoting health literacy while overcoming socioeconomic variation. Socioeconomic constraints are often seen in health promotion activities in the community. It was clear that a participatory health education programme was substantially effective and should be continued even when considering cost-effectiveness.

Table 10.10. Socio-demographic characteristics of the subjects

	INT group (n = 662) N (%)		REF group (n = 1361) N (%)		p<.01
Age					**
30–49	260	(39)	850	(62)	
50–59	402	(61)	511	(38)	
Monthly household expenses, in yen					
<200,000	65	(11)	164	(13)	
200,000–299,999	141	(25)	280	(22)	
300,000–399,999	152	(27)	336	(27)	
400,000–499,999	114	(20)	220	(17)	
>=500,000	96	(17)	266	(21)	
No answer	94		95		
Years of education					**
=<9	70	(11)	108	(8)	
10–12	335	(53)	594	(45)	
13–15	174	(27)	404	(30)	
>=16	55	(9)	224	(17)	
No answer	28		31		

Source: Yajima *et al.* 2001

Notes
INT group = intervention group; REF group = reference group
Both INT group and REF group were selected from females in greater Tokyo area
The difference between the REF group and the INT group was significant at p< .01(**) for the chi-square test comparison

Feedback and dissemination

Evaluation of the results of the community participation programme had been conducted through collaboration of community members of the programmes. Advantages of participation in the programme were quantitatively demonstrated. Both community participants as well as health professionals who support this programme were convinced of its positive influence on lifestyle change and improvement in health literacy. Evaluation results combined with substantial information served as a solid foundation for decision-making in health promotion policies.

Table 10.11. Lifestyle features, attention to a healthy lifestyle and interest in the relationship between food and health

	INT group (*n* = 662) N (%)	REF group (*n* = 1361) N (%)	p<.01
Lifestyle features			
Current non-smoker[a]	631 (95.3)	1139 (83.7)	**
Perform exercise at least once a week	359 (54.2)	441 (32.4)	**
Eat a meal regularly[b]	592 (89.4)	1047 (76.9)	**
Attention to a healthy lifestyle of food			
Nutritional balance[c]	260 (39.3)	367 (27.0)	**
Atmosphere[c]	97 (14.7)	144 (10.6)	**
Additive[c]	286 (43.2)	401 (29.5)	**
Interest in the relationship between food and health			
Interested[d]	617 (93.8)	1117 (82.7)	**

Source: Yajima *et al.* 2001

Notes:
INT group = intervention group; REF group = reference group

The difference between the REF group and the INT group was significant at p<.01 (**) for chi-square test comparison.

a   Those who answered 'I've never smoked' and 'I used to smoke before, but I don't smoke actually'
b   Those who answered 'I eat a meal three times a day regularly'
c   Those who answered 'I pay much attention to it'
d   Those who answered 'I'm interested in the relationship between food and health'.

Table 10.12. Comparison of the most important source of health-related information for individuals

	INT group N = 362 (%)	REF group N = 915 (%)	p<.05
Television and radio	37	42	
Magazines and newspapers	17	28	*
Books	10	12	
Friends and family members	8	11	
Health centre	22	4	*
Others	7	4	

Source: Yajima et al. 2001

Notes
INT group = intervention group; REF group = reference group

No answer was 33% for the REF group and 45% for the INT group, and were excluded in
the calculation of percentages

The difference between the REF group and the INT group was significant at p< .05 (*) for
the chi-square test comparison

Table 10.13. Comparison of satisfaction with the access to health-related
information

	INT group (n = 655) N (%)	REF group (n = 1348) N (%)
Very much satisfied	136 (20.8)	145 (10.8)
Fair	502 (76.6)	1136 (84.3)
Unsatisfied	17 (2.6)	67 (5.0)

Source: Yajima et al. 2001

Notes
INT group = intervention group; REF group = reference group
Statistical significance between the INT group and the REF group was shown at p< .05 for
the Kruskal–Wallis test comparison

Table 10.14. Factors associated with a healthy lifestyle and health literacy: results of multivariate log-linear analysis (n = 2024)

	Health-related behaviour			Health literacy		
	Physical exercise	Regularity of meals	Attention to nutritional balance	Attention to food additive	Interest in the relationship between health and food	Satisfaction with information
	Odds ratio (95%CI)	Odds ratio (95%CI)	Odds ratio (95%CI)	Odds ratio (95%CI)	Odds ratio (95%CI)	Odds ratio (95%CI)
Involvement in the model programme (INT/REF)	2.3 (1.9–2.9)	4.8 (2.0–11.1)	1.8 (1.4–2.2)	1.7 (1.4–2.2)	3.3 (2.2–5.0)	1.9 (1.5–2.5)
Age (middle/elder)	1.5 (1.8–1.2)	1.6 (1.0–2.8)	1.8 (1.4–2.2)	1.6 (1.3–2.0)	2.2 (1.6–3.0)	1.8 (1.4–2.3)
Educational backgrounds (high/low)	1.1 (0.9–1.3)	1.0 (0.6–1.7)	2.1 (1.7–2.7)	1.4 (1.1–1.7)	2.5 (1.9–3.4)	1.1 (0.8–1.7)
Monthly household expenses (high/low)	1.5 (1.0–2.1)	2.0 (1.0–3.9)	2.2 (1.4–3.3)	2.0 (1.3–2.9)	2.3 (1.4–3.8)	1.0 (0.7–1.4)
Monthly household expenses (middle/low)	1.2 (0.9–1.7)	3.0 (1.7–5.3)	1.9 (1.3–2.7)	1.6 (1.2–2.3)	1.7 (1.1–2.4)	1.2 (0.9–1.5)
X^2	20.1	12.0	24.7	18.4	24.5	20.5

Source: Yajima et al. 2001

Notes
Model: Involvement in the model programme + Age + Educational backgrounds + Monthly household expenses
(95%CI) = 95% Confidence Interval

References

Examples 1 to 5 summarised research results reported in the following publications and interpreted the background and research process, including feedback and dissemination, from the perspective of Healthy Cities research.

Example 1: Takano, T. and Nakamura, K. (2001a) An analysis of health levels and various indicators of urban environments for Healthy Cities projects. *Journal of Epidemiology and Community Health*, 55: 263–70.

Example 2: Takano, T., Nakamura, K. and Watanabe, M. (2002) Urban residential environments and senior citizens' longevity in megacity areas: the importance of walkable green spaces. *Journal of Epidemiology and Community Health*, 56: 913–18.

Example 3: Takano, T. and Nakamura, K. (2001b) The national financial adjustment policy and the equalization of health levels among prefectures. *Journal of Epidemiology and Community Health*, 55: 748–54.

Example 4: Kaneko, Y., Takano, T. and Nakamura, K. (2003) Visual localisation of community health needs to rational decision-making in public health services. *Health and Place, 9: 241–51.*

Example 5: Yajima, S., Takano, T. and Nakamura, K. (2001) Effectiveness of a community leaders' programme to promote healthy lifestyles in Tokyo. *Health Promotion International*, 16: 235–43.

Chapter 11

Baseline data in ASEAN member countries

Irene S. M. Lee

INTRODUCTION

According to United Nations' projections (United Nations [UN] 2001b), by the year 2030, more than half of the world's urban population will be living in Asia. In the face of this intensifying urbanisation and the emergence of the megacities in ASEAN, with the associated health and environmental issues, it is imperative that the Healthy City project is well established in the ASEAN member countries (AMCs).

The Healthy City concept advocates public health at the local level and the inclusion of health issues on the agenda for urban policy-makers. It has been realised that the biomedical approach alone is insufficient to solve human health problems and hence, a more holistic approach to health that takes into considera- tion the interrelation with social, economic and environmental aspects is necessary. Furthermore, there is a need to involve non-governmental players such as non-governmental organisations (NGOs), community-based organisations (CBOs), schools, universities, the private sector and the people as partners in pro- moting healthy cities (World Health Organisation [WHO] Regional Office for South-East Asia 2000).

The WHO Regional Office for the Western Pacific started consultations with countries in the region on urban health issues 11 years ago. Then, only Australia, Japan and New Zealand, the more developed countries, had the experience of implementing Healthy Cities projects. Since then, it has evolved into a dynamic movement and ten more countries, Cambodia, China, Fiji, Laos, Malaysia, Mongolia, Papua New Guinea, Korea, the Philippines and Vietnam have imple- mented or are planning to implement Healthy Cities activities (WHO Regional Office for the Western Pacific 2000). The Healthy Cities project was introduced in 1994 to the south-east Asian region (SEAR) member countries and since then, there are Healthy Cities programmes in place in Bangladesh, Thailand, Nepal, and Sri Lanka (WHO Regional Office for the South-East Asia 2000).

As such, the Healthy Cities project has gained a foothold within some of the rapidly urbanising AMCs. However, information or statistical data on some of the AMCs is scattered, not readily available or is sometimes inconsistent and outdated.

Therefore, a compilation of a set of consistent, up-to-date baseline data (which is defined as basic information to be gathered before a project begins) is necessary as the first step towards a good foundation. This data can be used later to provide a comparison for assessing the impact of the project.

OBJECTIVE

The objective of this chapter is to provide practitioners, researchers and those interested in the Healthy Cities project with a set of selected, current basic information for a country profile guideline and also baseline data, that is, a basic understanding of the AMCs in terms of statistics for beginning a programme, assessing and monitoring progress or implementing changes.

The focus of the data will be on the environment, health and urbanisation though other socio-economic data on the economy and education as well as data on geography, infrastructure, land use and population will be included. The ten AMCs comprise Brunei, Cambodia, Indonesia, Laos, Malaysia, Myanmar (Burma), the Philippines, Singapore, Thailand and Vietnam.

BASELINE DATA

Geography

The geographical data includes data on the total area, land area, water area, land boundaries, coastline, temperature range and elevation extremes.

The AMCs are located at the south-eastern part of the Asian continent. The equator runs through Indonesia and above this, in the northern hemisphere, are the other AMCs. Singapore has a latitude of 1°22′ north of the equator while Malaysia has a latitude range of approximately 2° to 6° north. Myanmar, Thailand, Laos, Cambodia and Vietnam are neighbouring countries clustered together further north while Brunei and the Philippines are to the east.

The total combined area of the ten AMCs is 4.4 million sq km. Indonesia is by far the largest, accounting for over 40 per cent of the total area. It is the world's largest archipelago with 13,667 islands and a total area of 1.9 million sq km. Singapore is the smallest at 648 sq km and is an island at the southern tip of the Malay peninsular. Likewise, the Philippines has no land boundaries and is an archipelago consisting of 7101 islands of which only 2000 are inhabited. At the other end of the spectrum, Laos has no coastline and is completely landlocked by Burma, Cambodia, China, Thailand and Vietnam. All the other AMCs have direct access to the sea. Brunei, the second smallest AMC after Singapore, has an area of 5770 sq km and is bordered by East Malaysia and the South China Sea.

The AMC climate is tropical and there are monsoons depending on the country location. In terms of topography, the highest elevation in Singapore is only 166 metres whereas Myanmar has the highest elevation of 5881 metres.

Table 11.1. Selected baseline data in ASEAN member countries

		Brunei	Cambodia	Indonesia	Laos	Malaysia
Geography						
Area	Total	5,770	181,040	1,919,440	236,800	329,750
	Land	5,270	176,520	1,826,440	230,800	328,550
	Water	500	4,520	93,000	6,000	1,200
Land boundaries		381	2,572	2,602	5,083	2,669
Coastline		161	443	54,716	0	4,675
Temperature range	Annual min	22.6	21	23	16.5	22.1
	Annual max	32.4	35	31	29	33.1
	Annual median	27.5	28	27	22.75	27.6
Elevation extremes	Lowest point	0	0	0	70	0
	Highest point	1,850	1,810	5,030	2,817	4,100
Land use						
Land use	Arable land	1	13	10	3	3
	Permanent crops	1	0	7	0	12
	Permanent pastures	1	11	7	3	0
	Forests and woodlands	85	66	62	54	68
	Other	12	10	14	40	17
Irrigated land		10	920	45,970	1,250	2,941
Population						
Population		n.a.	11,939,000	209,255,000	5,297,000	22,706,000
		343,653	12,491,501	228,438,870	5,635,967	22,229,040
Age structure	0–14 years	30.77	41.25	30.26	42.75	34.5
	Male	53,977	2,626,821	35,144,702	1,212,577	3,943,324
	Female	51,772	2,526,510	33,973,879	1,196,795	3,724,634
	15–64 years	66.52	55.28	65.11	53.94	61.35
	Male	121,601	3,253,611	74,273,519	1,494,927	6,828,670
	Female	107,007	3,651,129	74,458,291	1,544,851	6,808,623
	> 65 years	2.71	3.47	4.63	3.31	4.15
	Male	4,449	177,577	4,641,816	85,632	404,042
	Female	4,847	255,853	5,945,663	101,185	519,747
Population growth rate		2.11	2.25	1.6	2.48	1.96
Population density		59.6	69.0	119.0	23.8	67.4

Myanmar	Philippines	Singapore	Thailand	Vietnam	Year	Unit	Source
678,500	300,000	648	514,000	329,560	2002	sq km	4
657,740	298,170	638	511,770	325,360	2002	sq km	4
20,760	1,830	10	2,230	4,200	2002	sq km	4
5,876	0	0	4,863	4,639	2002	km	4
1,930	36,289	193	3,219	3,444	2002	km	4
17.9	20.9	24	20.8	21	2002	°C	3
37	34.3	31	34	27	2002	°C	3
27.45	27.6	27.5	27.4	24	2002	°C	Cal.
0	0	0	0	0	2002	m	4
5,881	2,954	166	2,576	3,143	2002	m	4
15	19	2	34	17	1993	%	4
1	12	6	6	4	1993	%	4
1	4	0	2	1	1993	%	4
49	46	5	26	30	1993	%	4
34	19	87	32	48	1993	%	4
10,680	15,800	0	44,000	18,600	1993–98	sq km	4
48,123,000	74,454,000	3,951,000	61,806,000	76,328,000	1999		4
41,994,678	82,841,518	4,300,419	61,797,751	79,939,014	2001		4
29.14	36.87	17.89	23.43	32.13	2000	%	4
6,245,798	15,547,712	397,124	7,380,273	13,266,585	2000		4
5,992,074	14,997,544	372,058	7,099,506	12,415,384	2000		4
66.08	59.45	75.16	69.95	62.44	2000	%	4
13,779,571	24,374,849	1,575,381	21,304,051	24,357,343	2000		4
13,970,707	24,873,595	1,656,838	21,921,383	25,556,187	2000		4
4.78	3.68	6.95	6.62	5.43	2000	%	4
895,554	1,355,046	130,815	1,796,325	1,722,094	2000		4
1,110,974	1,692,772	168,203	2,296,213	2,621,421	2000		4
0.6	2.03	3.5	0.91	1.45	2001	%	4
61.9	276.1	6641.6	120.2	242.6	2001	Pop/sq km	Cal.

		Brunei	Cambodia	Indonesia	Laos	Malaysia
Urbanisation						
Urban population		235,000	2,746,000	81,609,000	1,218,000	12,942,000
		n.a.	0.8	32.9	0.4	5.8
		0.2	1.8	82.5	1.2	12.9
		0.2	1.9	86.1	1.2	13.4
Urban population growth rate		3.0	4.6	4.2	5.1	3.3
Degree of urbanisation		72	23	39	23	57
Population in largest city		n.a.	44	18	n.a.	16
		n.a.	51	13	n.a.	10
Total recorded crime		n.a.	n.a.	219	n.a.	584
		n.a.	n.a.	80	n.a.	694
Economy						
Gross Domestic Product (GDP)	Purchasing power parity (PPP)	5.9	16.1	654	9	223.7
	Real growth rate	3	4	4.8	4	8.6
GDP per capita	PPP	17,600	1,300	2,900	1,700	10,300
GDP composition by sector	Agriculture	5	43	21	51	14
	Industry	46	20	35	22	44
	Services	49	37	44	27	42
Population below poverty line		n.a.	36	20	46.1	6.8
Household income /consumption	Lowest 10%	n.a.	2.9	3.6	4.2	1.4
	Highest 10%	n.a.	33.8	30.3	26.4	20.4
Inflation rate (consumer prices)		1	1.6	9	33	1.7
Labour force		0.144	6	99	1–1.5	9.6
Unemployment rate		4.9	2.8	15–29	5.7	2.8
Budget	Revenues	2.5	0.363	26	0.211	16.4
	Expenditures	2.6	0.532	30	0.462	17.8
Industrial production growth rate		4	n.a.	7.5	7.5	12.1
Education						
Literacy	Total population	88.2	65	83.8	57	83.5
	Male	92.6	48	89.6	70	89.1
	Female	83.4	22	78	44	78.1
Adult (>15 yrs) illiteracy rate	Male	5.4	20	8.1	35.9	8.6
	Female	11.9	43	17.9	66.8	16.5
Human development index (HDI)		0.89	0.42	0.68	0.46	0.83
		0.85	0.51	0.67	0.48	0.77
HDI ranking		32	136	109	140	61

Myanmar	Philippines	Singapore	Thailand	Vietnam	Year	Unit	Source
12,300,000	43,183,000	3,894,000	21,014,000	17,918,000	1999		3
8.1	18.1	2.3	7.9	10.3	1980	millions	6
12.3	42.8	3.9	12.8	15.2	1999	millions	6
13.2	44.3	4.0	13.1	18.8	2000	millions	7
2.6	3.7	1.4	2.5	1.8	1995–00	% p. a.	10
26	58	100	34	23	1999	%	3
27	33	100	59	34	1980	% of urban pop	7
33	25	100	56	30	2000	% of urban pop	7
n.a.	223	1441	424	n.a.	1980	/100,000 pop	5
n.a.	136	1833	464	n.a.	1997	/100,000 pop	5
63.7	310	109.8	413	154.4	2000	$ billion	4
4.9	3.6	10.1	4.2	5.5	2000	%	4
1,500	3,800	26,500	6,700	1,950	2000	$	4
42	20	0	13	25	1996–99	%	4
17	32	30	40	35	1996–99	%	4
41	48	70	47	40	1996–99	%	4
23	41	n.a.	12.5	37	1993–98	%	4
2.8	1.5	n.a.	2.5	3.5	1992–98	%	4
32.4	39.3	n.a.	37.1	29	1992–98	%	4
18	5	1.4	2.1	−0.6	1999–00	%	4
19.7	48.1	2.1	32.6	38.2	1995–00	million	4
7.1	10	3	3.7	25	1995–00	%	4
7.9	14.5	18.1	19	5.3	1996–00	$ billion	4
12.2	12.6	17.1	21	5.6	1996–00	$ billion	4
n.a.	4	14	3	10.7	1997–00	%	4
83.1	94.6	93.5	93.8	93.7	1995–99	%	4
88.7	95	97	96	96.5	1995–99	%	4
77.7	94.3	89.8	91.6	91.2	1990–99	%	4
11	4.5	3.7	2.8	4.5	2000	%	7
19.4	4.8	11.6	6.1	8.6	2000	%	7
0.48	0.68	0.9	0.84	0.56	1995		3
0.59	0.74	0.88	0.75	0.67	1998		3
125	77	24	76	108	2000		3

		Brunei	Cambodia	Indonesia	Laos	Malaysia
Environment						
Greenhouse gas	Carbon dioxide emissions	5404	513	238541	352	130844
	Carbon dioxide emissions/capita	16.82	0.05	1.22	0.07	5.79
	Carbon dioxide damage	n.a.	0.1	1	0.2	1
	Methane emissions	n.a.	n.a.	7,100	n.a.	640
Air pollution	Total suspended particulates	n.a.	n.a.	271	n.a.	85
	Particulate matter of 10 micron	15.75	n.a.	n.a.	n.a.	40
	Sulphur dioxide	4	n.a.	n.a.	n.a.	24
	Nitrogen dioxide	17	n.a.	n.a.	n.a.	n.a.
Water pollution	Organic water pollutant emission	n.a.	12078	347083	n.a.	166577
	/worker	n.a.	0.16	0.16	n.a.	0.12
	/capita	n.a.	96.69	151.94	n.a.	749.37
Industry shares of emissions of organic water pollutants	Primary metals	n.a.	0	2.8	n.a.	7.9
	Paper & pulp	n.a.	3.4	7	n.a.	13.7
	Chemicals	n.a.	3.3	7.1	n.a.	16.1
	Food & beverages	n.a.	59.2	55.3	n.a.	31.5
	Stone, ceramics & glass	n.a.	0.6	0.1	n.a.	0.3
	Textiles	n.a.	24.7	21.1	n.a.	8.6
	Wood	n.a.	5.8	4.1	n.a.	6.6
	Others	n.a.	3.1	2.5	n.a.	15.3
	Primary metals/capita	n.a.	0.00	8.05	n.a.	50.21
	Paper & pulp/capita	n.a.	3.29	28.87	n.a.	108.66
	Chemicals/capita	n.a.	3.19	15.95	n.a.	125.14
	Food & beverages/capita	n.a.	57.24	49.68	n.a.	238.30
	Stone, ceramics & glass/capita	n.a.	0.58	0.15	n.a.	2.25
	Textiles/capita	n.a.	23.88	36.01	n.a.	61.45
	Wood/capita	n.a.	5.61	4.56	n.a.	50.21
	Others/capita	n.a.	3.00	8.81	n.a.	113.90
Solid waste generation/capita		1	0.756	0.82	1.5	n.a.
Solid waste collection		333	838	6560	n.a.	n.a.
Solid waste collection/capita		0.97	0.07	0.03	n.a.	n.a.
Households with solid waste collection		n.a.	80	84	5	n.a.
Threatened species		128	86	763	83	805

Myanmar	Philippines	Singapore	Thailand	Vietnam	Year	Unit	Source
8493	74194	80276	208822	42485	1990–00	1000 tons of CO_2	10
0.17	0.9	19.51	3.47	0.5	1996	tons	9
n.a.	0.6	0.6	1	1	2000	% of GNI	7
n.a.	1,900	60	6,000	3,900	1991	1000 tons/year	1
n.a.	200	n.a.	223	100	1995	micrograms/ cu m	6
n.a.	n.a.	34	66.4	n.a.	1998–99	micrograms/ cu m	2 & 3
n.a.	33	20	11	n.a.	1998	micrograms/ cu m	6
n.a.	n.a.	30	23	n.a.	1998	micrograms/ cu m	6
4479	178239	33661	355819	n.a.	1998	kg/day	6
0.09	0.18	0.1	0.16	n.a.	1998	kg/day/worker	6
10.67	215.16	782.74	575.78	n.a.	1998	kg/day/ 100,000 pop.	Cal.
17.4	5.2	2	6.1	n.a.	1999	%	7
9	9.8	28	5.3	n.a.	1999	%	7
35.6	7.3	15.1	5.3	n.a.	1999	%	7
28.2	54.4	19.9	42.2	n.a.	1999	%	7
0.5	0.2	0.1	0.2	n.a.	1999	%	7
5	16.4	4	35.4	n.a.	1999	%	7
3	2	1.5	1.5	n.a.	1999	%	7
1.2	4.6	29.3	3.9	n.a.	1999	%	7
1.22	11.19	15.65	35.12	n.a.	1999	kg/day/ 100,000 pop.	Cal.
0.73	21.09	218.38	30.52	n.a.	1999	kg/day/ 100,000 pop.	Cal.
3.16	15.71	120.54	30.52	n.a.	1999	kg/day/ 100,000 pop.	Cal.
1.97	117.26	154.98	242.98	n.a.	1999	kg/day/ 100,000 pop.	Cal.
0.16	0.43	1.57	1.15	n.a.	1999	kg/day/ 100,000 pop.	Cal.
0.42	35.29	29.74	203.83	n.a.	1999	kg/day/ 100,000 pop.	Cal.
2.89	4.30	12.52	8.64	n.a.	1999	kg/day/ 100,000 pop.	Cal.
0.13	9.90	229.34	22.46	n.a.	1999	kg/day/ 100,000 pop.	Cal.
0.45	0.4–0.5	1.1	1.51	1.14	1993–98	kg/day	3
1510	4000	7780	8592	1370	1989–98	tons/day	3
0.04	0.05	1.81	0.14	0.02	1989–98	tons/day /1000 pop.	Cal.
32	15.8	100	90	72.5	1990–99	%	3 & 8
131	387	70	187	229	1990–00		10

		Brunei	Cambodia	Indonesia	Laos	Malaysia
Health						
Birth rate		20.45	33.16	22.26	37.84	24.75
Death rate		3.38	10.65	6.3	13.02	5.2
Net migration rate		4.07	0	0	0	0
Sex ratio	At birth	1.06	1.05	1.05	1.03	1.07
	< 15 years	1.04	1.04	1.03	1.01	1.06
	15–64 years	1.14	0.89	1	0.97	1
Sex ratio	> 65 years	0.92	0.69	0.78	0.85	0.78
	Total population	1.1	0.94	1	0.98	1.01
Infant mortality rate		14.4	65.41	40.91	92.89	20.31
Adult mortality	Male	n.a.	357	237	376	186
	Female	n.a.	309	186	320	113
Life expectancy at birth	Total population	73.82	56.82	68.27	53.48	71.11
	Male	71.45	54.62	65.9	51.58	68.48
	Female	76.31	59.12	70.75	55.44	73.92
Total fertility rate		3.4	5.2	2.8	5.6	3.2
Total fertility rate		2.44	4.74	2.58	5.12	3.24
Health services/disease prevention						
Health care	Total population	n.a.	n.a.	43	n.a.	88
Tetanus vaccinations		n.a.	31	78	32	71
Child immunisation rate	Measles	n.a.	63	71	71	88
	DPT	n.a.	64	64	56	89
Access to essential drugs		n.a.	30	80	n.a.	70
Tuberculosis treatment success rate		n.a.	94	81	55	69
DOTS detection rate		n.a.	50	7	32	70
Nutrition and risk factors						
Years lived in poor health	Males	n.a.	16	12	17	9
	Females	n.a.	14	12	17	12
Prevalence of undernourishment		n.a.	41	10	31	3
		n.a.	33	6	29	n.a.
Prevalence of child malnutrition	Weight for age	n.a.	47	34	40	20
	Height for age	n.a.	53	42	47	n.a.
Prevalence of overweight	Height for age	n.a.	n.a.	4	n.a.	n.a.
Prevalence of anaemia		n.a.	n.a.	64	62	56

Myanmar	Philippines	Singapore	Thailand	Vietnam	Year	Unit	Source
20.13	27.37	12.8	16.63	21.23	2001	births/1000 pop.	4
12.3	6.04	4.24	7.54	6.22	2001	deaths/1000 pop.	4
−1.84	−1.01	26.45	0	−0.49	2001	migrants/ 1000 pop.	4
1.06	1.05	1.08	1.05	1.07	2001	male/female	4
1.04	1.04	1.07	1.04	1.07	2001	male/female	4
0.99	0.98	0.95	0.97	0.95	2001	male/female	4
0.81	0.8	0.78	0.78	0.66	2001	male/female	4
0.99	0.99	0.96	0.97	0.97	2001	male/female	4
73.71	28.7	3.62	30.49	30.24	2001	1000 live births	4
n.a.	197	131	206	225	1998	/1000	3
n.a.	149	75	116	153	1997	/1000	3
55.16	67.8	80.17	68.86	69.56	2001	years	4
53.73	64.96	77.22	65.64	67.12	2001	years	4
56.68	70.79	83.35	72.24	72.19	2001	years	4
3.4	3.7	1.5	2	2.7	1999	children born/ woman	3
2.3	3.42	1.22	1.87	2.49	2001	children born/ woman	4
75	n.a.	100	59	75	1995–00	%	3
78	46	n.a.	81	83	1996–98	% pregnant women	7
85	87	86	94	93	1995–99	% children < 1 yr.	7
73	87	94	97	93	1995–99	% children < 1 yr.	7
60	95	100	95	85	1997	% of pop.	7
79	82	86	78	90	1990–97	% of cases	7
25	3	28	5	77	1995–97	% of cases	7
12	11	10	12	12	1999	% of lifespan	7
12	12	12	12	13	1999	% of lifespan	7
10	24	n.a.	31	28	1990–92	% of pop.	7
7	21	n.a.	21	22	1996–98	% of pop.	7
28	32	n.a.	18	37	1992–00	% of children < 5 yr.	3 & 7
42	32	n.a.	16	39	1992–00	% of children < 5 yr.	3 & 7
n.a.	1	1	1	1	1993–98	% of children < 5 yr.	7
58	48	n.a.	57	52	1985–99	% of pregnant women	3 & 7

		Brunei	Cambodia	Indonesia	Laos	Malaysia
Low birth weight babies		n.a.	18	15	60	8
Breast feeding	Exclusive breastfeeding <4mth	n.a.	n.a.	20	n.a.	n.a.
Consumption of iodised salt		n.a.	7	64	93	n.a.
Vitamin A supplementation	Children 6–59 months	n.a.	79	64	80	n.a.
Smoking prevalence	Male	n.a.	70	69	62	49
	Female	n.a.	10	3	8	4
Cigarette consumption		n.a.	912	n.a.	949	n.a.
Tuberculosis	Incidence	n.a.	539	285	167	112
	Prevalence	n.a.	101	1,606	17	30
Prevalence of HIV	Adults infected	n.a.	2.4	0.05	0.04	0.62
	People infected	n.a.	130,000	52,000	1,100	68,000
HIV/AIDS	Adult prevalence rate	0.2	4.04	0.05	0.05	0.42
	People living with HIV/AIDS	100	220,000	52,000	1,400	49,000
	AIDS deaths	n.a.	14,000	3,100	130	1,900
Health expenditure and services						
Health expenditure	Public	n.a.	0.6	0.8	1.2	1.4
	Private	n.a.	6.3	0.9	1.3	1.0
	Total	n.a.	6.9	1.6	2.5	2.5
Health expenditure per capita		n.a.	17.0	8.0	6.0	81.0
Physicians		n.a.	0.3	0.2	0.2	0.7
Hospital beds		n.a.	2.1	0.7	2.6	2.0
Infrastructure						
Urban households connected to	Water	n.a.	n.a.	15	95	n.a.
	Sewerage	n.a.	n.a.	0	0	n.a.
	Electricity	n.a.	n.a.	99	99	n.a.
Per capita water use		n.a.	n.a.	188	150	n.a.
Safe water	Total population	n.a.	13	62	39	88
Access to improved water source		n.a.	30	76	90	n.a.
Access to improved sanitation facilities		n.a.	18	66	46	n.a.
Access to improved sanitation facilitates	Urban	n.a.	58	87	84	n.a.
Sanitation	Total population	n.a.	n.a.	51	19	91
	Urban areas only	n.a.	n.a.	73	70	100
Energy	Energy consumption/capita	7582	17	388	32	1817
Electricity – production		2.445	0.147	78.674	0.792	59.044
Electricity – production by source	Fossil fuel	100	59.18	80.36	2.78	91.61
	Hydro	0	40.82	14.63	97.22	8.39
Electricity – production by source	Nuclear	0	0	0	0	0
	Other	0	0	5.01	0	0
Electricity consumption		2.274	0.1367	73.167	0.1736	54.872

Myanmar	Philippines	Singapore	Thailand	Vietnam	Year	Unit	Source
16	11	7	7	11	1992–99	% of births	3 & 7
n.a.	22	n.a.	4	1	1997–98	%	7
65	15	n.a.	50	89	1992–99	% of households	3 & 7
42	78	n.a.	n.a.	55	1998–00	%	3 & 7
71	75	27	39	73	1985–99	% of adults	3 & 7
52	18	3	2	4	1985–99	% of adults	3 & 7
n.a.	n.a.	5,110	2,140	730	1988–98	/smoker/year	3 & 7
171	310	48	142	189	1997	/100,000 pop.	3 & 7
20	481	2	142	124	1997	1000 cases	3 & 7
0.11	0.06	0.15	2.23	n.a.	1997	%	3 & 7
29,636	24,000	1,325	780,000	8,302	1997	number, all ages	3 & 7
1.99	0.07	0.19	2.15	0.24	1999	%	4
530,000	28,000	4,000	755,000	100,000	1999		4 & 7
48,000	1,200	210	66,000	2,500	1999		4
0.2	1.6	1.1	1.9	0.8	1995–99	% of GDP	7
1.6	2.1	2.1	4.1	4.0	1995–99	% of GDP	7
1.8	3.6	3.2	6.0	4.8	1995–99	% of GDP	7
97.0	37.0	678.0	112.0	17.0	1995–99	$	7
0.3	1.2	1.6	0.4	0.5	1990–99	/1,000 pop.	7
0.6	1.1	3.6	2.0	1.7	1990–99	/1,000 pop.	7
n.a.	95	n.a.	n.a.	80	1993	%	8
n.a.	80	n.a.	n.a.	40	1993	%	8
n.a.	86	n.a.	n.a.	100	1993	%	8
n.a.	n.a.	n.a.	n.a.	110	1993	litres/day	8
60	64.9	100	81	36	1995	%	3
68	87	100	80	56	2000	% of population	7
46	83	100	96	73	2000	% of population	7
65	92	100	97	86	2000	% of population	7
43	n.a.	97	70	21	1995	%	3
61	88	100	98	43	2000	%	3
71	374	7301	924	165	1990–00	kgs oil equiv.	10
4.813	40.745	27.381	83.991	22.985	1999	billion kWh	4
68.56	61.03	100	91.17	47.71	1999	%	4
31.44	18.68	0	3.81	52.29	1999	%	4
0	0	0	0	0	1999	%	4
0	20.29	0	5.02	0	1999	%	4
4.476	37.893	25.464	83.991	21.376	1999	billion kWh	4

		Brunei	Cambodia	Indonesia	Laos	Malaysia
Communication						
Telephones – main lines in use		0.079	0.0218	5.58831	0.025	4.5
Telephones – mobile/cellular		0.043524	0.08	1.07	0.004915	2.698
Radios		0.329	1.34	31.5	0.73	10.9
Televisions		0.2019	0.094	13.75	0.052	10.8
Internet users		0.028	0.006	0.4	0.002	1.5
Telephones/capita		229.88	1.75	24.46	4.44	202.44
Mobile telephones/capita		126.65	6.4	4.68	0.87	121.37
Radios/capita		957.36	107.27	137.89	129.53	490.35
Televisions/capita		587.51	7.53	60.19	9.23	485.85
Internet users/capita		81.48	0.48	1.75	0.35	67.48
Transportation						
Railways	Total	13	603	6,458	0	1,801
Highways (roads)	Total	1,712	35,768	342,700	14,000	64,672
	Paved	1,284	4,165	158,670	3,360	48,707
	Unpaved	428	31,604	184,030	10,640	15,965
	Total length /area	29.67	19.76	17.85	5.91	19.61
	Paved length /area	22.25	2.3	8.27	1.42	14.77
	Unpaved length /area	7.42	17.46	9.59	4.49	4.84
Ratio paved highways (roads)		75	11.64	46.3	24	75.31
Motor vehicles		606.8	6.0	25.0	4.0	200.0
		n.a.	2	14	1	69
Passenger cars		n.a.	5	14	3	170
Two-wheelers		n.a.	41	62	49	224
Fuel prices	Super	n.a.	0.61	0.17	0.41	0.28
	Diesel	n.a.	0.44	0.06	0.32	0.16
Waterways		209	3,700	21,579	4,578	7,296
Airports		2	19	453	51	115

Source:

1 First ASEAN State of the Environment Report (ASEAN Secretariat UNEP 1997)

2 Malaysia Environmental Quality Report 1999 (Department of Environment Malaysia, Ministry of Science, Technology and the Environment 2000)

3 Second ASEAN State of the Environmental Report 2000 (ASEAN Secretariat UNEP 2001)

4 The World Factbook 2001 (Central Intelligence Agency 2002)

5 Third to Sixth United Nations Survey (United Nations Crime and Justice Information Network 2002)

6 World Development Indicators (World Bank 2001)

7 World Development Indicators (World Bank 2002)

8 World Resources 1998–1999 (World Resource Institute 1998)

9 World Resources 2000–2001 (World Resource Institute 2000)

10 World Statistics Pocketbook (United Nations 2001a)

Myanmar	Philippines	Singapore	Thailand	Vietnam	Year	Unit	Source
0.25	1.9	1.928	5.4	2.6	1996–00	millions	4
0.008492	1.959	2.333	2.3	0.730155	1996–00	millions	4
4.2	11.5	2.6	13.96	8.2	1997–00	millions	4
0.32	3.7	1.33	15.19	3.57	1997–00	millions	4
0.0005	0.5	1.74	1	0.121	2000	millions	4
5.95	22.94	448.33	87.38	32.52	1996–00	/1,000 pop.	Cal.
0.2	23.65	542.51	37.22	9.13	1996–00	/1,000 pop.	Cal.
100.01	138.82	604.59	225.9	102.58	1997–00	/1,000 pop.	Cal.
7.62	44.66	309.27	245.8	44.66	1997–00	/1,000 pop.	Cal.
0.01	6.04	404.61	16.18	1.51	2000	/1,000 pop.	Cal.
3,991	492	39	4,071	3,142	1996–00	km	4
28,200	199,950	3,150	64,600	93,300	1991–00	km	4
3,440	39,590	3,066	62,985	23,418	1991–00	km	4
24,760	160,360	84	1,615	69,882	1991–00	km	4
4.16	66.65	486.49	12.57	28.31	1996–00	km/km^2	Cal.
0.51	13.2	473.51	12.25	7.11	1991–00	km/km^2	Cal.
3.65	53.45	12.97	0.31	21.2	1991–00	km/km^2	Cal.
12.2	19.8	97.33	97.5	25.1	1991–00	%	Cal.
5.8	31.7	164.0	110.4	0.7	1999–00	/1,000 pop.	6
2	11	170	97	n.a.	1999	/km road	6
1	10	119	28	n.a.	1999–00	/1,000 pop.	6
n.a.	14	41	174	45	1999–00	/1,000 pop.	6
n.a.	0.37	0.84	0.39	0.38	2000	$/litre	6
n.a.	0.28	0.38	0.35	0.27	2000	$/litre	6
12,800	3,219	0	4,000	17,702	2000	km	4
80	288	9	110	34	2000		4

Land use

The data for land use is divided into five categories namely, arable land, permanent crops, permanent pastures, forest and woodlands and other land.

Arable land includes land defined by the Food and Agriculture Organisation (FAO) as land under temporary crops (double-cropped areas are counted once), temporary meadows for mowing or for pasture, land under market or kitchen gardens, and land temporarily fallow. Land abandoned as a result of shifting cultivation is excluded. Permanent cropland is land cultivated with crops that occupy the land for long periods and need not be replanted after each harvest, such as cocoa, coffee and rubber. This category includes land under flowering shrubs, fruit trees, nut trees and vines but excludes land under trees grown for wood or timber. Other land includes uncultivated land, grassland not used for pasture, wetlands, wastelands and built-up areas – residential, recreational and industrial lands and areas covered by roads and other fabricated infrastructure (World Bank 2002).

The land use data indicate major differences in resource endowments and uses among the AMCs. Singapore is the exception with hardly any arable land, permanent crops, permanent pastures and forest and woodlands, and with 87 per cent of the land use falling under the other land use category. All the other AMCs have a very high percentage of forests and woodlands especially Brunei with 85 per cent. Malaysia, Cambodia and Indonesia have 68, 66 and 62 per cent of forest and woodlands respectively.

Population

The population data includes data on the total population, age structure, population growth rate and population density.

The total population of an economy includes all residents who are present regardless of legal status or citizenship – except for refugees not permanently settled in the country of asylum, who are generally considered part of the population of their country of origin (World Bank 2002). The data shown is for the years 1999 and 2001. The data on age structure shows the percentage of the total population, as well as the number of males and females, in specific age groups, namely 0 to14 years, 15 to 64 years and above 65 years. The population growth rate is the exponential change for the period indicated and the population density has been calculated by dividing the population by the land area in square kilometres.

From the data, the total population of the AMCs is about 540 million (2001). Indonesia has the highest population of 228,437,870 while Brunei has the lowest population of only 343,653. Indonesia has the fifth largest population in the world and accounts for more than 42 per cent of the total AMC population. Another 42 per cent of the AMC population is made up of the Philippines, Thailand and Vietnam with a combined population of nearly 225 million. The total population of the AMCs accounts for 8.6 per cent of the global population (2000) and is projected at 799 million by 2050 (ASEAN Secretariat UNEP 2001).

It can be gathered from the age structure data that the group of AMCs is not yet a predominantly aged population and that most of the population are in the 15 to 64 years range. Most of the AMCs have a population pyramid with an extended base and a tapered top. The more developed countries like Singapore have a heavy middle and narrower bottom. In terms of the population growth rate, Singapore is growing the most rapidly at a rate of 3.5 per cent and is also by far the densest, with a population density of 6642 persons per sq km while the population densities in the other AMCs range from only 24 persons per sq km (Laos) to 243 persons per sq km (Vietnam).

Singapore's rapid population growth rate can be attributed to government intervention. In 1990, Singapore had a population of only 2,705,115. In fact, for the period 1992 to 2000, Singapore had the lowest population growth rate in the AMCs, estimated at 0.9 per cent (ASEAN Secretariat UNEP 1997). The natural population increase began to fall when much of the population aged beyond child-bearing years. The decline in population growth rate was also attributed to the fact that as Singapore became more affluent and full employment was attained (ASEAN Secretariat UNEP 1997), the DINK (double income no kids) syndrome set in. As both spouses in families became gainfully employed under conditions of high wages, the tendency was towards smaller sized families. The government was concerned about the slow growth rate as this meant that increasingly fewer of the working population would have to support a growing elderly population, thus straining available resources for health care and other social services, and decided to step in by providing tax incentives to graduate mothers to have more children, to families with several children and also relaxing immigrations rules (All the Greatest Cities of the World 2002). Within a decade, by 2001, the population rose to 4,300,419.

Urbanisation
The urbanisation data includes data on the urban population, urban population growth rate, degree of urbanisation, population in largest city and social data on total recorded crime.

The urban population is the percentage of the population living in urban areas as defined according to the national definition used in the most recent population census, and depends on the boundaries chosen. Urbanisation is the process – including rural to urban migration, direct immigration from foreign countries, and natural population increase – by which cities capture an increasing proportion of the nation's total population (UN Centre for Human Settlements 2001). The population in the largest city is defined as the percentage of a country's urban population living in that country's largest metropolitan area (World Bank 2002).

From the data, it can be seen that the ten AMCs have varying degrees of urbanisation. The degree of urbanisation ranged from 23 per cent for Cambodia, Laos and Vietnam to 100 per cent for Singapore (1999). However, the urban population growth rate is the lowest for Singapore at 1.4 per cent as compared to the highest of 4.6 per cent for Cambodia. This can be attributed to the fact that urbanisation is an inherent characteristic of Singapore which is a city state. With the exception of Singapore and Brunei, urban population growth in the other AMCs is largely driven by rural-urban migration. The trend of urbanisation is expected to continue and the AMC's urban population is expected to increase from about 185 million in 1999 to about 249 million in 2010, with an annual average growth rate of 2.7 per cent (ASEAN Secretariat UNEP 2001). It has been recognised by the AMCs that escalating urbanisation brings about economic and environmental problems which will be discussed.

It is also interesting to note that the percentage of total recorded crime also increased with the degree of urbanisation. However, the sample size is deemed rather small to draw any definite conclusions. Furthermore, from the data source, there is a lack of information on the definition of recorded crime and the type of crime. Nevertheless, this relationship could be of interest for further research.

Economy

This includes data on the gross domestic product (GDP) – real growth rate, GDP per capita, GDP composition by sector, population below poverty line, household income/consumption, inflation rate (consumer prices), labour force, unemployment rate, budget – revenues and expenditures, and industrial production growth rate.

The GDP is the total output of goods and services for final use produced by an economy by both residents and non-residents, regardless of the allocation to domestic and foreign claims. It does not include deductions for depreciation of physical capital or depletion and degradation of natural resources (UN Centre for Human Settlements 2001). The GDP per capita is the gross domestic product divided by the midyear population. Growth is calculated from constant price GDP data in local currency (World Bank 2002). The purchasing power parity (PPP) attempts to calculate the actual purchasing power of money income received. At the PPP rate, one dollar has the same purchasing power over domestic GDP that the US dollar has over US GDP. PPP could also be expressed in other national currencies or in special drawing rights (SDRs). PPP rates allow a standard comparison of real price levels between countries, just as conventional price indexes allow comparison of real values over time; otherwise, normal exchange rates may over- or under-value purchasing power (UN Centre for Human Settlements 2001). The definition of poverty line depends on the country. The commonly used $1 a day standard, measured in 1985 international prices and adjusted to local currency using PPPs, was chosen for the World Bank's *World Development Report 1990: Poverty* because it is typical of the poverty lines in low-income countries. This has since been recalculated in 1993 PPP terms at about $1.08 a day (World Bank 2002).

From the data, the combined GDP (adjusted for purchasing power) for the AMCs in year 2000 was $1,960 billion. Indonesia had the highest GDP of $654 billion and the six largest economies, Indonesia, Thailand, the Philippines,

Malaysia, Vietnam and Singapore, had a combined 2000 GDP of $1,865 billion, accounting for 95 per cent of the AMC's 2000 GDP. In spite of the economic downturn in 1997, Singapore had a 2000 GDP real growth rate of 10.1 per cent while the lowest was that of Brunei at 3 per cent. The GDP per capita (adjusted for purchasing power) ranged from $1300 for Cambodia to $26,500 for Singapore. Brunei and Singapore are classified as high income countries, Malaysia as an upper middle income country, the Philippines and Thailand as lower middle income countries and Cambodia, Indonesia, Laos, Myanmar and Vietnam as low income countries.

In terms of the GDP composition by sector, agriculture was the dominant sector for Laos, Cambodia and Myanmar. The services and industry sectors played a more dominant role in the GDP composition of the other AMCs. Singapore, at the other extreme, had a GDP composition of 0, 30 and 70 per cent for the agriculture, industry and services sectors respectively.

From the data on the percentage of population living below the poverty line, Laos (46.1 per cent), the Philippines (41 per cent), Vietnam (37 per cent) and Cambodia (36 per cent) have a substantial percentage of population living below the poverty line. The inflation rate (consumer prices) ranges from 1 per cent for Brunei to 33 per cent for Laos (1999 to 2000). Indonesia has the largest labour force of 99 million while Brunei has the smallest labour force of 144,000. However, Indonesia also has the highest unemployment rate of 15 to 29 per cent as well as the highest budget revenues ($26 billion) and expenditures ($30 billion). Singapore has the lowest unemployment rate of 3 per cent and the highest industrial production growth rate of 14 per cent. Thailand has the lowest industrial production growth rate of 3 per cent.

Education

The literacy rate is defined as the percentage of people aged 15 and above who can, with understanding, both read and write a short, simple statement on their everyday life (UN Centre for Human Settlements 2001). The adult illiteracy rate is defined as the percentage of people aged 15 and above who cannot, with understanding, both read and write a short, simple statement about their everyday life (World Bank 2002). The Human Development Index (HDI) is a composite index developed by the United Nations Development Programme (UNDP) and has been used as a guide for allocating international funds for development cooperation with countries. It is based on three indicators: longevity, as measured by life expectancy at birth; educational attainment, as measured by a combination of adult literacy and the combined first, second and third level gross enrolment ratio; and standard of living, as measured by real GDP per capita (PPP$). Countries, with a few exceptions, are all rated from 0 to 1 along the HDI (UN Centre for Human Settlements 2001). In short, the HDI measures a country's achievements in terms of life expectancy, educational attainment and adjusted real income. The social development trends of a country can be roughly estimated by changes over time in the HDI. The UNDP has also calculated HDI rankings for all countries for which data is available, the highest being ranked 1 and the lowest currently 174. For the year 2000, rankings of 1 to 46 fall under high human development, rankings of 47 to 139 fall under medium human development and rankings of 140 to 174 fall under low human development (World Bank 2002).

According to the data, the AMCs with the highest literacy of total population are the Philippines (94.6 per cent), Thailand (93.8 per cent), Vietnam (93.7 per cent) and Singapore (93.5 per cent). In all the ten AMCs, the males have a higher percentage of literacy than the females. Singapore has the highest HDI (0.88) while Laos has the lowest HDI (0.48). In terms of HDI ranking, Singapore ranks 24 while Laos ranks 140. Singapore and Brunei fall well within the high human development category while Laos falls just within the low human development category and the other AMCs fall into the medium human development category.

Environment
The environmental data includes data on greenhouse gases (carbon dioxide emissions, carbon dioxide emissions per capita, carbon dioxide damage and methane emissions), air pollution (total suspended particulates, particulate matter of 10 micron, sulphur dioxide and nitrogen dioxide), water pollution (emissions of organic water pollutants and industry shares of emissions of organic water pollutants), solid waste (solid waste generation per capita, solid waste collection and solid waste collection per capita) and on threatened species.

The data on carbon dioxide (CO_2) emissions is defined as those stemming from the burning of fossil fuels and the manufacture of cement, and is from calculations derived from figures on fossil fuel consumption and world cement manufacturing. They include CO_2 produced during consumption of solid, liquid and gas fuels, and gas flaring. CO_2 emissions, largely a by-product of energy production and use, account for the largest share (60 per cent) of greenhouse gases which are associated with global warming (World Bank 2002). Deforestation is a contributory factor to global warming since it reduces the plant population that removes CO_2 or acts as a carbon sink (ASEAN Secretariat UNEP 2001).

CO_2 damage is estimated to be $20 per ton of carbon (the unit damage in 1995 US dollars) times the number of tons of carbon emitted, and is expressed as a percentage of the gross national income (GNI). For CO_2, the unit damage figure represents the present value of global damage to economic assets and to human welfare over the time the unit of pollution remains in the atmosphere (World Bank 2002).

Atmospheric methane (CH_4) comes primarily from the anaerobic decay of organic matter in natural wetlands, rice paddies, enteric fermentation in ruminants, landfills, biomass burning, natural gas production and transmission, and coal mining. The difficulty in quantifying emissions from these sources has been a major source of dispute between the industrialised nations and the developing, agricultural-based communities like ASEAN (ASEAN Secretariat UNEP 1997).

Total Suspended Particulates (TSP) refers to the smoke, soot, dust, and liquid droplets from combustion that is in the air. Particulate levels indicate the quality of the air people are breathing and the state of a country's technology and pollution controls (World Bank 2002). Particulate matter of 10 micron in size (PM10) and below is the component of TSP that is one of the 'criteria pollutants' in calculating the Pollutant Standards Index (PSI). Such particles below 10 micron (1 micron is a millionth of a mm or 100 micron is the width of a hair) are invisible to the naked eye, inhalable and can enter and be deposited in the respiratory system. Therefore, PM10 is very relevant to health consideration and is one of the criteria pollutants in air quality monitoring. The WHO guideline for permissible levels of TSP is 100 µg/cu m. The annual ambient air quality standard for PM10 in Brunei is 60 µg/cu m and 50 µg/cu m in Malaysia (Department of Environment Malaysia 1998), Singapore and Thailand (ASEAN Secretariat UNEP 2001).

The PSI is a system of reporting ambient air quality developed by the United States Environmental Protection Agency (USEPA) and the use of the USEPA guidelines is widespread throughout the world. The five pollutants designated as 'criteria pollutants' in the reporting of the PSI are dust or PM10, sulphur dioxide (SO_2), nitrogen dioxide (NO_2), carbon monoxide (CO) and ozone (O_3). The recorded levels of these pollutants are used to produce a single index (PSI) on a scale of 0 to 500. A PSI value of 0 to 50 is considered good, 51 to 100 moderate, 101 to 199 unhealthy, 200 to 299 very unhealthy and 300 and above, hazardous (Government of Brunei Darussalam 2002).

SO_2 is an air pollutant produced when fossil fuels containing sulphur are burnt. It contributes to acid rain and can damage human health, particularly that of the young and the elderly. Specifically, exposure to SO_2 can damage the respiratory system. It irritates the lung and causes chronic disorder and other complications. The environmental effects of SO_2 include: acidification of soils, lakes and rivers, damage to plants, corrosion of buildings and reactions with limestone deposits. In general, acid deposition affects human health, plant growth and aquatic life (World Bank 2002). The WHO guideline for permissible levels of SO_2 is 50 µg/cu m.

NO_2 is a poisonous, pungent gas formed when nitric oxide combines with hydrocarbons and sunlight, producing a photochemical reaction. These conditions occur in both natural and anthropogenic activities. NO_2 is emitted by bacteria, nitrogenous fertilisers, aerobic decomposition of organic matter in oceans and soils, combustion of fuels and biomass, motor vehicles and industrial activities (World Bank 2002). The WHO guideline for permissible levels of NO_2 is 50 µg/cu m.

The emissions of organic water pollutants are measured in terms of the biochemical oxygen demand (BOD) which refers to the amount of oxygen that bacteria in water will consume in breaking down waste. This is a standard water treatment test for the presence of organic pollutants. The emissions per worker is defined as the total emissions divided by the number of industrial workers. Industry shares of emissions of organic water pollutants refer to emissions from the following manufacturing activities: primary metals, paper and pulp, chemicals, food and beverages, stone, ceramics and glass, textiles, wood and other. Data on water pollution is more readily available than other emissions data because most industrial pollution control programmes start by regulating emissions of organic water pollutants. Such data is fairly reliable because sampling techniques for measuring water pollution are more widely understood and much less expensive than those for air pollution (World Bank 2002).

Municipal solid waste (MSW) refers to heterogeneous unwanted materials produced through daily activities of households, industry, offices and others. It consists mostly of decomposable organic materials, inert matter and sometimes smaller amounts of hazardous materials from hospitals and elsewhere (ASEAN Secretariat UNEP 2001). However, in the developed countries like Germany and the United States, MSW refers mainly to household waste which is a different category from office and industrial waste. Likewise, construction and demolition debris as well as hazardous waste from industry and hospitals are different categories of waste that are collected and disposed of differently.

Threatened species are the number of species classified by the International Union for Conservation of Nature and Natural Resources (IUCN) as endangered, vulnerable, rare, indeterminate, out of danger, or insufficiently known (World Bank 2002).

According to the data, Indonesia followed by Thailand has the highest level of CO_2 emissions whilst Laos and Cambodia have the two lowest levels. In terms of CO_2 emissions per capita, Singapore has the highest level (19.51 tons) followed by Brunei (16.82 tons). This can be attributed to the fact that among the AMCs, Singapore and Brunei are the most urbanised, have the highest incomes, have a high percentage of industry and a high percentage of energy consumption but have the smallest populations. The CO_2 emissions per capita of the other AMCs range from 0.05 to 5.79 tons. Cambodia (0.05 tons) and Laos (0.07 tons) have the lowest levels of CO_2 emissions per capita. The total emission of carbon dioxide in the AMCs is about 790 million tons a year, constituting 3.5 per cent of the total global emission. Though this figure is small, there is an increasing trend and in the last three decades, total emissions in the AMCs have increased almost ten-fold (ASEAN Secretariat UNEP 1997).

It is estimated that every year about 674 million tons of carbon remain in the atmosphere because the forests in AMCs that should have absorbed the gas were destroyed. Since land use change is irreversible, the capacity of forests to decrease carbon is permanently removed. The AMCs are currently addressing the problem of forest depletion as a means to reduce CO_2 emissions. Furthermore, since the AMCs economies are growing very fast, the rate of CO_2 emissions is expected to increase very rapidly unless intensity is reduced by promoting industrial efficiency and by making lifestyles less energy intensive (ASEAN Secretariat UNEP 1997).

The CO_2 damages of the AMCs range from 0.1 to 1 per cent of their respective gross national incomes. Cambodia (0.1 per cent) and Laos (0.2 per cent) have the lowest whilst Indonesia (1 per cent), Malaysia (1 per cent), Thailand (1 per cent) and Vietnam (1 per cent) have the highest amount of CO_2 damage. In most countries in the world, the CO_2 damage is below 1 per cent. However, certain countries like Mongolia (5.3 per cent) and Russia (4 per cent) have high CO_2 damage.

Among the AMCs, Indonesia (7.1 million tons) and Thailand (6 million tons) contribute the most CH_4 to the atmosphere followed by Vietnam (3.9 million tons) and the Philippines (1.9 million tons). Apparently, these countries with large agricultural bases contribute more to CH_4 emissions. Singapore contributes the least at 60,000 tons per year. Every year, the AMCs add 19.6 million tons of methane to the atmosphere, largely from agricultural activities, in particular, paddy rice growing. The AMCs contribute an estimated 21 per cent of the world's methane emissions that arise from wet paddy fields (ASEAN Secretariat UNEP 1997).

Data on TSP was only available for Indonesia, Malaysia, the Philippines, Thailand and Vietnam. Current TSP data does not exist for countries like Singapore and Brunei. In the 1980s, Singapore stopped recording TSP data, adopted the USEPA guidelines and is now recording PM10 data instead. Likewise, Brunei also records PM10 instead of TSP data. The TSP data of the AMCs is in the range of 85 µg/cu m to 271 µg/cu m (1995). Indonesia had the highest level of TSP (271 µg/cu m) followed by Thailand (223 µg/cu m), the Philippines (200 µg/cu m), Vietnam (100 µg/cu m) and Malaysia (85 µg/cu m). However, TSP levels in Indonesia, Thailand and the Philippines have exceeded, even doubled, the WHO guideline of 100 µg/cu m. The high TSP readings in Indonesia could have been due to the haze from the forest fires there. During haze episodes, the highest recorded pollutant was the PM10. PM10 data was available for the following AMCs – Thailand (66.4 µg/cu m), Malaysia (40 µg/cu m), Singapore (34 µg/cu m) and Brunei (15.75 µg/cu m). Except for Thailand, these all fell within the annual air quality standard of 50 to 60 µg/cu m for PM10. Neither TSP nor PM10 data was available for Cambodia, Laos and Myanmar.

The SO_2 levels in the AMCs range from 4 µg/cu m (Brunei) to 33 µg/cu m (Philippines) and hence fall within the WHO guideline of 50 µg/cu m. To reduce sulphur emissions, AMCs are shifting to the use of low-sulphur fuel (preferably less than 1 per cent) particularly for industries near urban centres. Meanwhile, the use of SO_2 removal technologies such as scrubbers that desulphurise flue gas is still limited due to prohibitive cost (ASEAN Secretariat UNEP 1997). Diesel fuel, used mainly by trucks and other heavy vehicles, is a major source of SO_2 particulate emissions. These can be effectively lowered through low sulphur diesel oils (ASEAN Secretariat UNEP 2001). The NO_2 levels in the AMCs range from 17 µg/cu m (Brunei) to 30 µg/cu m (Singapore) which fall within the WHO guideline of 50 µg/cu m.

Emissions of organic pollutants from industrial activities are a major cause of degradation of water quality and the polluting substances include organic matter, metals, minerals, sediment, bacteria and toxic chemicals (World Bank 2002). From the data, Thailand produces the most emissions of organic water pollutants (355,819 kg/day) followed closely by Indonesia (347,083 kg/day) whilst Myanmar produces the least (4479 kg/day). However, in terms of emissions of organic water pollutants per capita, Singapore produces the most and Myanmar the least. When the emissions are categorised according to the industry shares, the chemical as well as the food and beverages industries are found to be the most polluting.

From the data, it can be seen that in the AMCs, the MSW generated per capita ranges from 0.4 to 1.51 kg per day. However, the MSW collected has no relation to the MSW generated, hence the mountains of trash piling up in some AMCs. The amount of MSW collected for disposal varies among the AMCs and ranges from 5 per cent to 100 per cent. A reasonable goal for a well managed waste disposal system would be 85 to 95 per cent. Singapore and Brunei have the highest MSW collected per capita per day, with Singapore having 100 per cent of households with MSW collection. Improper management and disposal of waste can lead to public health hazards, soil pollution and water pollution.

Land disposal is the most commonly used method of MSW disposal for the AMCs. Singapore is the exception where 85 per cent of the MSW is incinerated. Singapore has one offshore landfill site and four incineration plants. Land disposal is used in most countries because land is available cheaply, requires a much smaller capital outlay and has low operating expenses compared to other alternatives. Composting is not widely practised due to the poor quality of the compost, limited market demand and low market value (World Bank 2002).

From the data on threatened species, Malaysia has the most at 805 followed by Indonesia at 763. Singapore has the least number of threatened species at 70. The other AMCs have a range of 83 to 387 threatened species.

Health

The health data includes data on the birth rate, death rate, net migration rate, sex ratio, infant mortality rate, adult mortality, life expectancy at birth and total fertility rate. The category on health services/disease prevention includes data on health care, tetanus vaccinations, child immunisation rate for measles and DPT, (diphtheria, pertussis or whooping cough and tetanus) access to essential drugs, tuberculosis treatment success rate and the directly observed treatment, short course (DOTS) detection rate. The category on nutrition and risk factors includes data on the number of years lived in poor health, prevalence of under nourishment, prevalence of child malnutrition, prevalence of overweight, prevalence of anaemia, low birth weight babies, breast feeding, consumption of iodised salt, vitamin A supplementation, smoking prevalence, cigarette consumption, tuberculosis, prevalence of HIV and HIV/AIDS. The category on health expenditure and services includes data on health expenditure, health expenditure per capita, physicians and hospital beds.

The crude death rate and crude birth rate are defined as the number of deaths and the number of live births occurring during the year, per 1000 population estimated at midyear. The difference between the crude death rate and the crude birth rate is the rate of natural increase, which is equal to the population growth rate in the absence of migration. The infant mortality rate (IMR) is the number of infants dying before reaching one year of age, per 1000 live births. The life expectancy at birth is defined as the number of years a newborn infant would live if prevailing patterns of mortality at the time of birth were to stay the same throughout the child's life. The total fertility rate (TFR) is defined as the number of children that would be born to a woman if she were to live to the end of her childbearing years and bear children in accordance with current age-specific fertility rates (World Bank 2002).

Tetanus vaccinations refer to the percentage of pregnant women who receive two tetanus toxoid injections during their first pregnancy and one booster shot during each subsequent pregnancy. Child immunisation rate is the percentage of children under one year of age receiving vaccination coverage for four diseases – measles and DPT. Tuberculosis treatment success rate refers to the percentage of new, registered smear-positive (infectious) cases that were cured or in which a full course of treatment was completed. DOTS detection rate is the percentage of esti-mated new infectious tuberculosis cases detected under the DOTS case detection and treatment strategy (World Bank 2002).

Prevalence of child malnutrition is defined as the percentage of children whose weight is more than two standard deviations below the median reference standard for their age as established by the US National Centre for Healthy Statistics, the US Centres for Disease Control and Prevention and the WHO. Incidence of tuber-culosis is the estimated number of new tuberculosis cases (pulmonary, smear positive and extra pulmonary). HIV prevalence refers to the percentage of people aged 15 to 24 who are infected with HIV (World Bank 2002).

The total health expenditure is defined as the sum of public and private health expenditure, plus, for some countries, external sources (mainly foreign assis-tance). It covers the provision of health services (preventive and curative), family planning activities, nutrition activities and emergency aid designated for health but does not include provision of water and sanitation. Hospital beds include inpatient beds available in public, private, general and specialised hospitals and rehabilitation centres. In most cases, beds for both acute and chronic care are included (World Bank 2002).

From 2001 AMC data on the birth rate and death rate, Singapore had the low-est birth rate (12.8 births per 1000 population) and also the lowest death rate (4.2 deaths per 1000 population). At the other end of the scale, Laos had the highest birth rate (37.8 births per 1000 population) and also the highest death rate (13.0 deaths per 1000 population). It can be seen that there is quite a difference between the AMC birth rates and death rates and that the AMCs are far from completing the demographic transition which is the point at which the birth rate is equal to the death rate and population growth levels off. Singapore also had the highest net migration rate (26.5 migrants per 1000 population) and Myanmar the lowest (–1.8 migrants per 1000 population). Singapore had the highest sex ratio at birth (1.08 males to females) and Laos had the lowest (1.03 males to females). Singapore had the lowest infant mortality rate (3.6 births) and Laos had the highest (92.9 births).

Likewise, Singapore had the lowest adult mortality rate and Laos had the highest for both males and females. Singapore had the highest life expectancy at birth (80.2 years) and Laos had the lowest (53.5 years). In 2001, Singapore had the lowest fertility rate (1.2 children born per woman) and Laos had the highest (5.1 children born per woman). Comparing 1999 and 2001 data, the fertility rate for all the AMCs has declined.

From the health services/disease prevention data, health care for the total population ranges from 43 per cent for Indonesia to 100 per cent for Singapore. Tetanus vaccinations range from 31 to 83 per cent of pregnant women. Neonatal tetanus is a main cause of infant mortality and it can be prevented through immunisation of mothers during pregnancy. There was no tetanus vaccination data from the high income countries Brunei and Singapore. Governments in developing countries usually finance immunisation against measles and DPT as part of the basic public health package. The access to essential drugs ranges from 30 (Cambodia) to 100 per cent (Singapore) of the population, and the tuberculosis treatment success rate ranges from 55 to 94 per cent of cases.

Under nutrition and risk factors, data on prevalence of under nourishment shows that there was the highest percentage of under nourishment in Cambodia and the least in Singapore. Low birth weight babies range from 7 per cent of births (Singapore and Thailand) to 60 per cent of births (Laos). From the data on smoking prevalence, it is interesting to note that male adults smoke far more than female adults in all the AMCs. The incidence of tuberculosis is the lowest in Singapore (48 per 100,000 population) and the highest in Cambodia (539 per 100,000 population). The prevalence of tuberculosis is also the lowest in Singapore (2000 cases) and the highest in Indonesia (1.6 million cases). The data on people living with HIV/AIDS is the lowest in Brunei (100) and the highest in Thailand (755,000) and the surrounding countries – Myanmar (530,000) and Cambodia (220,000).

From the health expenditure and services data, it can be seen that the health expenditure per capita is the highest in Singapore ($678) and the lowest in Laos ($6), a difference of one hundred and thirteen times. Likewise, Singapore has the highest percentage of physicians (1.6 per 1000 population) and the highest number of hospital beds (3.6 per 1000 population). Indonesia and Laos have the lowest number of physicians (0.2 per 1000 population) and Indonesia and Myanmar have the lowest number of hospital beds (0.7 per 1000 population and 0.6 per 1000 population respectively).

Infrastructure
The infrastructure data includes data on households connected to water, sewerage and electricity, per capita water use, safe water, access to improved water source, access to improved sanitation facilities, sanitation, energy consumption per capita, electricity production, electricity production by source and electricity consumption.

Under communication, data is given on main telephone lines in use, mobile or cellular telephones, radios, televisions and Internet users. Under transportation, data is given on railways, highways or roads, ratio of highways, motor vehicles, passenger cars, two-wheelers, fuel prices, waterways and airports.

Safe water should not contain biological or chemical agents at concentration levels directly detrimental to health. Safe water includes treated surface water and untreated but uncontaminated water such as that from protected boreholes, springs and sanitary wells. Untreated surface waters, such as streams and lakes, should be considered safe only if the water quality is regularly monitored and considered acceptable by public health officials (Uemura 2000). Access to an improved water source refers to the percentage of the population with reasonable access to an adequate amount of water from an improved source, such as a household connection, public standpipe, borehole, protected well or spring, or rainwater collection. Access to improved sanitation facilities refers to the percentage of the population with at least adequate excreta disposal facilities (private or shared, but not public) that can effectively prevent human, animal, and insect contact with excreta. Improved facilities range from simple but protected pit latrines to flush toilets with a sewerage connection. To be effective, facilities must be correctly constructed and properly maintained (World Bank 2002).

Electricity production is measured at the terminals of all alternator sets in a station. In addition to hydropower, coal, oil, gas and nuclear power generation, it covers generation by geothermal, solar, wind and the tide and wave energy as well as that from combustible renewables and waste. Telephone lines are telephone mainlines connecting a customer's equipment to the public switched telephone network. Internet users are people with access to the World Wide Web (Uemura 2000).

From the data on the percentage of the total population with safe water, Singapore has the highest (100 per cent) and Cambodia the lowest (13 per cent). Likewise, 100 per cent of the population in Singapore has access to an improved water source while only 30 per cent of the population in Cambodia has access. From the data on access to improved sanitation facilities, again 100 per cent of the population in Singapore has access while only 18 per cent of the population in Cambodia has access. The availability of safe drinking water supply is one of the essential requirements in primary health care. Access to reliable supplies or safe drinking water and sanitary disposal of excrement are two of the most important means of improving human health and protecting the environment (Uemura 2000).

The AMCs, in particular Indonesia, are endowed with abundant petroleum, natural gas, coal, hydropower, geothermal energy and biomass energy. Both Brunei and Indonesia have large oil reserves, while Vietnam, Malaysia and Myanmar have considerable potential. Indonesia, and to a lesser extent Malaysia, have sizeable gas and coal reserves. Myanmar and Indonesia have significant hydropower potential and most of the AMCs are well endowed with fuel wood, a common energy source for cooking and heating. Energy production and use can have profound environmental implications (ASEAN Secretariat UNEP 2001).

From the data, Brunei (7582 kgs oil equivalent) and Singapore (7301 kgs oil equivalent) have the highest energy consumption per capita while Cambodia (17 kgs oil equivalent) and Laos (32 kgs oil equivalent) have the lowest. An economy's production and consumption of electricity is a basic indicator of its size and level of development (World Bank 2002). The electricity production of the AMCs range from 0.147 billion kWh (Cambodia) to 83.991 billion kWh (Thailand). Data on electricity production by source shows that 100 per cent of the electricity in both Brunei and Singapore is produced by fossil fuel. None of the AMCs produced electricity by nuclear plants while all the AMCs except Brunei and Singapore also produced electricity by hydro sources. The electricity consumption in the AMCs is closely related to the production.

It can be seen from the data on communication infrastructure that the two high income AMCs, Singapore and Brunei, have the highest number of telephones per capita. Malaysia, an upper middle income country, ranks third, while the other AMCs have a much lower number of telephones per capita. Similarly, a direct relationship exists between the levels of income or GDP and the data on mobile telephones, Internet users and televisions per capita.

From the transportation infrastructure data, it can be seen that Singapore has the most highway or roads per area at 486.49 km/sq km. The other AMCs range from 4.16 km/sq km (Myanmar) to 66.65 km/sq km (the Philippines). Almost 100 per cent of the roads in Singapore, Brunei and Thailand are paved whereas Cambodia, Indonesia, Laos, Myanmar, the Philippines and Vietnam have high percentages of unpaved roads. Correspondingly, Brunei, Singapore, Thailand and Malaysia have a high number of motor vehicles per 1000 population.

INTERRELATIONSHIP OF INDICATORS

The data were analysed using various statistical analysis methods such as the Pearson correlation and Spearman correlation, scatter graph, multiple regression and interrelationship analyses.

Environment
The analysis of the data shows that there are significant, positive (bivariate) correlations between CO_2 emissions and PPP as well as electricity production and consumption. The result of regression analysis also shows a multivariate relationship between CO_2 emissions and the variables PPP and electricity production. Regarding CO_2 damage, there are also significant, positive correlations between the CO_2 damage and CO_2 emissions, GDP composition by industry, electricity production and consumption in the AMCs. That is, the CO_2 damage value will increase with the increase in value of any of these variables.

Further analysis shows that there are significant, positive correlation coefficients for CO_2 emissions per capita with the following indicators: energy consumption per capita, GDP per capita, degree of urbanisation, HDI ranking, motor vehicles, ratio of paved highways and electricity produced by fossil fuel. The result of regression analysis shows a multivariate relationship between CO_2 emissions per capita and the variables GDP per capita and energy consumption per capita. Another equation shows the multivariate relationship between CO_2 emissions per capita and the variables GDP per capita and motor vehicles.

The other environmental indicators TSP per capita, SO_2 per capita and NO_2 per capita have significant, positive correlation coefficients with motor vehicles. There are significant, positive correlation coefficients for TSP per capita with GDP per capita and paved highways per area but a negative correlation coefficient with HDI ranking. This makes sense since the GDP per capita has an inverse correlation with HDI ranking. However, it has to be pointed out that the sample size for these environmental indicators was small due to the limited data available.

Analysis of the data on emissions of organic H_2O pollutants per capita shows that there are significant, positive correlation coefficients for emissions of organic H_2O pollutants per capita with the following indicators: GDP per capita, electricity produced by fossil fuel, safe water, sanitation (urban areas) and life expectancy at birth. There are significant, negative correlation coefficients with HDI ranking and infant mortality rate. This means that as the value of the emissions of organic H_2O pollutants per capita increases, the values of the HDI ranking as well as the infant mortality rate will decrease, that is, AMCs with higher GDPs (and hence lower HDI rankings and infant mortality rates) emit more organic H_2O pollutants per capita. Further analysis of data shows that the industry shares of emissions of organic water pollutants per capita has the highest, significant correlation coefficients with the chemicals as well as the stone, ceramics and glass industry, showing that these two industries emit the most organic water pollutants per capita.

It is interesting to note that analysis of the AMC solid waste data shows that there is no significant correlation between the per capita solid waste collected per day and the per capita solid waste generation. However, there are significant correlation coefficients between the per capita solid waste collected per day and per capita GDP, per capita energy consumption, electricity produced by fossil fuel, degree of urbanisation, population density, population growth rate, highways per area, paved highways per area and per capita health expenditure. The result of regression analysis shows a multivariate relationship between per capita solid waste collected per day and the variables energy consumption per capita and paved highways per area. Obviously, the necessary infrastructure has to be in place before the solid waste can be collected.

It can be summarised that, for the AMCs, there is not only a strong linear relationship between these environmental indicators and the obvious economic indicators but also the health, urbanisation, infrastructure and social indicators, and that a change in the value of the health, urbanisation, infrastructure or socio-economic indicator will be accompanied by a change in the value of the environmental indicator.

Health

The analysis of the birth rate data shows that there are significant, positive correlation coefficients with the HDI ranking, urban population growth rate, infant mortality rate, low weight babies, total fertility rate and years lived in poor health, and significant, negative correlation coefficients with the data on electricity from fossil fuels, literacy of the total population and life expectancy at birth. The analysis of the death rate data shows that there are significant, positive correlation coefficients with the HDI ranking, infant mortality rate, low weight babies and years lived in poor health, and significant, negative correlation coefficients with the GDP per capita, energy consumption per capita, electricity from fossil fuels, literacy of total population, degree of urbanisation, access to improved sanitation and access to essential drugs.

The analysis of the infant mortality rate data shows that there are significant, positive correlation coefficients with the HDI ranking, inflation rate, low weight babies and years lived in poor health. There are significant, negative correlation coefficients with economic indicators such as GDP per capita and literacy of total population, with environmental indicators such as CO_2 emissions per capita and organic H_2O pollutants per capita, with urbanisation indicators such as the degree of urbanisation, with infrastructure indicators such as electricity produced by fossil fuel, energy consumption per capita, safe water, access to improved sanitation and ratio of paved highways, and with other health indicators such as child immunisation rate, access to essential drugs and number of physicians. The results of regression analysis show that the infant mortality rate is influenced by the GDP per capita and literacy of total population.

The analysis of the life expectancy data shows that there are significant, positive correlation coefficients with economic indicators such as GDP per capita and literacy of total population, with environmental indicators such as CO_2 emissions per capita and organic H_2O pollutants per capita, with urbanisation indicators such as the degree of urbanisation, with infrastructure indicators such as electricity produced by fossil fuel, energy consumption per capita, safe water, access to improved sanitation, per capita solid waste collected per day and ratio of paved highways, and with other health indicators such as child immunisation rate, access to essential drugs and number of physicians. There are significant, negative correlation coefficients between the life expectancy and the inflation rate, HDI ranking, low weight babies and years lived in poor health. The results of regression analysis show that the life expectancy is influenced by the variables GDP per capita and literacy of total population. Another equation shows that the life expectancy is also influenced by the variables degree of urbanisation and literacy of total population.

Analysis of the total fertility rate data shows that there are significant, positive correlation coefficients with the urban population growth rate, population aged 0 to 14 years and human development index, and a significant, negative correlation coefficient with the literacy of total population. In the AMCs, the total fertility rate is declining with the increase in the literacy of the total population. The results of regression analysis show that the total fertility rate is influenced by the variables literacy of total population, degree of urbanisation and population aged 15 to 64 years.

It can be summarised that, for the AMCs, there are significant relationships between the health indicators and the socio-economic, urbanisation and infra-structure indicators.

Urbanisation

The analysis of the degree of urbanisation data and socio-economic data shows that there are significant, positive correlations between the degree of urbanisation and the GDP per capita, CO_2 emissions per capita, energy consumption per capita, net migration rate, population density, population growth rate and recorded crime. Analysis of the degree of urbanisation data and health data shows that there are significant, positive correlations between the degree of urbanisation and the life expectancy at birth and the number of physicians but significant, neg-ative correlations with the death rate, infant mortality rate, smoking prevalence (male) and health expenditure per capita. Analysis of the degree of urbanisation data and infrastructure data shows that there are significant, positive correlations between the degree of urbanisation and safe water, sanitation, solid waste disposal (by incineration) and electricity produced by fossil fuel. However, there are sig-nificant but negative correlations with solid waste disposal (by dumping) and hydro-produced electricity. As the degree of urbanisation increases in the AMCs, solid waste is disposed of by incineration instead of dumping, and electricity is fossil fuel generated rather than hydro-generated.

The results of regression analysis show that the degree of urbanisation is influ-enced by the GDP per capita. However, the degree of urbanisation cannot be solely accounted for by the GDP per capita. Another equation shows that the degree of urbanisation is also influenced by the net migration rate and the death rate. Yet another equation shows the degree of urbanisation as being influenced by the number of physicians as one variable and the GDP per capita as another vari-able. Hence, it can be seen that urbanisation in the AMCs is interrelated with the health, infrastructure and socio-economic development of the AMCs.

CONCLUSION

This set of baseline data for the AMCs has been compiled from the most recent and reliable data where available. The selected data covers geography, land use, population, urbanisation, economy, education, environment, health and infra-structure though the emphasis is on the environment, health and urbanisation. Within each of these categories, the various indicators have been defined, com-parisons have been made and interesting facts or aberrations/confounding factors highlighted and explained. Hence, this chapter has been mostly descriptive.

It can be concluded from the analysis of the baseline data that there exist significant interrelationships between the environmental, health, urbanisation, infrastructure and other indicators. Hence, socio-economic, environmental, urbanisation and other conditions are important aspects which should be taken into account in formulating health policies, developing and implementing health programmes and evaluating the outcome of health action.

In closing, it is necessary to examine the AMCs in order to make comparisons and to draw conclusions for the whole group. However, true comparability of the data is limited by variations in definitions, statistical methods, the quality of the data collected and when it is collected. It is hoped that this set of baseline data has provided the reader with some basic information and understanding of the AMC profile which is essential for assessing the environmental, health, urban and socio-economic development of the AMCs and which can be used as a basis to set policies, introduce intervention priorities, monitor progress and evaluate results for any Healthy Cities project in the region.

References

All the Greatest Cities of the World (2002) *Singapore City-state.* <http://www.greatestcities.com/Asia/Singapore> (accessed July 2002).
ASEAN Secretariat (UNEP) (1997) *First ASEAN State of the Environment Report.* Jakarta: ASEAN Secretariat (UNEP).
ASEAN Secretariat (UNEP) (2001) *Second ASEAN State of the Environment Report 2000.* Jakarta: ASEAN Secretariat (UNEP).
Central Intelligence Agency (2002) *The World Factbook* 2001. <http://www.cia.gov/cia/publications/factbook> (accessed July 2002).
Department of Environment Malaysia, Ministry of Science, Technology and the Environment (2000) *Malaysian Environmental Quality Report 1999.* Kuala Lumpur: Department of Environment Malaysia, Ministry of Science, Technology and the Environment.
Government of Brunei Darussalam (2002) *Haze and the PSI,* <http://www.brunet.bn/gov/modev/environment/haze98.htm> (accessed July 2002).
Uemura, K. (ed.) (2000) *Practical Health Statistics: A SEAMIC Textbook:* Tokyo: Southeast Asia Medical Information Centre/International Medical Foundation of Japan.
United Nations (2001a) *World Statistics Pocketbook.* New York: United Nations.
United Nations (2001b) *World Urbanization Prospects: The 2001 Revision.* <http://www.un.org/esa/population> (accessed July 2002).
United Nations Centre for Human Settlements (Habitat) (2001) *The State of the World's Cities.* Nairobi: United Nations Centre for Human Settlements (Habitat).
United Nations Crime and Justice Information Network (2002) *Third to Sixth United Nations Survey.* < http://www.uncjin.org/Statistics/WCTS/wcts.html > (accessed July 2002).
World Bank (2001) *World Development Indicators.* Washington DC: The World Bank.
World Bank (2002) *World Development Indicators.* Washington DC: The World Bank.
World Health Organisation (WHO) Regional Office for the Western Pacific (2000) *Regional Guidelines for Developing a Healthy Cities Project: Healthy Setting, Document Series No. 2.* Manila: WHO Regional Office for the Western Pacific.

WHO Regional Office for South-East Asia (2000) *Strengthening Healthy Cities Projects in the South-East Asia Region: An Opinion Survey*. New Delhi: WHO Regional Office for South-East Asia.

World Resources Institute (1998) *World Resources 1998–1999: A Guide to the Global Environment: Environmental Change and Human Health*. Washington DC: World Resources Institute.

World Resources Institute (2000) *World Resources 2000–2001: People and Ecosystems: The Fraying Web of Life*. Washington DC: World Resources Institute.

Country and city experiences in Healthy Cities

The following appendices have been selected from papers presented at the International Conference for Healthy Cities and Urban Policy Research, 2000, Tokyo.

Countries
- China
- Lao People's Democratic Republic
- Mongolia
- Vietnam

Cities
- Canberra, Australia
- Haiphong, Vietnam
- Hue, Vietnam
- Illawarra, Australia
- Johor Bahru, Malaysia
- Kuching, Malaysia
- Malacca, Malaysia
- Olongapo, The Philippines
- Queensland, Australia
- Tagaytay, The Philippines

Appendix 1

Experience of national hygienic cities in China

Dr Gao Qifa

INTRODUCTION: NATIONAL PATRIOTIC HEALTH CAMPAIGN COMMITTEE

The Patriotic Health Campaign is a working style peculiar to China. It is a mass movement led by governments at all levels and participated in by sectors concerned and the community as a whole for the improvement of environmental hygiene in both rural and urban areas. The National Patriotic Health Campaign Committee (NPHCC) was first established in 1952 with the late Premier Zhou Enlai as its chairperson. The Patriotic Health Campaign has thus been launched in the whole country, centering on the mobilization of community, the change of unhygienic habits and customs, the observance of hygienic practice, and the prevention of diseases. The campaign has brought about an improvement of the health and sanitation feature of the country, both rural and urban. The density of rodents, mosquitoes, flies, and bedbugs has been reduced by a large margin. With regard to the agricultural production and farmer's livelihood, the activities of '2 controls and 5 improvements' (controls of drinking water sources and excreta, the improvement of water supply, latrine, cattle shed, kitchen stove and environment) have resulted in the improvement of environment sanitation and quality of life of farmers.

Since the implementation of policy of reform and opening to the outside world, the concepts and approaches of the Patriotic Health Campaign have undergone adjustment in line with the social and economic development. Its basic working principle has been formulated, namely, to be organized by the government, to be placed under the responsibility of local departments concerned, to be coordinated by sectors concerned, to be implemented by the community, to be administered in a scientific way and to be supervised by the society.

Its main responsibilities are as follows:

- To organize the activity of inspecting and evaluating cities' health status nationwide
- To implement the National Hygienic City Program
- To formulate the standard of rodent and vector control

- To be in charge of water supply and sanitation programs in rural areas
- To carry out a health education program, and
- To cooperate with WHO, UNICEF, WB and other international organizations as the national coordinator.

NPHCC consists of 26 ministries of State Council, social organizations and the media. Its executive office is located in the Ministry of Health. The Vice Premier of the country serves as its chairman, and the Minister of Health as vice chairman and the director of its executive office. From central to local governments, there are Patriotic Health Campaign Committees at all levels, and the organizational structures of them are similar to that of the NPHCC.

BUILDING OF A NATIONAL HYGIENIC CITY (NHC)

From the end of 1980s, NPHCC began to organize relevant ministries to inspect and evaluate the health status of cities all over the country every three years. The NPHCC preceded later on to build the National Hygienic City movement on the basis of this activity. NPHCC organized related sectors to formulate the *Standard of National Hygienic City* which included 10 aspects, such as environmental sanitation of the city, health education, environment protection, food safety, communicable diseases prevention and control, rodent and vector control, and so on.

OUTLINE OF THE STANDARDS OF A NATIONAL HYGIENIC CITY

1. Administration of PHCC organization: organization, staffing, funding, proper equipment, network of PHCC, action plan.
2. Health education: health education in schools, communities, hospitals and media, law enforcement on tobacco control.
3. Sanitation of the city: law enforcement on city administration, infrastructure construction, appearance of the city, greening, percentage of water closets in public places, markets management, construction sites management, and so on.
4. Environmental protection: air pollution control, noise control, drinking water protection, waste water management, sewage disposal, solid waste management, medical waste management.
5. Healthy public places and wholesome drinking water: environmental sanitation in public places (including airport, seaport, bus station, train station), employees' personal hygiene, health departments' monitoring and surveillance, water quality (physical and biochemical index).
6. Food safety: environmental sanitation, employees' personal hygiene, health departments' monitoring and surveillance.

7. Communicable diseases prevention and control: prevention of communicable diseases, report network of epidemic situation, immunization management, blood management.
8. Rodent and vector control: density of rodents, mosquitoes, flies, cockroaches, proper usage of pesticide.
9. Healthy communities and units.
10. Poll.

PROCEDURE OF BUILDING A NATIONAL HYGIENIC CITY

Phase 1: Self development
- characteristics of the city investigation and research
- objectives set and municipal government commitment won
- social mobilization
- accountability system set up between municipal government and related sectors and lower governments (sectors collaborating).

Phase 2: Provincial guidance, assessment, and supervision
Following a period of building NHC (maybe 1 year or 2), the PHCC of this city examines 10 aspects in term of the Standard of NHC. If they find out that the city almost meets the standard of NHC, they must submit a report to the Provincial PHCC. The provincial PHCC will organize specialists from every field concerned to assess the outcome, at the same time; they will provide counseling and guidance as well. If provincial PHCC considers the city has almost reached the standard of NHC, it will then submit the report to the NPHCC.

Phase 3: National guidance, assessment, and supervision
Upon receiving the report from the provincial PHCC, the office of NPHCC will organize specialists from related fields to evaluate the report, and investigate in the field. They will also provide counseling and guidance, or the office of NPHCC will organize specialists to inspect the city's status of environment in a secret manner. If the city passes NPHCC's investigation and inspection, the office of NPHCC will organize specialists to assess the outcome within 3 months. If the city passes the assessment, NPHCC will name the city National Hygienic City, if not, it will have to wait until the next round.

The title of National Hygienic City doesn't perpetuate. The office of NPHCC will often organize specialists to inspect the city's health status. If the status of environment reverses apparently, the office of NPHCC will criticize the city openly. If it happens twice, the office of NPHCC will revoke the city's title of NHC.

There is no end to the building of a National Hygienic City.

List of National Hygienic Cities

Total: 35 cities (668 cities in mainland China)
Liaoning Province: 1 city, Dalian.
Inner Mongolia Autonomous Region: 1 city, Chifeng.
Shandong Province: 11 cities, Weihai, Yantai, Bingzhou, Zibo, Laiwu, Laizhou, Taian, Jiaozhou, Qingdao, Qingzhou, Zhaoyuan.
Henan Province: 1 city, Puyang.
Anhui Province: 1 city, Maanshan.
Jiangsu Province: 7 cities, Jiangyin, Zhangjiagang, Kunshan, Wujiang, Changshu, Suzhou, Wuxi.
Zhejiang Province: 2 cities, Hangzhou, Xiaoshan.
Sichuan Province: 2 cities, Chengdu, Luzhou.
Xingjiang Uigur Autonomous Region: 1 city, Kuerle.
Fujian Province: 3 cities, Xiamen, Sanmin, Fuzhou.
Guangdong Province: 6 cities, Shenzhen, Zhongshan, Zhuhai, Foushan, Shantou, Nanhai.

List of Healthy Cities

Dongcheng District, Beijing (1994, selected)
Jiading District, Shanghai (1994)
Yuzhong District, Chongqing (1995)
Haikou, Hainan Province (1995)
Dalian, Liaoning Province (1996)
Baoding, Hebei Province (1996)

Appendix 2

Lessons learned from the implementation of Healthy Cities in Lao People's Democratic Republic

Dr Bounlay Phommasack

INTRODUCTION

Rapid urbanization has been observed in several provinces of the Lao People's Democratic Republic (Lao PDR) since the introduction of the new economic mechanism (NEM) from 1986 onwards. This is an economic reform mechanism the country had never experienced before, particularly after the year 1975, the period when the Lao People's Democratic Republic was established. The NEM has been proved to be an appropriate tool modifying and increasing living conditions of local people as well as generating the revenue of the state.

Various types of investments, either from external sources or under the forms of joint investments between the government and private have been set up in different big cities of Lao PDR, bringing an opportunity to all people, particularly those who are poor and living in rural areas, which represented the majority of Lao people who came to the cities seeking jobs.

As most cities in Lao PDR had no proper plan prepared for such a NEM, associated with the limited knowledge, skills and lack of experience among government staffs in dealing with the problems of urbanization, environmental health problems and other communicable diseases caused the most important issues to be solved by several cities of Lao PDR.

As a consequence, the disease such as dengue hemorrhagic fever (DHF) occurred in many cities in Lao PDR under the forms of outbreak, and subsequent epidemics. The amount of solid waste generated every day by the citizens, restaurants, markets and factories overloaded the capacity of government as well as private garbage companies to transport waste to the sanitary landfill, bringing finally the negative picture to the cities.

Motorbikes, cars, trucks increased drastically in the cities of Vientiane, Luangprabang, Khrammuane, Savannakhet and Champassak. Road congestion, particularly during and after working hours, and road accidents are now becoming an increasing public health problem in different cities, causing a high mortality rate as compared with other communicable diseases. There is a high percentage of disability among drivers, giving in consequence the increasing number of healthy years of life lost.

The number of street food vendors increased in the cities, bringing another workload and new challenges to the health service, by the fact that the latter is still young to deal with such new ways of selling food to the public. More importantly, the health staffs have a lack of skills and knowledge in organizing a network or structure for food inspection and prevention of risk of contaminated food prepared by those street food vendors.

The health system with its limited resources, during the 1980s, concentrated more on the improvement of the health of the rural people for improving productivity, through the strengthening of district health system based on primary health care. Recently, in the 1990s, in addition to the role of providing care to the rural people, the health sector has to deal with the health of the people in urban areas where problems are more complex and more difficult to solve, because some of the issues are beyond the capacity of the health sector to tackle.

HEALTHY CITIES IN LAO PEOPLE'S DEMOCRATIC REPUBLIC

Healthy Cities concept has been introduced into the Lao PDR since 1996, around the time the government started to solve the problems created by urbanization.

In September 1996, in collaboration with WHO, the Ministry of Health of the Lao PDR and the authorities of Vientiane Municipality, the workshop on Healthy Cities was first organized in Vientiane, the Capital of Lao PDR (total 18 provinces for the whole country). The workshop provided an opportunity to bring different stakeholders to understand the Healthy Cities concept, formulate the vision for the development of the city, discuss, share ideas, and together select priority issues they felt able to solve by their own efforts through their existing infrastructure and resources.

As the trend of urbanization among different major cities of Lao PDR is increasing, from the beginning of 1998, four provinces – namely Luangprabang, representing the north part, Khammuane, and Savannakhet provinces representing the central part, and Champassak province representing the south part of the country – expressed their willingness to implement Healthy Cities.

The objectives of the Healthy Cities approach in Lao PDR are:

1. Increase awareness and access to information on Healthy Cities concept by every citizen of Lao PDR.
2. Encourage local people, government officers, military, police and foreigners currently living in Laos to improve environmental issues in the cities, and in the villages where they live.
3. Promote intersectoral actions, and public/community involvement to identify and minimize different health hazards in their cities.

4. Cooperate with other urban development projects as complementary efforts, and with other non-governmental organizations, embassies and other external agencies currently implementing urban management projects.

The starting point for the implementation of Healthy Cities concept in Lao PDR is the orientation workshop on Healthy Cities, which is considered as an important factor for further involvement of different stakeholders in building up their cities to be clean, safe and Healthy Cities. Supported by WHO, during such workshops, district governors, directors of government departments and heads of the villages were asked to establish the vision for their own cities, and then identify the priority problems they thought the most important for further solving.

In implementing and putting Healthy Cities concept into practice, the government perceived that there is a need to focus on environmental health problems in markets, hospitals, schools and villages. Accordingly, the following healthy settings such as: Healthy School, Healthy Market, Healthy Hospital, Healthy Village, Healthy Working Place, Healthy Restaurant have been started in the above mentioned provinces.

RESULTS

From the year 1996–2000 (5 years), it may be too early to assess the impact of Healthy Cities concept to the real change of the city. However, one benefit that arose is that the concept of Healthy Cities was generally acceptable and gradually understood by a wide range of stakeholders from provinces, districts, villages and local communities.

The reasons could be explained as follows:

1. The concept of Healthy Cities was introduced into the country at the time when the Government was concerned more with environmental problems and other social issues due to urbanization.
2. The concept of Healthy Cities was introduced initially to provincial governors (highest level of administrative and authorities at province level), to district governors (highest level of administrative and authorities at district level), to village leaders (highest level of administrative and authorities at village level). The trigger points were accurately identified for introduction of Healthy Cities concept.
3. The characteristic administrative organization of the country could facilitate and accelerate the speed for putting Healthy Cities concept in place.

Generally speaking, the concept of Healthy Cities is widely disseminated in Lao PDR. Now every city, is first of all concerned about the future development of the city; cleanness, hygiene, and attractiveness, before introducing or building something new to the city.

To facilitate the long term strategy for city development, at central level, there was the establishment of an Institute for Development of Secondary Town, belonging to the Ministry of Communication, Transport, Post, and Construction and the establishment of a government body responsible for urban sanitation and solid waste management. Many governmental organizations such as Scientific Technology Environmental Organization (STENO) are responsible for environment management including environment impact assessment (EIA) as well as the control of water quality. In Vientiane, Urban Development Projects have been started, such as road widening, improvement of the drainage system, creation of a recreation park, setting up of a waste water treatment plant, construction of sanitary landfill, installation of public telephone boxes, and putting out public garbage containers. Recently in late 1999, there was Decree of Council of Prime Minister organized Municipal Managing Board for each province, which will facilitate the work of urban development.

There are many examples showing the active involvement of different stakeholders such as the Healthy Village Initiatives in Vientiane Municipality. In such initiatives, through the understanding of the concept, local people were committed to building their own villages to be clean, beautiful and healthy. The local people by their own efforts and strategies identified and tried to solve environmental health problems they thought harmful to their health. Such examples are being disseminated and replicated to other cities of Lao PDR.

There is a schedule established by the Education Department in Vientiane Municipality that brings school children to be involved in city cleaning, once every two weeks. Schools were asked to be responsible for the environment where the school is located nearby. To invest and introduce a new lifestyle for the young generation, model hygiene toilets, supported by WHO, UNICEF, Namphu Japan NGO, were built in many primary schools with the aims of introducing a healthy lifestyle to the young generation, in conjunction with the implementation of health promoting school concept. School children have been trained to use toilets, washing hands after using the toilets, washing before and after eating and cleaning their teeth after morning break.

In Vientiane Municipality, supported by CESVI, an Italian NGO, teachers at primary school have been trained as trainers for dengue control. These teachers were asked to train their students to collect and destroy aedes larvae before the holidays. Holiday period for school children in Lao is from June to August. This period is considered as high season for dengue virus transmission. The students then were asked to monitor aedes larvae in the water holding containers at their own houses during holidays. These events could significantly prevent the outbreak of dengue hemorrhages in Vientiane.

With the support of WHO, meat, fish and ready food sellers in different markets of Vientiane were trained on safety food security, particularly how to prepare and keep food safe for consumption. After training, an identity card was given to each seller. The main purposes are to facilitate the monitoring of food preparation, and at the same time identify who should be trained or retrained for handling food security.

In Savannakhet and Luangprabang provinces, teachers in selected primary schools were trained on the concept of health promoting at school. After the training, they could manage to formulate the Plan of Action which they think relevant for solving environmental health problems in their schools. In their POA, they could identify the different partners involved for solving environmental problems in the schools.

Many organizations, embassies, factories, enterprises and NGOs participated and supported the implementation of Healthy Cities in Lao PDR. Those organizations are cited as such: Australian Embassy, French Embassy, Japan Embassy, Malaysian Embassy Lao Beer Factory, Lao Garment Factory, Lao Electricity Enterprise, Namphu Japan NGO, Save Children Fund (UK).

PROBLEMS ENCOUNTERED

In implementing Healthy Cities concept from 1996–2000 in several provinces of the Lao PDR, problems mostly encountered were cited as follows:

1. There is a big misunderstanding among Healthy City members that Healthy Cities Project is similar to other vertical health program, where funds for implementing are available in big amounts within the framework of WHO.
2. The place of the organization of Healthy Cities within the health system is still in debate or unclear. Some provinces organized the office of Healthy Cities apart, but within the existing health system, although some activities of Healthy Cities are more or less similar to environmental sanitation activities (which belong to Environmental and Sanitation Unit).
3. As far as the concept of Healthy Cities has been disseminated to other sectors, there is a debate that activities of Healthy Cities should belong to the responsibilities of Department of Communication, Transport, Post, and Construction, or belong to Urban Development Project. Therefore, there is a need to establish real partnerships between different stakeholders for the common and mutual benefits.
4. Lack of knowledge and skills in preparing the Plan of Action (POA) for Healthy Cities at national, provincial and district level. Most activities planned in the POA are those dealing with various health determinants requiring a long term strategy for solving, and they are beyond the capacity of the health sector (or sometimes step on the work of other departments).
5. In preparing POA, some problems are relevant for Healthy City Team, but are not relevant for donors.
6. The network of Healthy Cities in Lao still does not yet officially include representatives of various sectors. The contact or communication with other relevant sectors was done informally. Most of the Healthy City Team members are within the health sector.

LESSONS LEARNED

For Lao situation, to be effective in any Healthy Cities Project, there is a need to:

1. Carefully introduce the concept to different stakeholders, either government or private as well as community, to rely on their own capacities and their existing resources for building up the Healthy City Project.
2. In introducing Healthy City concept, try to avoid as much as possible creating a new organization within the existing system for running specifically Healthy City activities, which require a lot of investment in terms of resources. In fact there are a series of health determinants that required the involvement of other sectors for solving environmental health problems and other related issues in the city.
3. As far as city planning belongs to local Council, or district authorities, there is a need to incorporate Healthy Cities concept to city planning.
4. As there is no specific model for implementing Healthy Cities, there is a need to accept the diversity of approaches that exist within the community for building up Healthy Cities.
5. There is a need to organize orientation workshops on Healthy Cities for heads of concerned ministries for further consolidating the plan for city development. Also orientation for village leaders, district authorities, and provincial governors, before starting the project.
6. Exchange of experiences and feed back lessons learned to newly implemented provinces could potentially make them understand the process and save time and speed up the process.
7. As the number of provinces implementing Healthy Cities Project increases, there is a need to organize the regular monitoring system from Ministry level to provincial level.
8. Illustrating examples of Healthy Cities activities such as organizing a health festival, Healthy Cities week or marathon run could make people understand the concept of Healthy Cities more deeply, and implement these activities at their home.
9. Setting up and conducting Healthy Family and Healthy Community projects could potentially bring more access to information on Healthy Cities to the community and then could involve them in solving the environmental health problems in their own areas, and incorporate their work in order to make the city clean and safe from hazards and wastes.
10. Exchange visits to villages or districts successful in implementing Healthy Cities could increase knowledge and capacity among Healthy City members.

CONCLUSION

Putting Healthy City concept into practice required a deep understanding of the concept among different stakeholders. In order to be able to keep up the results so far reached by the efforts made since 1996, there is a need to establish norms, regulations and laws as far as the city is growing up. To monitor the works at provincial level, there is a need to establish regular monitoring of the provinces.

To expand the network of Healthy Cities which will be composed of various ministries, there is a need to organize an orientation workshop for heads of concerned ministries such as ministry of education, ministry of communication, transport, post and construction, STENO, Trade and Tourism, Industry, Social Welfare Police. Through this orientation workshop, the head of each ministry will understand the concept and will delegate a responsible person to be involved in the National Healthy City Network.

Mongolian Healthy Cities Programme and prospect for the future

Dr Nagniin Saijaa

Mongolia is situated in the heart of Asia at the altitude of 626–1859 metres above the sea level. It has a harsh and severe climate with 4 seasons in a year and temperatures as high as 35 to 41°C in summer and as low as –49 to –51°C in winter, and the low precipitation makes the cool air dry.

The terrain consists of mountains, plains, sand deserts and the territory is about 1.5 million square kilometres in total. There are 21 aimags, about 360 soums, which are divided on baghs and khoroos, smaller administration units. At the end of 1999 the population was 2.3 million. Fifty-one per cent of the population were women, 38.2 per cent were children under 16 years of age.

Fifty-three per cent of the population live in urbanized areas, while 47 per cent has a rural lifestyle and is involved in agriculture and nomadic cattle farms. There are approximately 32 million livestock in Mongolia including cattle, camels, goats, horses, sheep, and others.

In recent years, urbanization has increased, and so has the number of people living in conditions with developed industry, service, businesses, transport, communications, energy, construction and other infrastructure. These conditions also change the lifestyle of people and contain many negative physical, chemical, biological effects, often in combinations, on the health of the population and serves as one of the leading factors for morbidity. In Mongolia in a year 21.64 children per 1000 population are born, 6.08 people die and the population growth rate is 15.06.

Morbidity of urbanized population is much higher than that of rural population. Therefore for improved hygiene and prevention of diseases it is essential to develop, start, and carry out all the stages of Healthy Cities Programme in urbanized areas of Mongolia.

OBJECTIVES OF 'HEALTHY CITIES' PROGRAMME MONGOLIA

1 Ulaanbaatar
Carry out urban development and planning policies in the light of the trends of the country's territorial, climatic and population distribution schemes, their

organization and the development tendency of the country with due regard to
the national progressive traditions regarding the urban development and architecture, based upon the common regularities of the world's urban development.
Developing in particular, the capital city as an ecological complex under the
schemes of the 'Healthy Cities' policies and creating a national system referring
to its territory with the aims of: reducing water, air and soil contamination
through developing a national infrastructure network; wider applying renewable
sources of energy; introducing smokeless fuel technologies and strengthening
ecological control over the operations of all kinds of motor vehicles and enterprises; improving the water supply of the population and perfecting the
characteristic of the water in terms of its hygiene and quality; applying appropriate technologies for the sorting out of wastes, their recycling, reprocessing and
liquidation; setting up waste disposal sites equipped with some certain amenities
and conveniences; improving drastically the waste transportation; creating a system to ensure the quality of foodstuffs and their safety guarantees; perfecting the
system of hygienic control and inspection.

2   *Darkhan*
With the support from the WHO, governmental and nongovernmental institutions,
and community itself, to implement the strategy 'Health for All': to develop new
health arrangements that best respond to the specific needs of the city and create
a favorable environment for the citizens.

3   *Erdenet*
Organize unique improvement of health conditions in work circumstances of the
local authority, public institutions, manufacturing and industry units, citizen partnerships and cooperation, assemble the healthy circumstances gradually creating
a resulting medical service and to improve the health of habitants.

CITY PROFILES

1   *Ulaanbaatar*

Established:	1639
Territory:	470,400 m^2
Population:	682,000
Year 'Healthy Cities' Programme started:	1997
Total morbidity:	4716.9 per 10,000
Mortality:	7.9 per 1000

2 *Darkhan*

Established:	1961
Territory:	78,000 hectare
Population:	87,800
Year 'Healthy Cities' Programme started:	1997
Total morbidity:	4072.4 per 10,000
Mortality:	6.86 per 1000

3 *Erdenet*

Established:	1975
Territory:	84,000 hectare
Population:	69,100
Year 'Healthy Cities' Programme started:	1999, October
Total morbidity:	3178.9 per 10,000
Mortality:	6.7 per 10,000
Average mortality for the country:	3940.8
Average morbidity for the country:	11.95

PRIORITY PROBLEMS IN MONGOLIA

1 *Ulaanbaatar*

- Urbanization, urban development and planning
- Air pollution
- Soil erosion and pollution
- Industrial waste disposal issue
- Water supply improvement
- Food safety
- Hygienic control and inspection system

2 *Darkhan*

- Implementation of general plan for developing of city
- Air pollution
- Soil erosion and sand movement
- Waste disposal issue
- Health education
- Food safety

3   *Erdenet*

- Dustiness and water pollution with Cu, Mo from 'Erdenet' Mining Corporation
- Dustiness from disposal of 'Erdenet' Mining Corporation
- Lack of capacity of sewerage water treatment plant
- Water supply in ger area
- Food safety

CRITERIA OF IMPLEMENTATION OF PROGRAMME IN ULAANBAATAR

Criteria	Measuring unit	Current level	Target level
1. Urban development and planning			
percentage of people living in an apartment against the total population	per cent	53.5	70
floor space per person living in an apartment	m² / 1 person	6.7	9
plantations of trees and shrubs per person living in an apartment	m² / 1 person	4.2	8
2. Air pollution			
SO_2 concentration in the atmosphere (annual mean value)	mkg / m³	5	3
NO_2 concentration in the atmosphere (annual mean value)	mkg / m³	19	12
CO concentration in the atmosphere (annual mean value)	mkg / m³	0.8	0.5
dust concentration in the atmosphere (annual mean value)	mkg / m³	129	80
3. Soil erosion and pollution			
eroded and overgrazed land	hectare	600	100
percentage of ger districts cesspits provided with protective shoring	per cent	–	–
4. Manufacturing water disposal			
waste of chemical origin	mg / l	120	80
waste of animal origin	mg / l	25	20

Criteria	Measuring unit	Current level	Target level
5. Solid waste disposal			
percentage of the disposed waste in comparison with the total amount of solid waste	%	44	100
amount of solid waste sorted out for recycling and reprocessing	%	0	50
6. Water supply			
Sufficiency of drinking water:			
in residential districts	L/1 person /	400	230
in ger districts	1 day	6	20
7. Food safety			
number of parameters used in chemical analyses of food	number	12	17
number of parameters used in bacteriological analyses of food	number	85	100
8. Hygiene control and inspection system			
Infectious disease rate	per 10,000 people	71 .005	70

CRITERIA OF IMPLEMENTATION OF PROGRAMME IN DARKHAN

No.	Criteria	Measuring units	1997	1998	1999	2000
1	Green grass	hectare	9	13	18	23
2	Solid waste land	hectare	47	20	7	7
3	Settlement noise	Db	44	44	43	42
4	Treatment of waste water	per cent	55	70	80	90
5	Sufficiency of drinking water in ger district	L/ 1 person per day	3–6	4–8	10–12	12–18
6	Decrease of occupa-tional disease	per cent	71.3	69.5	65.0	60.0
7	Life expectancy		63	63.5	64	64.5
8	Decrease of infectious disease	per 10,000 people	98.4	98.0	97.6	97.4
9	Death	per 1000 people	7.2	7.0	6.8	6.6

No. Criteria	Measuring units	1997	1998	1999	2000
10 Participants, who belonged in health training programs	number	14820	21000	27000	35000
11 Volunteers of health	number	51	250	450	650
12 Unemployment	number	9741	8000	7000	6000
13 Most poverty	number	10800	10000	9000	7500
14 New work place	number	300	1000	2000	3000
15 Institutions with estab- lished work condition	number	12	600	1000	1200
16 Public toilets	number	4	5	6	8
17 Healthy population	per cent	53.6	57.0	59.2	64.3
18 Protection zone	number		1	2	
19 Public bath	number	1	2	2	3

CRITERIA OF IMPLEMENTATION OF PROGRAMME IN ERDENET

Criteria	Measuring unit	1999	2000	2001	2002
Decrease of the infectious disease by oral way	Per 10,000 people	62.6	58.5	54.4	50.3
Sufficiency of drinking water in ger district	L/1 person per day	5–8	8–12	10–15	12–17
Public toilets	number	1	2	3	4
Public bath, sauna	number	2	2	3	4
Death caused by the heart, blood circulation sickness	per 10,000 people	28.6	28.0	27.5	25.0
Healthy population	per cent	20.0	30.0	40.0	50.0
Decrease of alcohol, cigarettes usage for adults	per cent				
Alcohol		12.5	11.5	10.0	8.0
Cigarettes		28.3	26.3	25.0	23.5
Decrease of tumor disease	per 10,000 people				
Sickness		28.1	27.0	26.0	25.2
Death		14.0	13.5	13.0	12.0
Innovation of construction technology at non-normal work condition			51.0	51.0	51.2

EXPECTED OUTCOMES OF THE PROGRAMME

1 *Ulaanbaatar*
- Establish proper conditions for the population of the capital city to live, work, and rest.
- Increase possibility of keeping ecological balance by reducing pollution of air, water, and soil.
- Improved water supply for the population.
- Possibility to solve the problem with eliminating of solid waste and industrial waste water.
- Increased safety and quality of food products.
- Improved hygiene control system.
- Established 'Healthy Lifestyle'.
- Decreased acute respiratory infections and diarrhea diseases caused by the environment.
- Improved living conditions of the population and balanced ecology.

2 *Darkhan*
- Corrections made to the General Plan of development of the city of Darkhan and improved planning for city constructions.
- Decreased respiratory diseases and cleaner air by wide usage of ecologically clean stoves G-G2 in ger districts of the city.
- Reduced dust in the air with improved protection of the soil and decreased sand migration by planting of grass and trees.
- Improved elimination of industrial disposals leading to decreased communicable diseases transmitted through soil.
- Improved knowledge of students in Healthy Schools will improve the general health status.
- Improved hygienic conditions of food markets will prevent diseases transmitted through food products.

3 *Erdenet*
- Reduced pollution with Cu, Mo from the Erdenet Plant will reduce diseases related to water and dusts with these metals included.
- Reduced dust from the DALAN and improved technology will improve health status of the population living below the DALAN.
- Improved capacity of the water cleaning plant will prevent diseases related to use of polluted water down the stream of Khangal and Orkhon rivers.
- Improved water supply in ger districts will improve hygiene conditions and prevent diseases related to polluted and/or contaminated water.
- Improved hygienic conditions of food markets will prevent diseases transmitted through food products.

Appendix 4

Master plan for Healthy Cities development in Vietnam 2000–2005

Dr Huy Nga Nguyen

SUCCESS AND LESSONS FROM HEALTHY CITIES PROJECT IN VIETNAM

Vietnam was not an exception of the developing direction of the world. It is estimated that in 2020 there will be over 40% of Vietnam population living in urban areas. In recent years, many provincial towns expanded to become cities. There are now 20 provincial cities and 4 central cities. Rapid urbanisation required integration in action various sectors to prevent the city from pollution and improve environment and human health, and to maintain sustainable development.

Healthy Cities concept was introduced into Vietnam by WHO in 1994. A Healthy Cities Project was carried out as a pilot in Hai Phong and Hue with the focus of involving sectors relating to environment and health into a sustainable development of the city. WHO has selected Ministry of Health to be the project coordinating body. On 8th May 1999, Ministry of Health signed the decision for establishment of Healthy City Management Committee and Vice Minister, Prof. Nguyen Van Thuong, was assigned to be the chief of the Committee.

With the technical assistance from WHO and Ministry of Health, Hai Phong and Hue have developed some healthy setting models such as Healthy Schools, Healthy Market-places, Healthy Work-places, Healthy Ward, and Healthy Community.

The result of the Healthy Cities Project in Hai Phong and Hue showed that the attention and involvement of city Government was a crucial factor for the success of the project. A Steering Committee for Healthy Cities Project has been established in both cities with the Vice Mayor of the city taking chief position of the Committee. It is important for the Committee to gather all sector representatives around the table for project. Aside from the technical and financial assistance from WHO, Hai Phong People Committee has supported one billion VND for cleaning and improving water quality in Quan Ngua lake; two hundred million VND for improving the Ga market (Hai Phong). Water supply and waste management in Ga market has also been improved by the contribution of a drainage and sewage company and water plant. Hai Phong also has a plan for bringing all vegetable and meat shops along streets into the Ga market. The public toilet in Ga market is being reconstructed. After 4 years of implementing Healthy Market project, Ga market has made a significant change from being a dirty and flooded market to becoming a clean and tidy one. In Hue, government has supported hundreds of millions VND for resettlement of more than 700 boat people and the building of hygienic latrines for poor households in suburban areas.

The success of the above two cities indicated the high socialisation of Healthy Cities Project. Any activities of the project had the involvement and cooperation at different levels of Agencies such as Department of Health Services, Science Technology and Environment, Agriculture and Rural Development, Urban Environmental Company. The participation of community and social associations also contributed to the success of the project: Parental Association participated in Healthy School activities and contributed money for sanitation improvement of the school; Woman's Union and Youth Union were involved in sanitation and water supply education.

The success of Healthy Cities Project in Vietnam has been highly appreciated by WHO consultants. After 4 years, the Ga market (Hai Phong) and Dong Ba market (Hue) had significant changes: no flood, all waste collected, water supply to each shop, market re-arrangement, roof repaired by vendors themselves, increase of knowledge on food hygiene and safety for consumers and vendors. In the primary schools of Phu My (Hue) and Nguyen Dinh Chieu (Hai Phong) health protection activities for students were well organised (particularly in dental sector); sanitation was improved; toilets were rebuilt; students were educated to practice hand washing before meals and after defecation. Working environment in some enterprises and traditional handicraft villages was improved, workers' health was better cared for, many enterprises paid a big sum of money for installing heat preventing system, air exhausters and provision of personal protection equipment.

THE IMPORTANT SUPPORT OF WHO

Since introduction of Healthy Cities concept into Vietnam, WHO has supported techniques and finance to help Vietnam in developing this project. WHO sent many technical consultants in various fields to Vietnam to discuss and conduct training courses for key persons in project areas:

- December 1995: Mr Brent Powis and Mr Jim Ireland conducted a workshop on environmental health and discussed the development of Healthy Cities Project.
- June 1996: Dr Hisashi Ogawa conducted a training course on environment and Health Strategy.
- October 1996: Training course on Food Hygiene and Safety by Mr Deon Mahoney.
- October 1998: Two workshops on Healthy Cities in Hai Phong and Hue by Prof. Frances Elaine Baum and Prof. Takehito Takano.

- July 1999: Reviewing Healthy Cities Project and conducting workshop on Healthy Cities in Hai Phong and Hue by Prof. Takehito Takano.
- September 1999: Training course on introduction and application of HACCP system in Healthy Market-places project in Hai Phong and Hue by Mr Anthony Roy Hazzard, Dr Gerald Moy and Dr Maria Nystrom.

Aside from the technical assistance, WHO also support finance for Hai Phong and Hue to conduct training courses for project participants and print education communication materials. WHO support and cooperate with Ministry of Health and local government to organise 19 workshops and training courses on Healthy Cities, Healthy Districts, environment pollution monitoring, Healthy Market-places, Healthy School and Healthy Work-places. More than 30 persons have trained abroad or participated in overseas workshops/conferences.

THE IMPORTANCE OF DEVELOPING A MASTER PLAN FOR DEVELOPMENT OF HEALTHY CITIES IN VIETNAM

The rapid urbanisation and industrialisation require the improvement of health protection for urban citizens. The health of city dwellers would be improved by the interaction of health services with other sectors. Urban people are affected by more environmental factors than those living in rural areas. They live closely with pollution sources and under high pressure of socio-economic conditions. Each member of a family can be impacted by various working or studying environments. Therefore health services and the creation of a supportive environment for health are more complicated and difficult than that in the rural area.

The results of Healthy Cities Project in Hai Phong and Hue are still the preliminary success and are evaluated by local people and through the review of international consultants because there are not yet criteria for evaluation. Therefore the setting up of evaluation criteria is one important task in future.

Development of a Healthy City is not only creating healthy settings but also including other activities. In Vietnam there are many National programs that can contribute its part for the environmental and health improvement and city development. Many cities have plans for improvement in water supply, sewage system, solid waste disposal, roads, etc. All these projects aim to improve environment and human health of city and they should be integrated with Healthy Cities Project.

Healthy Cities development is included in the national strategy for health care to the year 2000 and 2020 of Vietnam Government. The Resolution 37/CP of Government showed that 'Active and intensive prevention must be well understood and practiced in creation of healthy lifestyles, ensure of a working, living and studying environment that supports diseases prevention and health promotion, actively prevent health hazards in the process of industrialisation and urbanisation'. Healthy Cities development is the strategy of Ministry of Health in health care and promotion for city dwellers. Healthy Cities is a holistic approach for health.

OBJECTIVE

- Reduce and prevent health risks associated with changes in physical and social environments and promote healthy lifestyles through an interactive approach in environmental and health protection which will be an integral part of development plan.
- Improve social and physical environment for health through development of healthy setting in urban areas.
- Increase the awareness of community in hygiene and sanitation, promote healthy practices, and improve health service system.
- Promote interaction between ministries and branches in health policy development.

STRATEGIES

1. Reduce and prevent health risks associated with changes in physical and social environments and promote healthy lifestyles through an interactive approach in environment and health protection which will be an integral part of development plan:

a) Develop a national coordination system from centre to localities with effective mechanisms for Healthy Cities Project.
b) Collect basic data in physical and social environment, living standards, and health status of city dwellers in cities and urban areas.
c) Develop a master plan for city development in which health is one of major issues. Health of people is considered in all development policies and strategies. Include Healthy Cities activities into the national five-years planning.
d) Prepare and introduce the guideline for Healthy Cities development in Vietnam.

2. Improve physical and social environments for health:

a) Conduct survey and gather relating data to determine indicators of relation between health and urban environment including:
   – Health indicators
   – Health services indicators
   – Environmental indicators
b) Select and implement appropriate healthy settings:
   – Healthy School
   – Healthy Market-places
   – Healthy Work-places
   – Healthy Hospital
   – Healthy Tourism
   – Healthy Island, etc.

c)   Improve infrastructure:
– Drainage and sewage system
– Water supply
– Public works
d)   Renew and develop legislation and standards:
– Solid and liquid waste treatment
– Air quality standard
– Water quality standard
– Food Law
– Application of HACCP in food safety

3.   Increase knowledge and carry out healthy practices of people in hygiene and sanitation, and introduce healthy lifestyles:

a)   Introduce environment and health education curricula in school
b)   Launch campaigns for 'environment clean' and giving up unhealthy practices

4.   Establish monitoring and evaluation system for a Healthy Cities Project:

a)   Establish monitoring system
b)   Develop evaluation criteria and indicators
c)   Implement evaluation

5.   Host an international conference on Healthy Cities to increase the exchange of experience between cities worldwide.

ACTION PLAN

2000–2005 stage

1   Establish a coordinating mechanism from centre to localities

a)   Establish the Central Office for Healthy Cities:
This office is located in the Department of Preventive Medicine, Ministry of Health. Office staff are part time officers from the Department. Tasks of the office include:

• Assist Healthy Cities Management Committee to guide local cities implementing the project;
• To be the contact office between local cities with WHO and other NGOs support for project;
• Help local cities in making action plan for development of healthy settings
• Monitor and evaluate activities of cities.

Equipment for the Central Office for Healthy Cities: 1 photocopier, 4 computers, 2 laser printers, 1 telephone, 1 fax, 1 car.

b)   Establish National Network for Healthy Cities:
This issue has been addressed in the Healthy Cities workshop held in Hai Phong in 1999. Hai Phong, Hue and some other cities agreed the necessity of a Healthy Cities Network and the coordination of the Ministry of Health.

- Liaison body of the network will be in Central Office for Healthy Cities. Through this office local, Cities exchange information and experiences;
- Cooperate with the Vietnam's Cities Association and keep contact with city governments for the project;
- Set up a website for all cities in Vietnam and contact with collaborating centre for Healthy Cities in regions and the world.

2   Collect basic data on environment and health

Although Hai Phong and Hue have implemented some healthy setting projects, the basic data is still necessary to compare in evaluation. The data include:

- Community health status
- Infrastructure of the city
- Environmental quality
- Living environment and housing
- Participation of community in environmental and health protection
- Lifestyles and activities for prevention of health hazards
- Health care, health services and environmental health
- Health education and communication
- Industrial development and employment
- Living standard and average income
- Local economy
- Population growth
- Education.

For the cities that are going to join the project, it is important to have the data in all above issue to be used for making plan and priority identification.

Building of a Master Plan for city development with the involvement of various sectors and health is considered as an important issue.

Integrating Healthy Cities activities into the National Five-year Plan encourages cooperation with other Ministries in Healthy Cities.

3   Document Healthy Cities guidelines for Vietnam

The documents include concepts, objectives of Healthy Cities; the application of Healthy Cities in Vietnam including the experience from two pilot cities (Hai Phong and Hue). Central Office for Healthy Cities is responsible for preparation of the documents.

The documents may contain some main sections as follows:

- Introduction of the history of the Healthy Cities
- Concept and objectives of Healthy Cities Projects
- Healthy setting
- Application of Healthy Cities in Vietnam
- Results and lessons learnt from International and National Healthy Cities Project
- The steps for implementation of Healthy Cities Project
- Monitoring and evaluation of Healthy Cities Project

4   Continue to implement healthy settings in Hai Phong and Hue

4.1 Complete models of healthy settings

a) Healthy Market-places: Ga market (Hai Phong) and Dong Ba market (Hue):
- Rearrange shops in the market, bring vegetable and meat shops along streets into the market
- Rebuild public toilets in the market
- Strengthen food inspection in the market and control food quality before brought into the market
- Conduct training courses on food safety for food vendors
- Educate and communicate consumers in food safety

b) Healthy School: primary school Nguyen Dinh Chieu (Hai Phong) and primary school Phu My (Hue). Beside the works that have been done, these schools continue to:
- Implement model of school health designed by Ministry of Health
- Arrange and build a play-year for students in the school

c) Healthy Hospital: Select one hospital in Hai Phong and one in Hue:
- Conduct training courses on preventive medicine and sanitation for hospital staffs
- Improve hospital waste management: hazardous waste collection and categorisation in hospital
- Improve drainage and sewage system of hospital

4.2 Continue health education and communication activities and carry out some new activities

Hai Phong:
- Implement An Duong healthy market, Le Chan district
- Expand Healthy Schools in 24 schools in Ngo Quyen and 3 pilot schools in 3 other districts
- Expand Healthy Work-places in 15 new enterprises. Conduct training courses on various subjects. Develop criteria, method and steps for monitoring and valuation of Healthy Work-places project (health promotion at work-places)
- Improve infrastructure of hospitals, health services and waste management

- Implement old people health care project in Hai Phong
- Organise motivated groups for on-site old people health care
- Organise entertainment activities, sport
- Conduct a workshop on occasion of the 'International Day for old people'

Hue:
- Apply HACCP in Dong Ba market, rearrange food shops, and improve sewage system in the market. Expand to at least another market in Hue
- Implement health promotion at work-places programme at 10 enterprises and traditional handicraft villages
- Develop model of school health following the guidelines of the Ministry of Health

5 Expand Healthy Cities in other cities and towns
Vung Tau, Can Tho, Nha Trang cities and Ha Dong town – Ha Tay province
- Conduct a workshop on introduction of Healthy Cities and method of making a master plan for healthy settings project
- Establish provincial Steering Committee for Healthy Cities. Organise a meeting with the participation of various sectors to address the integration and identify priorities
- Start implementing healthy settings

6 Expand the project in 3–4 cities

Year	Cities
2001	Hai Duong, Da Nang, Vinh
2002	My Tho, Phan Thiet, Dak Lak, Ha Long
2003	Long Xuyen, Da Lat, Ha Noi, Thanh Hoa
2004	Dong Nai, Quy Nhon, Pleiku, Thai Nguyen
2005	Ca Mau, Ho Chi Minh City, Viet Tri, Nam Dinh

The following activities will be implemented in each city (or town):

- Establish city steering committee for Healthy Cities
- Workshop on introduction of Healthy Cities and making plan with the participation of different sectors and identify priorities
- Collect basic data in health, environment, socio-economy, infrastructure
- Implement some pilot healthy setting activities
- Expand healthy settings throughout the city

7   *Develop a pilot Healthy Island-tourism in Cat Ba (Hai Phong) and Phu Quoc islands*
- Cooperate with General Department of Tourism and island government to conduct a workshop on introduction of Healthy Cities, Healthy Island
- Reinforce food safety activities at restaurants in tourist areas and beach
- Conduct training courses for food vendors on food hygiene and safety
- Educate and communicate community on HIV/AIDS prevention with the focus on Bar-Karaoke, cafe, sauna massage centre
- Improve solid waste management and sewage system
- Involve people in protection of natural environment and prevention of pollution at tourist areas and beaches

2002–2005 stage

8   *Continue to expand project*

a) Healthy market-places:
- Continue improving market floor and sewage system, water supply, solid waste collection and disposal, and the toilets in the market area
- Food safety education, introduction and application of HACCP system
- Food inspection in the market

b) Healthy school:
- Sanitation and food safety education in school
- Implement school health model under the guidelines of Ministry of Health
- Encourage the participation of parental association to the project
- Improve water supply system and sanitation of the school
- Organise contests on knowledge in Healthy Cities, sanitation, food safety

c) Healthy work-places:
- Conduct training courses on primary health care for health staff and 'hygiene volunteer' of enterprises
- Occupational health record

d) Healthy hospital:
- Improve solid and liquid treatment system
- Educate hospital staff in sanitation and preventive medicine

e) HIV/AIDS education for community, schools and work-places:
- Distribute leaflets, posters on HIV/AIDS to community, students and workers
- Organise discussion meeting and forum on HIV/AIDS

f) Combine with some national programmes:
Sanitation, malaria prevention, dengue prevention, health for all family, etc. to launch campaigns on environmental sanitation and disease prevention.

9   *Legislation system*
- Develop or renew water quality standard, air quality
- Issue the food law

- Guideline for application of HACCP in food processing enterprises
- Application of air quality guidelines, waste treatment, hospital waste management of WHO

10 Increase the awareness of community in sanitation and promote healthy lifestyles

- Launch campaigns 'clean up environment', 'use tapped water', 'drink boiled water'
- Encourage community to organise 'wedding, festival without cigarette smoke'
- Educate school children in hygienic practices such as washing hands before meals and after defecation, drinking only boiled water, and eating only cooked food

11 Management, monitoring and evaluation of project activities

- Central Office for Healthy Cities keep the contact regularly with steering Committee for Healthy Cities project of cities and towns to exchange information
- City/town steering committees send quarterly and annually project progress report to Central Office for Healthy Cities
- At least every six months, management committee for Healthy Cities send staff to cities to review and assist local activities
- Develop a list of evaluation criteria on health, environment, infrastructure improvement and changes of awareness, habit and practice in sanitation and hygiene
- Evaluate the project with above criteria

12 Set up an information network among cities

Each city that takes part in the project will be provided with a computer. A website will be set up on the Internet to link all project cities to exchange information and experience. The Central Office for Healthy Cities will link with some Healthy Cities collaborating centres in the region and the world.

13 Integrate with National Medical Programmes:

- Use mass media for propagandising sanitation environment protection, clean water supply at the immunisation points
- Integrate the 'day', 'week' of clean water and sanitation with mosquito larvae kill and elimination of ditch-water containers to prevent the living environment for larvae growth
- Strengthen the collaboration of local sectors in food safety check and environmental sanitation within market area in 'Month of action for food safety'
- Collaborate with the National Malaria Control Programme to detect and treat all malaria cases in the city and urban area

- Involve the National Committee for HIV/AIDS prevention in HIV/AIDS prevention education and communication with focus on high risk areas (tourist, city centre, etc.).

EXPECTED OUTCOMES

- A central office for Healthy Cities Project will be established at the end of 2000 and effectively operated. The office can provide update information in Healthy Cities for all cities. A Vietnam Healthy Cities collaborating centre will be hopefully established in 2003.
- Develop and issue guidelines for Healthy Cities implementation in Vietnam in 2001.

To 2005 (for urban area):
- At least 50% of markets implementing healthy market-places and all food will be checked before brought into market; all animals will be killed in slaughterhouses under the quality examination of veterinary staff.
- Over 80% of women and 95% food vendors in markets understand and practice 10 golden rules for food safety of WHO.
- 60% of food processing premises apply HACCP system.
- 70% of markets have hygienic latrines and water supply for food shop.s
- 50% of markets have drainage and sewage system, and solid waste collection
- Reduce considerably diarrhoea and communicable diseases in children.
- 100% of schools implement model school health of Ministry of Health. All students will access to dental care and primary health care.
- 90% of schools have hygienic latrines and enough water supplies.
- 70% of factories apply working environment protection measures and provide health care for workers.
- Improve sanitation, water supply and environment of cities.
- 75% of hospitals have solid and liquid treatment systems that meet the standard of WHO.
- Awareness of community on clean water, sanitation, and food safety is significantly increased.
- 50% of old people will be provided with health care at home.

RESPONSIBILITY OF INSTITUTIONS

- Ministry of Health is the contact body in Healthy Cities for all cities and international organisations. Ministry of Health looks for the collaboration of other ministries and the support from Central Government to develop a national programme of Healthy Cities and include Healthy Cities activities into national five-years planning.

- Involve Ministry of Science Technology and Environment, Ministry of Agriculture and Rural Development, Ministry of Transportation, Ministry of Construction, General Department of Tourism, etc. in Healthy Cities Project; invite representatives from these ministries to take part in Management Committee.
- Local government: City People Committee directs Healthy Cities Project and integrate project activities into development plan of the city.
- City Department of Health Services is the 'champion office' to involve other departments, social associations of the city in the project.
- Women Union and Youth Union stimulate experience and skills in community education and communication for the project.

Canberra – a healthy capital: Australia

Mr Michael Moore and Dr Shirley Bowen

The City of Canberra is in the Australian Capital Territory. Canberra has a population of 308,659 people and a land area of 2,400 km^2. It is located 306 km from Sydney, 655 km from Melbourne and 8,062 km from Tokyo.

CANBERRA

- is the seat of the Australian Federal Government;
- has outstanding national education and research facilities such as the Commonwealth Scientific and Industrial Research Organisation (CSIRO), Australian National University and the John Curtin School of Medical Research;
- has national institutions such as the High Court of Australia, the National Gallery and the National Library of Australia.

Planned city
- Over 53% of the total area is nature parks and reserves.
- The metropolitan structure is decentralised town centres separated by urban bushland.
- The residential, commercial, industrial areas and community facilities are balanced with rural and urban open spaces.

Housing
- Canberra provides public housing for low income households which is integrated in almost all suburbs (10% of households are publicly owned).
- Types of housing include: detached houses (79%), semi-detached townhouses and units (12%) and apartments and flats (8%).
- The average house size is 161m^2.

There is purpose-built housing for older residents.

Economy

- Canberra has the highest workforce participation rate and the 2nd lowest unemployment rate in the country.
- The unemployment rate is 5.6%.
- The average weekly earnings in Canberra are approximately $100 higher than the national average.
- There was a 5% growth in the economy over the last year.

Air and water quality

- Nitrogen dioxide, carbon monoxide, lead and ozone levels monitored regularly.
- The ACT has a Greenhouse Strategy which outlines initiatives for reducing greenhouse gases.
- Canberra has clean and safe drinking water.

Waste management

- The Lower Molonglo Water Quality Control Centre is the major treatment plant; treated wastewater is discharged into natural waterways.
- There is a 98% participation rate for kerbside recycling.
- The ACT has a 'No Waste by 2010' strategy.

Harm minimisation strategies in health

- First Australian jurisdiction to enact smoke-free legislation to reduce harmful effects of cigarette smoke.
- Prostitution is legal but restricted to industrial areas.
- Drug policy is based on harm minimisation and includes needle exchange, supervised injecting room and decriminalisation for the personal use of cannabis ($100 fine).

Health indicators

- ACT residents compare favourably with the Australian averages on all main health indicators.
- Cardiovascular disease and cancer are the main causes of death in the ACT.
- Lowest infant mortality rate in Australia (3.8 per 1000 live births compared with the Australian average of 5.3 per 1000 live births).
- ACT has a higher participation rate in sport than national average (73% compared with Australian average of 59%).
- 93% of children under three years are breastfed (Australia average is 86%).
- High rates of immunisation for childhood diseases (89% of children 12 months fully immunised, the Australian average is 86%).
- The mortality rate is 10% lower than the Australian average (ACT rate is 5.4 deaths per 1000 people; the Australian rate is 6.0 deaths per 1000 people).

- There are fewer than average admissions to hospital (ACT has 182 hospital separations per 1000 people; the Australian average is 198 per 1000 people).
- Mental illness is the major cause of long hospital stays (with an average length of stay of 12 days).

Hospitals and health services
- Canberra has two major public hospitals and four private hospitals.
- The Community Health Care Program provides a range of services for people at home or in clinics.
- There is approximately one doctor per 770 people in the ACT.

HOW CANBERRA RATES AGAINST WHO HEALTHY CITIES PRINCIPLES

Easily accessible health services
- Canberra has high child immunisation rates (89% of children at 12 months)
- There are high participation rates in health screening programs
- Canberra residents have a high overall health status

A sustainable ecosystem
- Canberra recently introduced energy rating legislation for domestic dwellings
- There is an ACT Greenhouse Strategy to reduce greenhouse gas emissions

Meets the basic needs of inhabitants
- The ACT has clean air and water
- A range of housing options
- A high proportion of students completing secondary education

A strong community
- High participation in cultural activities
- Many interest groups and clubs
- Cultural diversity

Involves the community in government
- There is an emphasis on involving the community in decisions
- There are many opportunities for community consultation and input

Offers access to many experiences and interactions
- Easy access to the natural environment
- Range of sports and interest clubs
- National Capital attractions

Promotes historical and cultural heritage
- Preservation of cultural heritage
- Many festivals
- Multicultural backgrounds are celebrated
- A diverse, innovative economy
- Unemployment lower than national average
- Low inflation
- Growing small business sector

Emerging challenges and opportunities
- The ACT is 1.7% of the Australian population
- ACT has a younger population than the national average (32.1 years compared with 34.6 years for Australia)
- It is the 2nd youngest jurisdiction
- The proportion of people aged over 65 years is expected to triple by 2051
- The average life expectancy is greater than for the rest of Australia (81 years for females and 77 years for males)
- Implementation of mental health strategies for depression and adolescent suicide
- Illicit drug use – implementation of broad ranging harm minimisation strategies
- High risk alcohol consumption – especially young people
- Obesity and cardiovascular disease – promoting physical activity
- Neighbourhoods, physical and social health of older people and physical infrastructure
- Impact of work on family life

Appendix 6

Activities on healthy workplace in the city of Haiphong: Vietnam

Dr Ta Quang Buu

Haiphong, the third largest [city] with big harbor in Vietnam, is located in the northeast of Vietnam. Metropolitan Haiphong covers approximately 1503 km² with a population of approximately 1.7 million including 0.7 million of urban dwellers. It has thirteen administration areas involving four urban districts, one town, six districts and two island districts.

HAIPHONG WITH THE HEALTHY CITIES PROJECT

In 1994, Haiphong received the Healthy Cities Project from WHO and MOH of Vietnam. A research team on environmental health issues was established.

In 1995, a report about the environmental health status of three urban districts of Haiphong was compiled. In the report, there were five initial priorities identified: to increase awareness of environmental health and the importance of persuading the community to assume responsibility in this area; food safety in the markets; adequate water supply and sewerage; cleaning up air pollution; and effective solid waste disposal. Then an action plan was given.

Following the action plan, Haiphong people are implementing a series of projects:

- Supply water project
- Improving sewerage project
- Building a new dump site
- Monitoring air pollution project
- Healthy district project
- Healthy commune project
- Healthy school project
- Healthy market project, and
- Healthy workplace project

HEALTHY WORKPLACE PROJECT IN HAIPHONG

Industries in Haiphong

Scale	No. of enterprises	No. of workers
Large	229	95,864
Medium and small	750	51,907
Official	152	40,564
Home	38,684	59,489
Total	39,815	247,834

Most enterprises with backward technology are located in the crowded dweller areas. Therefore, the development of the healthy workplace movement is very important for implementing the Healthy Cities Project.

Activities on healthy workplace in large factories
- Taking part in environment impact assessment (EIA) and environment risk assessment (ERA)
- Enterprises have to invest for resolving pollution, change technology or will be expelled
- Enhance the effect of laws and regulations (labor law, law for people's health protection, law for environment protection, etc.)
- Monitoring pollution emission resources
- Control hazards
- Organizing work appropriately

Activities on healthy workplace in medium and small-scale enterprises
In these enterprises, the negative health effect has largely resulted from ignorance and mismanagement of environmental hazards. There is an urgent need for our government and community action to control industrial pollution and provide a healthy and safe workplace. The challenge is to keep to a minimum the adverse health and environmental effects, while promoting and sustaining economic development. Here the first problem is that legislations which contain incentives for industry to reduce release of pollutants are not covered comprehensively to both employers and employees. So, what approach is suitable and acceptable to solve the problem? To answer this question, we have implemented the healthy workplace project in medium and small-scale enterprises.

The actions below have been taken to implement the project

- Set up a steering committee in the city level
- Set up a steering committee in the district level
- To open the project the MOH assisted Haiphong to investigate the need of health of medium and small scale-enterprises in Ngo Quyen district. The project originally was implemented in only four small enterprises in Ngo Quyen district: Duc Thang; Quang Hung; Dai Phong and Phuong Vien. Using the slogan 'Higher productivity and better place to work', this project was very successful. Then, in 1999 the project was expanded to 11 other enterprises with the new slogan 'workplace health promotion'
- Set up a working group to directly help enterprises during implementation of the project
- Training course on healthy workplace issues for owners, managers and representatives of workers
- Enterprises participants made their action plan and then owners signed their commitment to participate in the project
- Training course on rescue of the victim for 50 participants who came from 15 enterprises implementing the project
- Training course on healthy workplace issues and laws and regulations for 650 workers of 15 enterprises
- In June 1999, the MOH of Vietnam assisted Haiphong to open a conference to review the activities of the project. Dr Benjamin Vitasa, a consultant from WHO opened the conference
- In December 1999, we organized a healthy workplace festival in Ngo Quyen district. The festival included a competition for owners and their workers in order to promote realization about healthy workplace issues and evaluate the participants understanding of it. After the competition three winning enterprises were chosen and prizes were given for first, second and third place. Observers of the competition were experts from MOH and the national institute on occupational health and environmental hygiene and other departments and sectors of the city
- To review the project, an investigation was launched and then its report showed:
  - Each enterprise has a person responsible for the mission of safety and hygiene in the workplace
  - Improvement of 'green clean beautiful action' changes the view of enterprises
  - More than 80% of employees were trained on health promotion and hygiene in the workplace
  - Each enterprise has 'a health corner' where the owner and workers can pick up paper, handbooks, documents, and leaflets. These documents help them to learn how they can prevent and prove health themselves and other knowledge

- Each enterprise identified at least two priorities for action in order to improve the conditions for employees
- Based on the checkpoint survey to evaluate the project, the report indicated:
  - No accidents
  - 100% of workers feel more confident, energetic, alert, etc.
  - 56% of smoking workers have given up smoking
  - Decrease injuries and backache
  - 100% of owners know well:
        'Work environment = key determinant of employees health'
        'Healthy workers are productive workers are healthy businesses are sustainable development', and they are happy to offer setting for health promotion programs
  - Monitoring the workplace environment and workers health
  - Risk factors are reduced
  - Improved quality of life for workers and their families
  - 100% of 642 workers answered in favor of continuation of implementing the project

CONCLUSION

- Implementing the healthy workplace project in medium and small scale-enterprises is suitable and acceptable.
- The government authorities at all level supported this pilot project, by many sectors and departments in Ngo Quyen district.
- All members of enterprises agreed to participate and assume responsibility in this project.
- The project was very successful.
- It is necessary to develop the project.

Appendix 7

Community participation and urban policies on health and environment of the city of Hue: Vietnam

Dr Nguyen Nhien

OVERVIEW

The Programme 'Healthy Cities', initiated by the World Health Organisation many years ago, has now received the support of most of the countries in the world, all of which have in common the goal of creating an effective and healthy working and living environment.

Like many cities around the world, Hue has participated in this programme. However, because of its special contexts and its own characteristics and difficulties, Hue has been part of the programme for only 3 years.

1. Overview of the development process of Hue:

• Like many other cities of Vietnam, Hue has experienced two long wars with much lasting damage to the infrastructure and environment. Various ancient architectural structures and many of the green trees throughout the city were severely damaged.

During war time, the environment of the city was harmed not only by the use of toxic chemicals but also by human behavior. A typical example of the problems which have resulted from people's behavior has been the environmental pollution generated by squatters, by people living in houses in and around historic sites, and by boat people emigrating from rural areas to live along the Huong River in the city. In addition, the municipal management of the environment is not yet well organized, and pollution, especially the river pollution, is becoming more and more serious and badly affecting the local people's health.

• With a population growth of 100% in only 25 years after the wars, urbanization has created many problems and demands for housing, activities of daily life, and employment, while the urban infrastructure, public work projects and policies have been inadequate to meet these demands. As part of urbanization, many industrial zones as well as public works (hospitals, markets, commercial areas) have been built and developed within residential areas without any master plan. The waste treatment system has been in bad condition or non-existent. As a result, the population's health has been seriously affected.

- The municipal budget has given priority to overcoming the consequences of the wars but has also been very limited; thus, policies for health care and environmental protection have not yet been given sufficient attention.

2. In dealing with the existing problems of the city, which is recognized as a national tourist attraction and a world cultural heritage site and has an average of 1000 visitors per day, decision-making which involves human health care and improvement of the environment must reflect the goal of achieving a healthier city. The importance of decisions affecting the environment and health of the people should be recognized in every community programme initiated by the city. In the past few years, the city has made several significant efforts to solve these problems and has also drawn up plans and policies for the years ahead.

OBJECTIVE

- Promoting the Healthy Cities Programme with many policies and activities that will improve the environmental conditions of the city and community health.
- Recognizing the important role of the community and the necessity for coordination between the authorities and the local population in order for this programme to be successful.

EVALUATION

Nature of the problem
- The measures and policies that the local government adopts to deal with urban issues should be suitable for the development trends for a city with tourism potential such as Hue.
- The importance of dealing with environmental problems should always have high priority. However, due to severe regional weather conditions, natural disasters often occur, causing many serious consequences for the environment and affecting directly the health of the community. Measures and policies for these problems are insufficient or have not been implemented.
- Ever year, the city has to experience 4–5 floods, in addition to many other natural disasters.

Community participation
- Once policies and programmes related to health and the environment are introduced, the population, which follows the guideline of 'the state and population in cooperation', pays much attention and participates in them. The population contributes not only labour but also finance. According to annual evaluation figures, the people's contributions to the budget for programmes

as well as public works account for 30–40% of the total budget. The role of the population is truly important.
- With their contributions to programmes, the population has more awareness of the value of protecting and restoring what they own and achieve.

LONG-TERM SOLUTION AND POLICY

1. Master planning of Hue:
- Identifying and establishing new residential areas for squatters, for people living in and around historic sites, and for people living in slums under bridge foots, in markets and bus stations, etc.;
- Planning and building new commercial areas and stabilizing activities within markets while solving the environmental and health problems of the market workers;
- Developing new industrial zones located far from residential areas and planning to relocate factories currently operating in densely populated areas;
- Promoting the collection and treatment of garbage and improving operation of waste treatment plants.

2. Developing community health care:
- Accelerating measures to improve food safety;
- Strengthening primary health care programmes and health care for the elderly;
- Dealing with the physical environment: dredging the drainage system, solving problem of pollution of the drinking water supply, and cleaning streets in the city.

3. Propagation and education:
- Printing leaflets and posters to publicise these programmes in order to increase the awareness of the community about the value of Healthy Cities.
- Mobilising and encouraging the participation of the community.

4. Supporting the development of a specific action plan and coordinating implementation among the relevant agencies.

5. Participating in the national network for implementation of the Healthy Cities Programme.

6. Properly promoting and allocating the budget.

7. Promoting foreign affairs attracting and consolidating external resources interested in the programme.

8. Adopting specific policies for relevant agencies.

CONCLUSION

For Hue, it is both important and necessary to implement such a programme. And it is also important for every city in the world to pursue a similar one. In the process of programme implementation, existing weaknesses, needs and urban problems can be fully identified, thus leading to long-term action policies for the sustainable socio-economic development of the city.

This is a programme that every city should consider as a strategy for its sustainable development.

Appendix 8

Using community action to stimulate and implement healthy urban policy: Illawarra, Australia

Dr Pat Mowbray

What has the greatest effect on health? The air we breathe, the water we drink, the food we eat, the income we have, our pride in our culture, the quality of our lives and the sustainability of this earth, its natural systems and biodiversity. Yet many of these essential factors for our health are under threat and the general community is becoming increasingly concerned for the future.

Healthy City Illawarra has recently completed a Municipal Planning Process with Kiama Municipal Council where it has harnessed that concern in a visionary and action process that brings together the whole community to dream, identify problems, plan and implement solutions. Already Council policy has been changed and a number of outcomes have been achieved.

Healthy City Illawarra has also formed a strong association with Futureworld, the National Centre for Appropriate Technology being developed in Wollongong.

Futureworld is a demonstration centre of appropriate technologies for industry, business, and the general community such as solar power, wind power, water, energy and waste conservation, permaculture, land rehabilitation, and healthy, safe and sustainable housing, buildings, products and processes.

In addition Healthy City Illawarra has been one of the key players in the establishment of a community based Environmental and Heritage Information Centre which brings together policy makers and the community to stimulate action and has given strong support to community activist groups such as those involved in the campaign to lower dioxin emissions from a major local industry.

Healthy City Illawarra gives Annual Business Awards for Environmental Management and Healthy City Awards to organisations and individuals who have implemented the principles of the Ottawa Charter.

It is our belief that Healthy Cities everywhere must attempt, in co-operation with others, to play a key role in all main factors affecting both the public health and the environment on which we depend.

Towards a Healthy City Johor Bahru

Incorporating community action: Malaysia

Dr Daud Abdul Rahim

INTRODUCTION

Johor Bahru lies at the southernmost part of Peninsular Malaysia, thus making it the southern gateway to the Peninsular. Its population, according to the 1995 census, was 490,000, with a population density of 185 per km^2. The population is skewed towards the young: 40% under 20 years and only 6% over 65 years. Johor Bahru town was formerly managed by the Johor Bahru Municipal Council. It was officially proclaimed a city in January 1994. The Johor Bahru City Council as the Local Authority Board is responsible for the administration, planning, and development of the city. Although Johor Bahru is a small city, it is going through a phase of rapid urbanization and 20 major townships are expected to mushroom around it in the next 10 years. The population is expected to increase to one million by the year 2020. This rapid urbanization will give rise to basic problems of urbanization.

TOWARDS A HEALTHY CITY

The mission of Healthy Johor Bahru City 2005 is to improve the health and quality of life in the community by making the city a better place to work and live in. Underlying this mission is a strong political will and commitment, with multisectoral collaboration, and full support and participation of the community.

'Vision of a Healthy City' which includes environmental, social economical aspects, was formulated.

Our declaration and pledge are: A Healthy Johor Bahru City will be one where:

- There will be a mature, democratic, community oriented society, strong in religious, spiritual, moral values and enjoying a high and optimal level of health.
- The population will live in a healthy aesthetic environment, free from pollution with ample open green spaces and sufficient opportunities for leisure and recreation.

- There will be a thriving and resilient economy with emphasis on high technology, capital intensive industry, commerce, and information technology, taking full advantage of its strategic location in the region.

To achieve the above mission and vision, the objectives are:

- To improve the environment through increased awareness amongst the community
- To enhance participation and roles of city council, government agencies, private sector and community through collective responsibility
- To improve the ability of the city authority in providing an effective service
- To widen the role of the city authority in order to achieve 'Health For All'.

INCORPORATING COMMUNITY ACTION

In 1994, the city of Johor Bahru took the global challenge to participate in the Healthy Cities initiative put forward by the World Health Organization. The Plan of Action was developed and some projects had already been started.

In the aspect of community participation, Johor Bahru Healthy City Committee has formulated and embarked on several projects. Among them are:

Gerak Tumpu (the clean-up campaign)

Johor Bahru City Council has enlisted the help of 24 community associations in its year-long clean-up campaign, which was launched in 1997. The purpose of this campaign is to inculcate a sense of belonging among residents in their respective housing estates. The community associations have been assigned to help people in their areas to dispose rubbish and garden waste in an orderly manner.

The program also covers tree planting, in which only certain tree species are planted in each designated area, to give it a unique identity and image. This campaign acts as a pro-active measure to boost the image of the various areas in the city. With active participation from the community, the residents would appreciate their residential areas, help put a stop to vandalism and activities that pollute the environment. The idea is to inculcate a healthy mentality among the community to take care of public property.

Other than the activities stated, at each launching there were cultural shows, health exhibitions, a 'one stop' information centre and dialogue sessions between the authorities and local community.

This program has activated the participation of the local community as well as some associations and organizations in the community with regards to the cleanliness of the city.

Neighbourhood Watch

Several residents' associations were set up since 1998 in response to the worrying increase in the number of break-ins, robberies, and petty thefts in the neighbourhood. Their immediate priority was the implementation of a neighbourhood watch program by the residents on a voluntary basis. Nightly patrols have been carried out by the residents, both on foot and in vehicles.

They believe that these night patrols have helped to prevent crime in the area. In fact, during the first few months, they have been virtually crime free. Recognising that a voluntary set-up needs a fair amount of motivation, members of the police force have made visits to their respective areas and have joined the residents on their night patrols.

The community has incorporated other social activities into this program. These include forming a special committee that became the core in finding solutions to problems relating to social, physical and environmental issues within their neighbourhood.

Dengue free UDA

UDA is located in the midst of rapid urbanisation within the Johor Bahru City Council. It recorded an increase of dengue cases over the past 4 years with 11 occurrences of epidemic outbreaks and 2 deaths. Various action and strategies were executed but with dismal outcomes. Several contributory factors were identified for the occurrence of dengue in UDA. Commenced in early 1998, concerted efforts were rallied to address the prevailing problem in the area with joint participation from the health authority, related government agencies, private sectors and the UDA community at large. The local community combined efforts in setting up a team to search and destroy mosquito breeding areas. They also conduct awareness programs such as dialogues, lectures and exhibitions, throughout the year. Subsequently, the number of dengue cases recorded a tremendous decrease. This scenario bears testimony to the success of the efforts by all quarters to stamp out the disease from UDA.

Thus, from this achievement, the UDA community and the private sectors are becoming more proactive towards lending any effort particularly in the control of dengue, and other initiatives in the near future.

'Meet people on Saturday'

Johor Bahru City Council declares a working Saturday as a 'no meeting' and 'no function' day to ensure that the heads of departments are able to meet the people. On such days, the community can meet the heads of department directly, without any appointment and without intermediaries. They are assured of a warm and cordial reception, and immediate attentions are given to their queries and grievances. 'Management Meets the People day' enables heads of departments to be accessible to the public, who would thus be able to obtain accurate information and solutions to their problems. City council staffs gain vital feedback towards improving departmental efficiency and performance.

This program has been running successfully, and without fail on every working Saturday since January 1998. It received tremendous support from various levels of community. It became the most important channel which enabled the community to provide feedback to the city authority and vice versa.

Health Advisory Panel

Forming the Health Advisory Panel at every Health Clinic is another strategy to increase the participation of the local community in health matters concerning the community. It is about empowering the community to identify health problems and the needs of the community and plan for activities to achieve 'Health for All'. Members of the Health Advisory Panel consist of voluntary individuals from the community and most of them are active members of the society. This panel will provide the channel of communication between the Public Health Department and the community, as well as providing a more cost effective way of health information distribution to the community.

Currently about 12 Health Advisory Panels have been formed in the city, and hopefully they can identify and promote more volunteers in the community to work towards the well being of the community.

Maju Jaya Healthy Community Kitchen

The Healthy Community Kitchen Project in Maju Jaya, which is located at the outskirts of Johor Bahru City, is a joint project of the Department of Health and the State Government, in smart partnership with the community. It is a facility made available in the community to enable participation and hands on training of housewives as well as female teenagers and students, in healthy food preparation and cooking methods, in developing skills and testing healthy recipes, in practicing food and personal hygiene, and also in maintaining kitchen safety and cleanliness. Consequently, the facility can be expanded into a model kitchen, and centre of health and nutrition promotion for women. In addition, the facility can serve as feeding centres for children, women, the aged and those with diet-related chronic diseases. An important feature of the Healthy Community Kitchen is that it emphasizes community participation. The daily activities at the facility are planned and carried out by the target groups themselves, volunteer groups and local women's group under the supervision of the local community nurse. The procurement of food items is by the participants and donors from the local community, food company, and vendors. Bulk purchase of goods and kitchen needs as well as food production and processing are encouraged.

Our initial experiences suggest that the project is well accepted by the community. We attribute this to the broad-based nature of the project which appeals to and meets the expectations of the community. Its success is also due the smart partnership approach that we have applied. The approach has also generated a greater sense of ownership, belonging and responsibility.

CONCLUSION

Involving the community in the various social, economic and environmental activities is not something new in our society. In fact, it is a natural trend within the community themselves. With a comprehensive program or project, the community would be attracted to joining in and involving themselves for their own good and benefit.

To succeed in the Healthy Cities initiative, there must be leadership. This has to come from city councils that run the cities. They will provide the commitment, coordination, and direction to facilitate the program in order for it to succeed and be sustained.

The Healthy Johor Bahru is a continuing initiative. It needs support and co-operation from all sectors, and a more practical and holistic approach. To achieve its vision, involvement of and contributions from the public and private sectors, non-governmental organizations and community is much needed in realizing the council's ambition in making Johor Bahru a Healthy City.

Bibliography

WHO (1997) *Case Report Study on Healthy City Johor Bahru. Healthy Cities* – Healthy Islands Document Series No. 2, WHO WPREC, Kuala Lumpur.

WHO (1995) *Building A Healthy City: A Practitioners' Guide*. Geneva: WHO Plan of Action. First Interagency Conference Report 1995, Johor State Health Department.

Developing Healthy City Profile Second Interagency Conference Report 1997. Johor State Health Department.

Azmi, Daud. The Healthy Community Kitchen Project Report 1998, Johor State Health Department.

Healthy City Kuching

Intersectoral collaboration in
Healthy Cities: Malaysia

Dr Yao Sik Chi

INTRODUCTION

The implementation of Healthy Cities Programmes around the world has emerged as an effective means for improving urban health and the urban environment. The development of the programme has taken different paths in different regions. However, there are perhaps two common key concepts that help define the Healthy Cities Programme: intersectoral collaboration (used interchangeably with intersectoral action and intersectoral collaboration for health), and supportive environments (WHO 1995).

However, intersectoral collaboration is not a panacea. Not everything that needs to be done to enhance the quality of life of people in the city is suitable for intersectoral collaboration. Indeed it may be more a hindrance than a help if it is applied to the wrong type of problem. The purpose of this paper is to discuss the factors that have to be taken into consideration before intersectoral collaboration is used to solve problems in the context of Healthy City. Some examples of inter-sectoral collaboration and action from Healthy City Kuching will be presented.

Kuching (see Note 1 [page 289] for a brief description of the city) joined the Healthy Cities movement in 1994. Since then the Healthy City concept has been adopted as a way of planning for the city, and all the other urban areas of the State.

The Healthy City Kuching steering committee defined a Healthy City as one that would continuously enhance the quality of life of its citizens. In order to achieve that, two things had to be done simultaneously. One was to solve existing problems that affected the quality of life of the citizens. The other was to improve the conditions in which its people live, work play and dream.

DIMENSIONS AND SECTORS OF HEALTHY CITIES
PROBLEMS AND ISSUES

The problems and conditions, as well as actions that need to be taken to solve or improve them, involve one, two or all three of the following dimensions: social, physical and economic. The agencies and groups whose efforts are necessary to solve the issues may come from various sectors such as health, agriculture, commerce, and so on. The organisations and agencies involved may be government and other public agencies, non-government organisations, private businesses, and the community. Further, the organisations may be operating at local, national, regional or multinational levels.

FACTORS TO CONSIDER WHEN CHOOSING ISSUES AND TASKS TO BE TACKLED USING INTERSECTORAL COLLABORATION

Among the factors to consider before embarking on solving issues and problems using intersectoral collaboration are: a) number of disciplines and sectors involved, b) complexity and politicality of the issues, c) task characteristics, and d) the pros and cons of adopting the intersectoral approach.

Number of disciplines and sectors involved

Many of the issues and problems facing cities and other urban areas are usually complex. There is a need to identify the major dimensions, sectors and disciplines involved in the issues and problems. The solutions will also require the expertise and efforts of individuals, groups, communities, agencies, departments and organisations in those sectors. All these efforts will need proper coordination so that they will enhance and not negate the effect of each other's efforts.

Complexity and politicality of the issues

In addition to the number of sectors that the issues impinge on, the complexity and politicality of the issues should be taken into account to determine whether intersectoral and interdisciplinary efforts are needed.

Problems may be classified into three grades based on their complexity and politicality (Noorderhaven 1995).

The most complex and most political issues are classified as *vortex* because they tend to suck many decision-makers into swirls of activity. Less complex and non-political issues are classified as *tractable,* because they are non-controversial and more malleable. The least complex and only mildly political issues are classified as *familiar* because they are normal and recurrent,

Based on this classification, intersectoral collaboration is best suited for solving vortex and tractable issues and problems. One example of a vortex issue is squatters. One example of a tractable issue is the 'pedestrianisation' of streets.

Task characteristics

Another very important aspect of issues and tasks that will determine whether they are suitable for intersectoral collaboration is the task characteristics. For instance, the performance of groups of agencies relative to that of individual agencies depends, among other things, on the question of whether the task permits the group to pool their resources. If the task allows pooling of resources, like in a tug-of-war, recycling activities to reduce solid wastes, 'love the river', groups do better than individuals. If on the other hand the task requires very precise coordination, like driving a car, enforcement of laws such as fire safety of buildings, environment quality laws, 'Healthy Market', 'Healthy Hospital', individuals/individual agencies do better.

Based on the task characteristics, intersectoral collaboration is most suitable for tasks that are:

a) *divisible* in the sense that they can be divided into subtasks that can be performed by different group members, such as recycling activities,
b) *maximising*, in the sense that performance rests on sheer quantity, such as tree-planting, recycling activities,
c) *optimising* (right output), e.g. issue of licences for public transport (buses, taxis),
d) *judgmental* in nature, where there is no demonstrably correct answer.

Possible types of solution to problems

There are two possible types of solution to problems faced.

a) Intellectual task, where there is a demonstrably correct answer, such as solutions for traffic jams, reduction of solid waste and resettlement of hawkers.
b) Judgmental in nature, where there is no demonstrably correct answer, such as land area adequate for public recreation places and public parks and homes for the elderly.

PROS AND CONS OF INTERSECTORAL COLLABORATION

From the point of view of decision-making, bringing diverse disciplines and sectors to bear upon issues has the potential for a) more varieties of skills and specialized knowledge can be brought in, b) multiple and conflicting views and approaches can be aired and considered, c) beliefs and values can be transmitted and aligned, d) more organizations and their members will be committed to the decisions and actions, since they have participated in the process.

During the implementation phase, intersectoral collaboration will bring about a) critical mass, b) better coordination leading to more efficiency, c) time saving, d) comprehensive solution, e) more resources, f) more credibility, and so on, leading to g) more effectiveness.

The intersectoral collaboration approach should not be taken lightly because the decision-making process: a) can be more time consuming, b) may lead to feeble compromises, c) may conversely lead to more risky decisions, and d) may stifle creativity.

Furthermore during the implementation phase, intersectoral efforts may suffer from coordination losses, when agencies and groups cannot combine their efforts in an optimal way, and motivation losses, when agencies and groups exert less effort when working in a group than if they work individually (Noorderhaven 1995). Thus intersectoral efforts need to have a strong lead agency and secretariat to get the group together initially, and to maintain and sustain the efforts of the group later on.

SOME EXAMPLES ON INTERSECTORAL COLLABORATION IN HEALTHY CITY KUCHING

Healthy City Kuching

Healthy City Kuching Programme itself is one example of intersectoral collaboration. Involving 28 agencies, Healthy City Kuching has been successful because the concept has been modified to suit the local administrative culture and the development needs of the State. The Healthy Cities concept is seen as a way of thinking and planning for the State. Other success factors include:

a)   strong and visible support of the top politicians and policy makers (from the Chief Minister downwards) and top administrators and implementers of government policies (such as the State Secretary who heads the steering committee at state level);

b)   the harmonious relationships that exist at all levels and sectors in the city. This overall harmony is reflected in the close rapport that exists between public and private agencies and the politicians, and between the agencies. In such a climate, it is relatively easy and pleasant to get things done;

c)   the presence of a core team as prime movers;

d)   the spirit of give and take and the belief that 'anything can get done if we do not care who gets the credit'; and

e)   study visits, conferences, seminars as avenues for continuous learning, exchange of ideas and recognition for those involved.

In the context of intersectoral collaboration and action, Healthy City Kuching steering committee usually meets at the beginning of the year to decide what issues to tackle during that year. These issues are usually complex and involve many dimensions and sectors. They would form the theme for the annual inter-agency conference on Healthy City as well as for the Healthy City week. Some of the past issues that were taken up were vandalism, law enforcement, and illegal trading in residential areas.

Simple, mundane issues that single agencies can deal with on their own were left with the relevant agencies to tackle.

Safety, health, and environmental coordinating committee

Another example of Intersectoral Collaboration is the Safety, Health, and Environmental Coordinating Committee (SHECCOM). It was one of the first intersectoral working committees that were set up as part of Healthy City Kuching. In retrospect, the need for such a committee to visit the factories in the city should have been obvious.

Prior to the existence of Healthy City Kuching, a factory in the city would be visited by many agencies such as the Health Department, Department of Occupational Safety and Health, Labour Department, Department of the Environment, the Local Authority, and so on. The visits were not coordinated and each agency only reported on the issues within its purview. Thus the reports were not comprehensive and the factory's operations might be disrupted many times because of the many visits. After the formation of Healthy City Kuching, the relevant agencies formed SHEC-COM and the committee planned the visits. Members of the committee go together and they are able to provide more comprehensive advice and solutions to whatever problems there are in the factory during one visit. The multi-agency visiting team also produces and sends just one joint report of the visit to the factory.

This is a situation where intersectoral collaboration brought in a variety of disciplines and expertise, and legal backing to tractable issues that are: a) divisible (the inspection of different aspects of the factories can be divided into subtasks that can be performed by different group members with the relevant expertise), b) maximising, in the sense that performance rests the number of factories that had complete inspections done, c) additive in which the committee's output is the sum of the individual contribution of the members from different disciplines, and d) judgmental in the sense that there are many possible solutions to problems that were present in the factories' face.

Committee on illegal businesses and small-scale industries in residential areas

In Sarawak, it is illegal for anyone to carry on businesses and industries in residential areas because they will be a form of nuisance to the neighbours. Yet it is very common to find people setting up small businesses using their houses and compounds as business premises.

Such businesses include motor vehicle repair and slaughtering of chicken for the market. The neighbours staying near such premises would complain of the nuisance to the Local Authorities, the Land and Survey Department the Health Department and so on.

The Local Authority would request the Land and Survey Department to take action because the misuse of land is under the jurisdiction of the Land and Survey. The Land and Survey Department would in turn say that the abatement of such nuisances is the responsibility of the Local Authority.

This issue was discussed at one of the Healthy City Kuching conferences. A multi-agency committee was set up to study the issue. A survey was done to determine the locations, types of trades, number of premises involved, and so on. As a result, the Land Code (1957) was amended with the passing of the Prescribed Activities Amendment (1997) to address the issue.

However, it is not possible to enforce the law just like that. By the very nature of these trades, the alternative sites should not be too far away from their customers. One of the difficulties that have to be overcome in finding the solution to the issue was to find alternative sites for the trades to move to. This is an example of a vortex issue. It is very complex and highly political. It has to be tackled with due care. Even with many agencies involved in trying to find a solution, the issue is not going to be solved overnight, but at least the city now has data on its magnitude.

CONCLUSION

While intersectoral collaboration has been considered as one of the strategies to be adopted by Healthy Cities, it must be used only to address complex issues and problems which single agencies or sectors cannot tackle on their own. Factors that need to be considered before recommending the intersectoral approach include the: a) number of disciplines and sectors involved, b) complexity and politicality of issues, c) task characteristics, and d) pros and cons of adopting the intersectoral approach. When using intersectoral collaboration, steps must be taken to minimise coordination and motivation losses.

Bibliography

Dengeling P. and Apthorpe R. (1992) Can intersectoral cooperation be organised? Uncovering some implications of 'sectors' in calls for 'intersectoral' cooperation, 26 November 1992. As quoted in: WHO (1997) *Think and Act Globally and Intersectorally to Protect National Health.* Geneva: World Health Organization.

Hancock T. (1994) A healthy and sustainable community: the view from 2020. In Chu, C. and Simpson, R. (eds) *Ecological Public Health: From Vision to Practice.* Nathan, Queensland: Griffith University, Institute of Applied Environmental Research.

Noorderhaven, N. G. (1995) *Strategic Decision-making.* Wokingham, England: Addison-Wesley.

WHO (1986) *Intersectoral Action for Health: The Role of Intersectoral Cooperation in National Strategies for Health for All.* Geneva: World Health Organization.

WHO (1995) *WHO Healthy Cities: A Programme Framework, A Review of the Operation and Future Development of the WHO Healthy Cities Programme.* Geneva: World Health Organization.

WHO (1997a) *Think and Act Globally and Intersectorally to Protect National Health.* Geneva: World Health Organization.

WHO (1997b) *Intersectoral Action for Health: Addressing Health and Environment Concerns in Sustainable Development.* Geneva: World Health Organization.

NOTE 1

Kuching

Kuching is the state capital of Sarawak, one of the 13 states in Malaysia. Historically, Kuching was a revering settlement and trading post about 12 kilometres up the Sarawak River. From the 1840s to the mid 1970s, Kuching had very slow growth. This gradual growth did not appear to give rise to any serious congestion or pollution. Since then the picture has changed.

Today Kuching has grown to a city covering an area approximately 431 square kilometres, reaching right out to the South China Sea on the north. Terrain-wise the populated part of the city, which covers about a third of the city, is flatter. The remainder of the areas are swampy or mountainous.

Kuching was officially proclaimed as a city on 1 August 1988. It is divided into two administrative areas: Kuching North and Kuching South. The former is managed by Kuching North City Hall and has an area of 369 square kilometres, with a population of 122,000. Kuching South is managed by the Council of the City of Kuching South and has an area of 61.5 square kilometres, with a population of 130,000.

Kuching joined the Healthy Cities movement in August 1994. There are now about 30 agencies in the programme. More information may be obtained from the homepage at <http://Sarawak.health.gov.my>

Healthy City Malacca

The community's expectation, satisfaction and contribution: Malaysia

Dr Rosnah Ismail

BACKGROUND Healthy Cities concept was taken by Malaysia in 1994 and Malacca State has initiated this project in late 1997 and launched in September 1998. The aim of the project is to find ways of achieving a better quality of urban life.

OBJECTIVE To assess the views and responses of Melaka Tengah community with regards to the existing facilities and services rendered in the district. The responses will be incorporated to the ideas of the policy makers and planners in developing Malacca into a Healthy City.

METHODOLOGY Three methods were used to collect data. Questionnaires were given to the community of Melaka Tengah District. The 988 respondents were selected by multistage sampling and simple random sampling. Observation was carried out at selected public places to assess the community's practices and contribution. Ten focus group discussions were conducted consisting of health staff and the public to discuss on environmental, social, physical and economic issues of Malacca.

FINDINGS AND DISCUSSION There were 3 sectors that had mean scores above 3 (the cut off level for being satisfied). They were health, housing, and environment. In terms of dissatisfaction, there were 4 sectors scoring below 3. These include domestic waste disposal, road system, public transportation, and recreational park. Meanwhile 70% of the respondents felt that the social indiscipline was well contained. The community expected the services to be improved especially in terms of cleanliness. They agreed to contribute in their own way in developing the sectors discussed except for public transportation, wet market, and food premises which were beyond their control. Observation showed that some of the community had bad behaviours that could contribute to an unhealthy city.

CONCLUSION The community expected efficient and quality services. They agreed to contribute in making Malacca a Healthy City.

Olongapo City healthy program implementation: the Philippines

Mayor Katherine H. Gordon

HISTORY

Olongapo has struggled to develop under harsh circumstances that strengthened its people. It was the last piece of Philippine territory surrendered by the US to the country in the 1950s. It was the first chartered city and highly urbanized city in its province. It rose from a 'sin city' in the 1960s and 1970s to become a model city in the 1980s and 1990s. It has survived extreme political reversals, the withdrawal of the bases and the greatest volcanic eruption of the century. It built the Subic Bay free port from its vision and now seeks to extend the free trade regime to its people. The resulting culture of volunteerism built a hardy and resilient people that remain Olongapo's most enduring resource.

FACTS AND FIGURES

Land area	185 square kilometres (17 Barangays)
Population	250,000 (1999 estimated)
Growth rate	2.14%
Households	50,000 (1999 estimated)
Average household size	5 persons
Population density	1,240 persons per sq km
Urban density	10,513 persons per sq km

SOCIAL SERVICES

Education

1. **Public elementary ratio**
- Classroom   1:40
- Teacher   1:35

2. Public secondary ratio
- Classroom   1:51
- Teacher   1:24

3. Literacy rate = 98%
- Elementary   97.31%
- Secondary   99.52%

4. Graduation rate
- Elementary   98.87%
- Secondary   91.12%

5. Programs
- City Scholars: 1737 (67 colleges, 590 high schools, 1080 elementary schools)
- 113 computers donated to all high schools
- Operates the (OCC) Olongapo City Colleges
- Funded 73 seminars for teachers
- Constructed Division of Schools Building

Sports and recreation

To keep our children active and healthy, there are 28 basketball grounds in 17 barangays, and 9 parks established for their recreational activities. The City also has an athletic field of 1.5 hectares, and a Sports and Civic Center.

Welfare services

The delivery of welfare services encompasses individuals from preschool age, to adolescents, to persons with disabilities, up to the elderly.

1. Child Minding Center – only child minding center in Region III
2. Day Care Centers/Feeding Centers 49
3. Rehabilitation Center – for victims of drug abuse, vagrancy, child exploitation and abuse, victims of calamities
4. Women's Desk
5. Adult and Community Education Program
6. Office of the Senior Citizen

Protective services

Olongapo City is one of the most peaceful cities in the country. Members of the City's police force have been consistent awardees for the last several years. In 1998, it was awarded the Best City Police Force in Region III. Likewise, its female officers were awarded the Best Police Woman of the Year in 1998. There are 213 policemen in the service with a police to population ratio of 1:844, which is better than the national standard of 1:1000. It has a crime solution efficiency of

96.3%. It enjoys the full support of the City which provides it with 40 handheld radios, 14 vehicles, 100 leather pistol belts, as well as cash bonuses, secondary education, insurance and free hospitalization.

Fire Protection – The City augments this with its own resources. The KHG Fire-Rescue Team is composed of 25 specially trained personnel who provide the City emergency response capacity during fires, floods, earthquakes and other disasters.

Public Safety – as a measure to safeguard the public from crimes, the color-coding system in public transportation was introduced in 1997. These included the wearing of uniforms of drivers, with name tags and vehicle body numbers prominently displayed for easy identification.

Environmental protection

Olongapo City is proud to be the first to pioneer the award winning Integrated Garbage Collection System in the country. This system was started in 1989 and replicated by other cities and provinces, both locally and internationally. It has been very successful in improving the sanitary conditions of the City.

To minimize the incidence of air pollution in the City annual inspection of public utility vehicles is being conducted.

Infrastructure and utilities

The City distributes power through its Public Utilities Department (PUD), which is operated as a revenue-generating arm of the local government. Ninety per cent of the City is served.

The first privatization of a water works system occurred in Olongapo City with the aid of the World Bank. The Olongapo City Water District has been privatized effectively since April 1997 into a joint venture named Subicwater, where the City, SBMA, D.M. Consunji and Biwater of the U.K. are now shareholders. Eighty per cent of the City is served.

Health and nutrition

The implementation of health programs and services is a combination of interagency collaboration and coordination between the government and the private sector. The Local Government Code of 1991 mandates the transfer of health services, facilities, powers, and responsibilities to the local government units. This was meant to contribute to a more effective delivery of health services to the people by the local government units, thus enhancing the quality of life of the individuals.

The medical needs of the community are being met by a city funded tertiary hospital which boasts a CT Scan, dialysis machines, ultra-sound machines and other modern equipment. The promotive and preventive aspects of health care are being taken care of by 17 barangay health centers and 4 health stations. The City also has eight well equipped ambulances.

Barangay Health Workers and Barangay Nutrition Scholars are community leaders who undergo training on primary health care and nutrition, and assist the delivery of services in the community.

The national standards are met by the health personnel in terms of the ratio of medical personnel to the population being served.

Important indicators of impact programs are the following:

- Fully immunized children (FIC): 99.81% (5,864)
- Crude birth rate: 25.41 per 1000 pop.
- Crude death rate: 4.15 per 1000 pop.
- Infant mortality rate: 12.32 per 1000 live births
- Maternal mortality rate: 0.63 per 1000 live births
- Nutrition: operation Timbang (preschoolers)
- Severely underweight: 0.62% (223)
- Moderately underweight: 3.14% (1,133)
- Mildly underweight: 16.19% (5,842)
- Normal: 69.6% (25,106)
- Overweight: 10.44% (3,768)
- Malnutrition prevalence rate: 1998 = 4.3 and 1999 = 3.75

The most common cause of diseases is still infectious, as shown by the prevalence of respiratory illness, diarrheas, tuberculosis and pneumonias. Mortality causes, on the other hand, are shifting from the infectious to the non-infectious types, like heart diseases, hypertension, malignancies, and diabetes.

INTERSECTORAL COLLABORATION AND COMMUNITY PARTICIPATION: THE OLONGAPO EXPERIENCE

Primary health care and the community volunteer health workers

Primary health care as an approach remains as the core strategy in the implementation of all health programs. It calls for greater community involvement; intersectoral collaboration and the use of appropriate technology in health care delivery, including indigenous ones, to make services more effective, affordable, accessible and culturally acceptable.

Community organizations, through their leaders and other volunteers, share the responsibility for promoting and maintaining community health. Health volunteers in the communities composed of Barangay Health Workers (BHW), Barangay Nutrition Scholars (BNS) and Male Family Planning Motivators, work hand in hand in bringing health care closer to the people through:

a)   service delivery – weighing of preschoolers, micronutrient supplementation; follow up and referral of patients to health facilities;

b)   capability building – conduct of health and nutrition classes; motivation and
      counseling;
c)   advocacy and social mobilization – coordination with Barangay Council, the
      Local Government Unit, and NGOs/private sector; networking and establish-
      ing linkages with GOs and NGOs;
d)   community organizing – organizing the community into various committees,
      e.g. health, education, peace and order;
e)   monitoring – continuous observation of the community's health situation.

With the institutionalization of the Primary Health Care approach, however, the
over-all health situation improved as shown by the following key indicators.

	1988		**1999**	
1. Crude birth rate per 1000 population	29.48		25.41	
2. Crude death rate per 1000 population	5.74		4.15	
3. Fetal mortality rate per 1000 live births	14.40		10.03	
4. Neonatal mortality rate per 1000 live births	20.22		8.56	
5. Infant mortality rate per 1000 live births	39.39		12.32	
6. Maternal mortality rate per 1000 live births	0.70		0.63	
7. Fully immunized children	44%		99.81%	
8. Tetanus toxoid immunization for pregnant women	21%		75.42%	
9. Nutrition (Operation Timbang)	**Number**	**%**	**Number**	**%**
Severely underweight	675	2.97	223	0.62
Moderately underweight	2,705	11.91	1,133	3.14
Mildly underweight	9,530	41.95	5,842	16.19
Normal	8,961	39.45	25,106	69.6
Overweight	845	3.72	3,768	10.44
Total	22,716	–	36,072	–
Percentage coverage	–	62.04	–	92.26
Malnutrition prevalence rate (MPR)	3,380	14.87	1,356	3.75

Clearly, the people have transcended their role as mere recipients to active participants and major players in health improvement. Even the relationship between
the government and non government organizations took a new light. NGOs have
become regular participants in government processes, at the level of policy and
decision making, program planning, implementation, monitoring and evaluation.
      The numerous prestigious awards received by the City and the City Mayor
show that intersectoral collaboration and community participation are dynamic
and essential factors in good governance.

Considering all the outstanding achievements in health, sustaining and maintaining this harmonious combination of intersectoral collaboration and community participation is still a big challenge to the people of Olongapo City.

Major impact programs
a)   Expanded Program on Immunization/Maternal and Child Health/Nutrition
     – Control of Acute Respiratory Illnesses
     – Control of Diarrhea Diseases/Family Planning
b)   National Tuberculosis Program
c)   Dental Services
d)   STD and AIDS Control

Community volunteers organization
The program aims to provide a holistic approach in providing services and assistance to the various barangays of the City. There are complementary efforts by different government agencies and concerned NGOs in bringing services and assistance to the targeted communities.

The general objective of the program is to mobilize and energize the joint efforts of the local leadership and people and to serve as a catalyst of change and positive medium in the delivery of basic services. Through the establishment and active participation in the Community Volunteers Organization (CVO), which is a major program component of Olongapo CARES, we are effectively empowering the people to have an active part in the affairs of their community.

Sectors which are involved in information dissemination and implementation of the program include, but are not limited to, the following:

a)   City Government Officials/employees
b)   Urban poor
c)   Day Care Center Parents Committee
d)   The Philippine National Red Cross
e)   Barangay Health Workers
f)   Outreach Workers and Male Motivators of the City Population Office
g)   Sangguniang Kabataan and other youth group
h)   Senior citizens
i)   Olongapo City Police Office/PNP
j)   Schools and educators
k)   Vendors
l)   Various NGOs
m) Women's groups

While the program may also serve as a feedback mechanism and establishes/ enhances dialogue and rapport with the people, it is, first and foremost, a government service delivery system.

The following are major service components of the project:

a) Health and environmental services
i. Medical/ Dental; ii.Community Hygiene; iii. Immunization;
iv. PTB (Treatment and Prevention); v. Hospitalization; vi. Population
Education; vii. Nutrition

b) Philippine National Red Cross
i. Blood-Typing; ii. Blood-Letting; iii. CPR Training/Orientation

c) Disaster management and rescue
i. Orientation and Training; ii. Emergency Response

d) Youth and sports
i. Summer Sports Activities; ii. Little League; iii. Dramatic Guild and
Performing Arts; iv. Dance Troupe

e) Technical and infrastructure
i. Power and Electrical; ii. Roads and Drainage; iii. Infrastructure Projects

f) Peace and order
i. Barangay Neighborhood Watch; ii. Illegal Drugs; iii. Campaign Against
All Forms of Crime

g) Education
i. Reading Centers; ii. Remedial classes; iii. Truant Officers

h) Social welfare
i. 'Bantay Bata' Child Watch; ii. Battered Wife/Women; iii. Hospital/Health
Referral

This program is also being used effectively as a vehicle to share the administration's vision and accomplishments. It is also utilized as an opportunity to promote
the culture of success and an excellence as against the culture of victimization and
mediocrity.

After organizing the communities in the various barangays, volunteers are
recruited according to their specific fields of interest. The recruitment will be a continuing process involving the widest participation of the citizens in the community.

With the community volunteers organized into sectors/areas of concern, they
serve as conduits in bringing about the plans and programs of the city in the
neighborhood level. Directly and indirectly, they participate and/or are effectively
used in the various programs of the city which include health and sanitation,
peace and order, education, social welfare and others. In health programs,
barangay health workers serve as a vital cog in monitoring the health conditions
of their community. They also serve as sources or retrievers of information for
planning purposes and help carry out health programs and projects in their
respective neighborhoods.

Recruited volunteers undergo scheduled sectoral training to equip them with the required knowledge and methodology in carrying out their responsibilities. The reporting system as part of feedback mechanism must be fully institutionalized.

Subsidized health insurance for indigents

Recent data consistently show that around 50% to as high as 76% in 1992 of national government funds were being used for the operation of public hospitals. Although the proportion of national government health funds spent on public health increased from 24% in 1991 to 39% in 1993, the P3.406 billion ($85,150,000) allotted to public health seemed to be still very inadequate to meet such needs of the people.

The City Government of Olongapo recently launched a health insurance program for indigent families in coordination with the Philippine Health Insurance Corporation.

The City is the first local government unit in the whole Central Luzon to initiate such project. Under this program, urban poor residents of the City can enjoy the benefits of a health insurance.

The concept of intersectoral collaboration was utilized in involving the various government departments and the non-government organizations (NGOs) to:

a)   disseminate information to the general public;
b)   identify qualified families;
c)   conduct survey on the family profile using the minimum basic needs (MBN) checklist;
d)   conduct social work validation; and
e)   collate data.

The annual contribution of each family amounts to P1,188.00 ($29.00). Half of this will be paid by the city government and half by the PHC under its Indigence Component Program. The health insurance coverage is effective for 1 year and is renewable. The program promotes self-help health care through its eventual expansion to all citizens of the community. Families will then be able to pay a higher amount as their counterpart in the program.

Criteria for qualification set by the PHC and the City government of Olongapo includes:

a)   the household income of the family each month should not exceed P5,000.00 ($122),
b)   families with three children or more, with ages 20 years old and below; and
c)   families who are able to pass the validation conducted by the City Social Welfare and Development Office.

Increasing the level of awareness of people on health care will be a continuous priority activity which will in turn improve community participation. This growing awareness and desire for self-help health care will lead to a more meaningful people empowerment.

AWARDS/RECOGNITIONS

1. Recognition for Excellence – Special Recognition for Partnership with the World Bank under the CDS, February 26, 2000
2. Child Friendly City, Regional Level, December 15, 1999
3. Clean and Green National Award, December 1999
4. National Award Hall of Fame for Lupong Tagapamayapa Barangay STA. RITA (Presidential Trophy) December 14, 1999
5. Konrad Adenauer Local Government Award, December 1, 1999
6. Presidential Scroll of Honor, December 1, 1999
7. Plaque of Recognition – Konrad Adenauer Stiftung and LOGODEF
8. Awarded 1999 Plaque of Recognition for International Understanding awarded by the Konrad Adenauer Stiftung and the LOGODEF
9. National Award Hall of Fame for Lupong Tagapamayapa Barangay Old Cabalan (Presidential Trophy)
10. National Awardee Lupong Tagapamayapa Barangay Old Cabalan
11. City Police Office of the Year 1999
12. Best Police Woman of the Year (February 1999)
13. Non Commissioned Police Officer of the Year (February 1999)
14. Traffic Enforcer of the Year Region III (February 1999)
15. Award of Excellence – Second Runner-up and National Finalist Presidential Awards for the Cleanest Greenest Local Government Units of the Philippines (December1999)
16. Most Prepared City Disaster Coordinating Council in the Region (December 15, 1999)
17. Dilg Plaque of Exemplary Leadership (June 25)
18. Kalinisan Award of Excellence for Healthy Market Olongapo Public Market (June 24, 1999)
19. Healthy Street of Region III Award, given by DOH Rizal Avenue (June 24, 1999)
20. Woman Distinction Award given by the Soroptomist International
21. UNESCO Cities for Peace Prize for Asia-Pacific Region – (March 31, 1998)

Municipal public health planning

Queensland's experience: Australia

Mr Peter Davey

INTRODUCTION

The Healthy Cities Movement began in Europe in 1986 as a way of implementing the Ottawa Charter health promotion actions at the local level. The Healthy Cities work in Queensland provides a socio-ecological approach aimed at urban and rural planning for healthy and sustainable communities.

In 1994 funding from Queensland Health allowed Health Cities and Shires, Queensland to initiate 'encouragement grants' to nine local governments to facilitate Municipal Public Health Planning demonstration projects. A Healthy Cities and Shires project coordinator supported these projects. Lessons learnt through these projects and previous Healthy Cities work in the local setting assisted the project to develop an overall framework, resource guide and published case studies for the development of 'Municipal Public Health Plans' (MPHP).

The key principles of the Healthy Cities movement are to ensure public urban and rural planning includes intersectoral collaboration, interdepartmental collaboration and community participation in decision making about health agenda.

Central to the development of these plans was the changing role of local governments as facilitators of collaborative planning within a community. Partnerships between sectors of governments, non-governments and the community were formed to identify and address factors affecting the health of the particular community.

As mentioned previously Municipal Public Health Planning takes a socio-ecological perspective of health, these projects consequently also take on a role of assisting the community to view health in terms of more than illness and to consider the priority physical, social, economic and environmental factors determining the health of their community.

This paper will discuss the history and changing focus of planning for healthy communities and review the planning process and provide some case study examples of MPHP: Queensland's experience.

THE CHANGING FOCUS OF PUBLIC HEALTH, AND LOCAL GOVERNMENT'S ROLE

Health is a valuable human resource, which requires protection and maintenance. In times of increasing urbanisation and industrialisation, and of dramatically shifting social and economic patterns, traditional public health services can no longer be viewed as adequate to address the complex range of factors which determine people's health and well being. A much more integrated and holistic approach to health is needed to provide physical, social, and economic environments, which promote and maintain the health of populations, and the sustainability of the natural environment. This approach has been termed the 'new public health' which takes a socio-ecological view of health.

Local Municipal Government in Queensland, Australia has a long history of involvement in the provision of services and programs designed to protect and maintain public health. Clean water, a safe food supply, immunisation and waste disposal programs are some traditional responsibilities of local government which have helped to reduce the spread of diseases to maintain healthy and sustainable communities.

Local government has the opportunity to continue to be a key player in the prevention of disease and maintenance of health by applying a socio-ecological approach to urban and rural administration. It is difficult to identify one program area within local government boundaries that does not impact on physical, social or economic environments. However, local government does not have sole responsibility for the planning and development of healthy and sustainable communities.

Population health gains rely on policies and interventions that impact positively on the determinants of health, and administrative responsibility for many of these determinants such as transport, housing and education, lies both with other levels and sectors of government, private enterprise and the community. These key stakeholders must therefore be involved in planning and action to create healthy and sustainable communities.

THE HEALTHY CITIES APPROACH AS A SETTINGS APPROACH

The idea of Healthy Cities began in 1986 when the World Health Organisation in Europe decided that a focus on the city setting would be a way of consolidating and localising the very broad health promotion strategies of the Ottawa Charter. This approach would allow the social, economic and environmental conditions which foster healthy and sustainable communities to be realistically attempted. Since 1986 the Healthy Cities approach has spread internationally to include more than 1500 cities and communities in both developed and developing countries. This growth of the Healthy Cities approach is more than evident in Australia with the first pilot cities being established in 1987. This has grown to include more than 20 cities and communities.

According to the philosophy of the Healthy Cities Project, any city can be a Healthy City. A Healthy City is defined by its commitment to improve health and the structures and processes it establishes to achieve it. This does not remove improved health outcomes as part of the Healthy City goal. However, the emphasis is on the process of setting locally appropriate goals and health indicators and securing ongoing approaches to achieve these goals.

But what do these new commitments, structures and processes mean in real terms at the city level? In practical terms, it means that the strategies for health promotion as set out in the Ottawa Charter are adopted and implemented. In this way, improved co-operation and involvement between sectors and levels of government as well as greater community participation in decision-making is developed.

In more philosophical terms, it also means organisational, cultural and value changes. Applying the strategies of the Ottawa Charter to the city and the shire (shires are rural communities) setting means that cities and shires must be managed and organised differently. Traditionally cities and shires have been managed with a top down approach where professionals have made most of the decisions within discrete departments or sectors. Healthy Cities advocates a new approach which:

'Cut[s] across the old departmental lines and indeed across different sectors – public, private, voluntary and community. None [health issues] can be addressed by one department of government alone, nor indeed by city government alone. The whole community has to be mobilised and the effort of all sectors and departments has to be combined and focussed. In this new approach, power has to be wielded by influence more than authority and health advocates have to learn to share power with people rather than wield power over people... The structures that are implemented should be more collegial and less hierarchical. These structures and processes should enhance collaboration rather than competition, analyse issues holistically rather than sectorally'.

(WHO 1991)

THE MUNICIPAL PUBLIC HEALTH PLANNING DEMONSTRATION PROJECT

In Queensland, the Healthy Cities and Shires State Network has been actively involved in this process of change since 1992, with funding support from Queensland Health since then. In 1993, Queensland Health, through the Health Advancement Branch, provided funding to the Healthy Cities and Shires Project to develop nine pilot projects in Queensland. The experiences and learning from these projects produced a resource guide that will assist all local governments, other Government sectors and the community to plan for healthy and sustainable communities.

Municipal Public Health Plans can best be described as both a product and a process. One product of the planning process is a dynamic co-ordinating document that represents the best efforts of the local government and its community to develop goals and strategies that respond to local public health and sustainability priority issues.

Of equal importance is the process of developing the plan. Unlike many strategic planning exercises, Municipal Public Health Plans in their formulation, implementation and evaluation must involve the local community. The key principles of the Healthy Cities approach to urban and rural planning emphasise a shared responsibility for health between the local government, other sectors, community groups and community members. The test of the plan will be how well these new partnerships are developed and maintained over time. Municipal Public Health Plans represent a new focus on a policy of goal directed administration of public health that will both complement and enhance the traditional regulation driven administrative approach.

By early 2000, some 11 Local Governments have completed 3 year MPHP, with another 7 communities commencing the process in 2000; this represents over half the population of Queensland (QLD has a population of approx 3 million) that will be influenced by the planning model at this point in time.

LINKS WITH QUEENSLAND HEALTH'S POPULATION HEALTH FOCUS

Queensland Health's activities, which seek to protect and promote the health of the population, are all placed within its Population Health Services. The key objectives of the program, particularly those of improving the capacity of the physical and social environment to support good health, a commitment to health equity, and participation in health decision making, are in harmony with the goals and strategies of the Municipal Public Health Planning process.

Similarly, the strategic principles of the Population Health Services are consistent with the Municipal Public Health Planning Process, both of which focus on an ecological approach to health, looking at the organisational, structural and individual determinants of health, and creating programs for specific settings using community development/organisational development approaches.

In fact the Local Government Association of Queensland has developed a protocol with Queensland Health to work together on MPHP state wide in 2000. Griffith University is working collaboratively with these stakeholders to broaden the MPHP program reach.

THE MPHP RESOURCE GUIDE AND CASE STUDIES

A resource guide that has been published consists of two manuals. Part A consists of three sections and is concerned with the theory and process of developing a Municipal Public Health Plan to implementation stage, along with the provision of some general resource and presentation material to assist local government health planners. Part B assists local government health planners to further confront some of the challenges faced in developing a MPHP by sharing in the case study experiences of the three pilot local governments; Cairns City Council, Banana Shire, and Brisbane City Council.

CASE STUDIES IN MPHP

Case studies, which highlight the achievements of local governments in Municipal Public Health Planning, offer insights into the ways in which local governments can work co-operatively with other sectors of government and the local community to ensure the development of healthy and sustainable communities.

During 1994/5 for the period of approximately twelve months, three local governments in Queensland (Brisbane City Council, Banana Shire Council and Cairns City Council) have participated in a pilot project to develop Municipal Public Health Plans within a Healthy Cities and Shires framework. This essentially required Council project teams to facilitate and nurture local partnerships for the purposes of investigating local health needs and implementing strategies to address them. The alliances formed included other levels and sectors of government, non-government agencies, together with the local community. In 2000 eight more communities have developed and are implementing MPHP.

The case studies presented in the resource guide offer local governments who may be intending to develop a Municipal Public Health Plan the opportunity to hear about and share in the experiences of the project teams/officers. Each project team has written its own story to emphasise the rich detail of the 'highs' and 'lows' of developing a participatory health plan for their local communities.

The geographic separateness and demographic diversity of the three communities has ensured that each of the case studies has offered different approaches and strategies to ensure participation in the process. Additionally each community contributed to the identification of a broad spectrum of issues and needs which required discussion and prioritisation.

The issues raised by communities were common to the degree that they encompassed what would be regarded as having a traditional health focus such as the quality of water supplies, air and noise pollution, and the incidence of skin cancers, as well as issues that deal with the determinants of whether a community will be healthy and sustainable such as access to public transport, affordable housing and access to social networks, and meaningful recreation and work. Another six case studies are being documented by the project team at Griffith University.

Interestingly, despite the obvious diversities amongst the communities, many of the themes or categories of issues were similar. For example, all communities saw the need to address, in a proactive way, the maintenance of the viability of the natural environment through protection of water supplies, reduction of industrial pollution and attention to waste management. The connection between human health and the health of the natural environment was highlighted.

A concern for youth health related issues was also important for each community, as were aspects of creating and maintaining a healthy social environment for residents. The key themes arising from each planning process highlight these similarities. For example, Brisbane City Council identified four themes within their plan:

- public health and safety; which considered such issues as pedestrian safety for youth and aged, safety in residences and disease protection;
- healthy lifestyles; encompassing food quality and nutrition, skin cancer prevention, youth alcohol and drug misuse;
- community health networks; involving issues of social isolation, and sport and recreational opportunities;
- environmental protection.

Cairns City Council in their Municipal Public Health Plan will address the key areas of skin cancer prevention, youth health, intersectoral collaboration, waste management, cultural diversity, and community consultation, while Banana Shire Council and its community saw the need to focus on the areas of community safety, community services and development, health services and health promotion, the preservation and protection of the physical environment.

DEVELOPING A 'MUNICIPAL PUBLIC HEALTH PLAN'

The process steps identified, through the pilot projects and other research, in the resource guide include:

1. Doing the Groundwork: awareness raising and gaining commitment
2. Managing the Project
3. Needs Assessment: internal analysis, community profile, and community consultation
4. Determining Priority Issues
5. Developing Strategies
6. Writing the Draft Plan
7. Monitoring, Review and Evaluation of the Plan.

Case Study: The Next Evolutionary Step in Municipal Public Health Planning: Regional Management – Local Implementation

Due to Local Governments having the facilitation and coordinating role in the pilot projects there was very much a focus on the development of partnerships between local government and other stakeholders to identify and seek solutions to priority health issues.

Since 1998 there has been an evolutionary shift towards regional management and local implementation of community health planning.

Public Health Units, Queensland Health are the second tier of government in Australia, which has public health as a focus and works intimately with local communities. Public Health Units are concerned with the health promotion and environmental health needs of local communities in regional settings.

Consequently in May 1998, the Queensland Health – Wide Bay approached the Hervey Bay City Council and Maryborough City Council to participate in a proposed public health planning. Both Councils had been and were interested in conducting public health planning projects, however the issues of money, skills and available time were identified as major barriers. The ensuing discussions and dealings led to an agreement of involvement and money contributions from all three parties. Skills and the accompanying time requirements were still a concern, however the pooling of money had been seen as a means to accessing outside skills. The group approached Healthy Cities and Shires, Griffith University and a working relationship for project guidance and support was established.

The public health model had evolved to a level where the management team had expanded to include vested interests of major players in local health issues. The benefits here included the development of collaborative partnerships for the facilitation, ownership and management of the project, the breadth in the expertise and skill base of the management and the strength of the support structure, which developed through the project.

Benefits of this regional management model include:

- Less duplication
- Better use of Local Government staff resources
- Better use of non government staff who were servicing both communities
- Support for Local Government through the process
- Affirming relationship between Public Health Unit and the Local Governments/Councils
- Coming together of Councils/overcoming some political separation issues
- Timetabling
- Ability to bring in an external project officer
- Skilling Environmental Health practitioners in health planning
- The bringing together of internal organisational staff to work on one project
- Identified as a method of increasing the number of people working in a community on health promotion goals

- Communication between the parties was maintained
- Sharing of money.

SUMMARY

One learning from this experience may well be that despite apparent diversity amongst communities in Queensland, many of the indicators of a quality of life amongst communities and the values that they have about healthy and sustainable communities for themselves and their children are remarkably similar.

The process of planning and implementation is continuing and being evaluated to access health impacts for communities. The project is now focusing on integrating MPHP into existing planning and organisational frameworks to optimise on health impacts and outcomes overtime.

Finally, a National Environmental Healthy Strategy developed by the Commonwealth Department of Health and Aged Care has recognised Health Planning as an important process towards developing healthy communities. It is important to have both 'top down' support and 'bottom up' action to plan for health and implement programs at a local level.

The project is co-ordinated by Mr. Peter Davey, Senior Lecturer in Environmental Health at Griffith University, Brisbane, Australia (see <www.gu.edu.au>).

Acknowledgements

Thanks to Zoe Murray at Griffith University and members of the project team in Queensland especially Mal Price, Darren Hauser, Brian Barker.

Tagaytay City welfare in progress

Action planning and community-based activities: the Philippines

Mayor Francis N. Tolentino

SIGNIFICANCE OF THE CASE

The rapid pace of urbanization is a global concern. It is a call for an urgent and decisive action among our leaders in meeting the challenge of the present times. Several studies would show the adverse effects brought about by urbanization such as poor health conditions, degradation of the environment and inequality of access to basic social services, etc. These are but some concrete manifestations that have to be addressed immediately. However, finding the best solutions to the problem is not the sole responsibility of the leaders concerned. The people in the basic sectors of society should also actively take part and participate even in the action planning process.

THE VISION

'A natural and institutional City utilizing its full potential through a sustainable ecological tourism-based, adequate infrastructure support system, character building and accessible pro-people social services'.

Programs under review
- Health Insurance 'Para sa Barangay'
- Tagaytay Housing Program
- Nutrition Program
- Day Care Program
- Barangay Health Worker
- Lingap sa Bayan: A Rolling Store
- Ospital ng Tagaytay
- Clean and Green
- Peace and Order
- City of Character
- Developing Healthy Lifestyle

LGU profile

- Basically a resort city
- Population: 40,000 (1998)
- Land area: 6,615 Has.
- Topography: mixed and rugged
- Main economic activities: tourism and agriculture
- No. of barangay (villages): 34
- No. of families: 6,747

BACKGROUND

Demographic situation

Tagaytay is a component city within the province of Cavite where the Philippine Republic was born in 1898. It is located in the southern part of the province, about 60 kilometres south of Manila. It has a total land area of 66.15 square kilometres and is politically subdivided into 34 barangays.

As of December 1998, the city's total population is 40,000,

- with a population growth rate (PGR) of 3.89%
- most of which belong to the younger age which contribute the dependency ratio of 1:3.

The city's labor force is 19,960 (15–55 years of age), mostly belonging to the school age bracket.

Emerging issues and concerns

The city's health facilities are sometimes inadequate, particularly in terms of providing health care services in the remote barangays. Services cover only first-aid, pre/post-natal check up and family planning. Hence, patients with serious illness that need emergency medical attention have to be brought to the adjoining towns (Silang, Dasmariñas, Trece Martirez City and as far as hospitals in Metro Manila). In short, such inadequacy may be due to lack of medical facilities/equipments as well the ratio of the medical personnel against the number of population to be served which is relatively below the standard as set forth by the Department of Health (DOH). Another consideration would be the topographical location of some barangays that are quite inaccessible to any types of motor vehicles.

Agricultural production, which has been the traditional and main economic base of the city, declined into a certain level due to the sudden shift of development activities from agricultural to tourism and real estate business. Such shift had somehow contributed to the increasing number of squatters (who were indiscriminately displaced in the course of development), thereby resulting in housing problems. In a 1997 survey, there were 1,791 urban poor families registered by the City Government. These include caretakers of lands owned by the rich people based in Metropolitan Manila. They usually resort to squatting on available lands when the land they occupy is sold by the owners and subsequently developed into subdivisions, townhouses and the like.

Malnutrition, specifically among children, has also been one of the major concerns of the City Government.

The last but not the least is the economic difficulty of the city's populace brought about by external factors such as inflation and the effects of the Asian currency crisis.

THE PROGRAMS ON THE 'GO'

Out of the relentless effort and steadfast commitment of the city government in providing various basic social services to the city's populace the following programs have been put in place, to wit:

Tagaytay housing program

The program directly addresses housing problems and squatting in the city. It is a provision of decent and affordable housing units to qualified beneficiaries (mostly homeless and squatter families, adversely affected by the city's on-going development). As of December 1999, the city has awarded a total of 334 housing units and is expected to accommodate more in the near future. The city government on Nov. 28, 1997 created its own Tagaytay Housing Office tasked to formulate rules and coordinate programs relative to providing socialized housing to Tagaytay homeless residents.

Another feature of the housing program is the use of 'sweat-equity hours' wherein beneficiaries selected by a task force (Habitat) coming from the cross-section of the community contribute their physical resource through manual labor in building their own homes.

Health Insurance Program

HIP started in 1997. It is a provision of health insurance coverage to indigent families. Beneficiaries of the program are entitled to avail of as much as 48% discount to accredited hospitals in case of confinement (even to other hospitals outside of the city). As of this year, there are 2,400 indigents beneficiaries from the 34 barangays (villages) benefiting the program. The City Government pays for the health insurance coverage premium.

Plingap sa Bayan: a rolling store

Amidst economic crisis besetting the entire Philippines (brought about by external factors of inflation and unabated oil prices increases) the City Government of

Tagaytay searched for ways and means on how to cushion the adverse effects affecting the very lives of the people. As an urgent response to the need, the rolling store program has been established through selling of basic commodities at very low prices to poor families, in the future, to include basic over-the-counter medicines. At the village level, immediate beneficiaries are being identified by village leaders, social workers and other volunteers.

City nutrition program

The program is a relentless effort of the city government in eradicating malnutrition cases in the entire city. It is under the direct supervision of the City Nutrition Council (CNC) chaired by the City Mayor himself. To ensure its proper implementation, the city involved the services of Barangay Nutrition Scholars (BNS) from the 34 villages. Among the tasks of the BNS are: Operation Timbang (weighing of children to determine the degree of malnutrition), home visitation, home and community food production, micro-nutrient supplementation, nutrition education and food assistance. Public schools are likewise being assisted through a supplemental feeding program among school children. BNS are expected to submit status reports regularly to the City Nutrition Office for proper monitoring and evaluation. This program has earned for the City various regional and national nutrition awards.

Day care service

The program is directly supervised by the City Social Welfare and Development Office (CSWDO). It is the provision of supplementary parental care to 0–5-year-old children of parents who find it difficult to fully take care of their children during part of the day because of work and some other reasons. It is also an integral component of the child's basic rights to survival, protection, participation, and development.

At present the city has 23 Day Care Centers with average enrollees of 450 annually. Day Care Workers receive only monthly honorarium, taken from the budget of the city and barangay, respectively. Some of the workers receive allowances provided by community residents who realized the need to support to this service.

Clean and Green Program

Amidst rapid pace of development, the present administration has been able to implement various activities relating to environmental conservation/preservation. Among these activities are tree planting in open spaces and denuded areas; 'linis bayan' – participated in by city employees and Non-Government Organizations (NGOs). Creation of 'Task Force Kalikasan' is also one of the major components of the program. It is held responsible for garbage collection, bush cutting along major thoroughfares, etc. The city has been successful in its implementation. In fact, the city received a series of awards/recognitions as one of the Cleanest and Greenest Cities in the Philippines. In fact, one of its initiatives in 1994, the Youth Green Brigade (youth helping in environmental protection), has been adapted as a national project by the Central Government in 1999.

Peace and Order
Peace and Order situation in the entire city is relatively peaceful. Official records of the Tagaytay City Component Police Force show that the crime rate for the last five years is relatively low as compared to other component cities in the country today. Nevertheless, the city's vigilance against the proliferation of crimes does not cease, in fact, the city has been trying to intensify its campaign against criminality such as illegal drugs by encouraging active participation of the local residents. The City's Peace and Order Council, with members coming from various sectors of the society (including NGO and the religious) vigorously plan and pursue an integrated community peace and order program for the city with members heading various teams aimed at meeting yearly pre-set targets concerning law enforcement. Bantay Lungsod (City Watch Team) was also created under the Tagaytay Office of Public Safety (TOPS), to augment the efforts of the Philippine National Police (PNP) particularly in traffic management and environmental protection. Just recently, the city formed/organized the Mounted Police (the country's first) – an auxiliary police force mounted on trained horses, tasked in apprehending suspected criminals in the remote villages of the city. As a positive indication of this effort and based on the recent evaluation/survey conducted, PNP-Tagaytay has been rated number one in Cavite Province while the PNP-Cavite had also received the same rating in the entire Philippines.

Barangay Health Workers (BHWs)
To further promote health care services being rendered by the LGU, BHWs from the 34 barangays (villages) were selected and provided proper training prior to registration/accreditation as being required by the DOH. As health care providers, they are supposed to render primary health care services to the members of the community by 1) referring patients with complications and those suspected to have communicable disease to the appropriate health centers or hospital; 2) monitoring the health status of the household members under his/her area of service coverage; 3) keeping records of health activities in the community and the health station; and 4) ensuring the proper maintenance of the health station and the safe custody of equipments, basic medical supplies and health records of community members. They also assist various government agencies such as the Agriculture Department in anti-rabies campaign, etc. and NGOs providing supplemental health services such as the NGO-initiated Project Health, among others.

Hospital in Tagaytay

The delivery of basic health care services to the general public is basically one of the primordial concerns of the city. The City Government of Tagaytay established its very first public city-owned hospital in 1997 aimed at providing health services charging the minimum amount particularly to underprivileged patients. It started with only 10-bed capacity. And after a period of about two years, the hospital can now accommodate 25 in-patients serving other adjoining towns as well. The said hospital serves as a glaring example on how some affluent transient residents of the city and new migrants share their talent and resources by serving as hospital directors and consultants (without pay) in order to serve the needs of the indigent local families of their new city. The hospital board tasked with running the hospital is composed of the religious sectors, NGO members, local residents and other transient residents of the city.

Notwithstanding the city's financial conditions, the present administration through the City Health Board with the other community residents' assistance has been able to sustain the usual operation of the hospital.

Developing healthy lifestyles

Undeniably, technological advancement has, in a certain extent, changed the very lifestyle of the people, some tend to depend on what the technology can offer: televisions and computer systems, for instance, are now being operated through the use of remote controls; 'instant food' is readily available in the grocery stores; communication becomes easier by using cell-phones and the Internet, and so on and so forth. As measures in maintaining health conditions, some activities have also been incorporated in various programs of the city such as yearly sports festival and weekly physical exercise aimed at ensuring good health, physical fitness and readiness among the city's constituents. In fact, the City Government enacted ordinances relating to health and environment (City Ordinance # 98–123 – amending City Ordinance 89–16 and Ordinance 93–16 known as the Anti-Littering Ordinance of Tagaytay City enacted on December 10, 1998 and City Ordinance # 99–139 – prohibiting smoking in Government Offices within the Tagaytay City Centrum, the city's business center – enacted on August 9, 1999, respectively).

Moreover, farmers are also being encouraged to use organic fertilizers as an alternative in producing 'chemical free' agricultural products. As part of this effort, and in order to preserve the natural beauty and landscape of the city, pollutive industries such as factories are not included in the formulated land use plan and zoning ordinance.

THE PROCESS

The mandate of localizing Agenda 21 has been brought to the concern of every nation. It further mandates that every city in the world should carry out various programs to the fullest extent in response to the alarming trend of rapid urbanization.

The City of Tagaytay institutionalized community welfare initiatives, way back about five years ago, and is being given priority concern by the present administration. It is hoped that the city's effort shall greatly complement the drive in uplifting the living conditions of poor families, as the City's landscape is transformed further into a rapidly growing tourism area.

Moreover, such situation further prompted the Local Chief Executive to determine and define the most viable implementation mechanism – i.e. 'Action Planning and Community-Based Activities Initiatives'. An example of this type of mechanism is the creation of various local task forces such as a Tourism Council as program implementers. Among their tasks is to raise awareness of the stakeholders and people actively involved in the program. They are held responsible as well in the coordination process, mobilization of program resource, formalization of rules, work flows, documentation, and reporting/monitoring processes.

The community activities run smoothly as the manpower involved are always kept in touch in the work plan. The system of coordination became effective which mobilizes the participation of all sectors in the community. Moreover, the collaboration of various government agencies has been proven effective for an efficient delivery of basic services to the community. Eventually these activities were tapped as a medium by the city in rendering services and thereby build a sort of confidence among the citizens in the sincerity of the government in carrying out genuine development programs.

As laid out by the City Mayor, the overall goal is to achieve a City of Character (another project to be launched by April 2000) wherein city residents will share common dreams and aspirations by practicing good attitudes (such as cleanliness, discipline, respect for the environment, etc.) daily in their homes, schools, workplaces, government offices among others, to arrive at a fusion of both the physical and spiritual components of a truly 'livable' city.

RESULTS

Improved living condition
Through the community welfare program, the City of Tagaytay has been able to improve the socio-economic condition of the poor families by providing access to basic health and other social services.

Maximized utilization of resources (manpower, financial and time)
Improved the city's capability in mobilizing, budgeting, and utilizing available resources intended for development services. Innovative practices on fiscal administration and income generation were likewise devised to meet the growing needs of the city residents. Planning implementation has become the city's standing policy in the overall management/operation of various programs and projects.

Established good rapport with the community
Well-organized community activities being initiated by the city government have paved the way in restoring the trust and confidence of the people in the government. 'Gaps' between new residents and original city residents are slowly being bridged. The community and the basic sectors are now actively participating and supporting the efforts of the city in attaining the common vision towards a so called 'City of Character'.

CHALLENGES

Influx of immigration – the rapid pace of urban development encourages immigration of families from nearby congested growth centers to seek livelihood and employment opportunities. Moreover, the vast tracts of lands owned by the rich/transient families also invite migration of settlers/squatters in the city. Based on the belief that people are a part of development, undeniably, the city is caught in a situation and practically left no other choice/option but to face the challenge squarely and find possible solutions in addressing the problem.

Escalating Cost of Living – the rapid price increases of basic commodities as well as poor access to basic services brought about by the uncontrolled oil prices in the world market have left a devastating effect among the poor in terms of meeting their minimum basic needs. Amidst this situation, it is therefore imperative that the city should adopt mitigating measures and introduce innovative strategies in enhancing the general welfare of the poor families in the community.

Uniting Various Political Interest – indeed, upholding the mandates of the Constitution and the provisions of the (1991) Local Government Code by the incumbent government officials is a pre-requisite in empowering and protecting the general welfare of the people regardless of political belief, interests and affiliation.

Strategic Location for Tourism – Considering that the City of Tagaytay has been gaining popularity as one of the major tourist destinations in the country today, influx of local and foreign investors is, indeed, inevitable. Thus, the city is now being challenged to protect the existing landscape by strictly implementing the City Land Use Plan and Zoning Ordinance.

LESSONS LEARNED

On Management Systems – the establishment and localization of the existing service delivery systems in the community had been proven to be effective in fast tracking various programs and activities considered to be more responsive and suitable to local settings and conditions. An example of this is the establishment of Barangay Health Workers (BHWs), Bantay-Lungsod (City Watch Team) and Barangay Nutrition Scholars (BNS) wherein provisions of the needed services are readily available within the community.

On the Process of Planning of Project Implementation – constant practice of the process hastens the city's implementation of various programs and community activities. The essential components (action plan, organizational structures, coordination procedure and formalized-rules and work-flows) diminish possible irregularities, maximize time and effort and ensure success of the project. The project's goal has to be shared by all participants.

On Community Activity – the process of project implementation becomes easier when the program beneficiaries themselves are actively involved in various activities. New partners or participants (through the new city migrants – the poor who have to be shown concern and affluent who have to be involved) are needed to be integrated into the mainstream process to make the effort truly collaborative such as in the case of the Hospital in Tagaytay. They are willing to spend time and effort provided they are given proper orientation and right motivation by the project implementers.

Index